Women as Weapons of War

Women as Weapons of War

Iraq, Sex, and the Media

KELLY OLIVER

Columbia University Press   *New York*

Columbia University Press
Publishers Since 1893
New York   Chichester, West Sussex
Copyright © 2007 Columbia University Press
All rights reserved

Library of Congress Cataloging-in-Publication Data
Oliver, Kelly, 1958–
Women as weapons of war : Iraq, sex, and the media / Kelly Oliver.
p   cm.
Includes bibliographical references and index.
ISBN 978–0–231–14190–1 (cloth : alk. paper) — ISBN 978–0–231–51245–9 (ebook)
1. Women and the military—Iraq. 2. Iraq War, 2003—Press coverage—United States.
3. Feminist theory. I. Title.

021.75.043 2007
956.7044'3082—dc22
2007027467

Columbia University Press books are printed on permanent and durable acid-free paper.
This book was printed on paper with recycled content.
Printed in the United States of America

c 10 9 8 7 6 5 4 3 2 1

For Melvin Aaberg

1913–2005

Recipient of the Purple Heart for bravery
at the Battle of Normandy in World War II
…and my grandfather

Contents

Preface

Like many people, when I saw the photographs of abuse at Abu Ghraib, I couldn't shake the combination of horror and fascination that drew me to those images. Here, gleefully abusing Iraqi prisoners, were girls like the ones I had known growing up in rural Idaho and Montana. Like me, maybe, these girls grew up around the woods, eating wild game shot by their fathers and learning to cook from their mothers. Like me, some of them reportedly dreamed of becoming teachers when they grew up. (I remember that I declined an ROTC scholarship that would have allowed me to attend an Ivy league college and instead went to the local Jesuit school, in part because I couldn't wrap my head around war... or wearing that ugly uniform.) For most of these girls, however, unlike me, joining the military was their only hope of fulfilling their dreams. Did I identify with these girls from rural Pennsylvania and West Virginia? Or did I see in their lives the path not chosen... "there but for the grace of God"? I couldn't imagine doing what they had done, but could they have imagined it before they enlisted?

I think too of my students at West Virginia University (where I had my first full-time teaching position), many of them first-generation college students, daughters of coal-miners, hoping for a better life; girls who demanded to know what philosophy had to do with their fathers' black lung disease. I kept asking myself, who were these girls at Abu Ghraib, girls capable of such violence? But it wasn't the violence that haunted me. It was the joy on their faces—they were so happy, they were having fun, they seemed so innocent. Why did these girls enjoy hurting others? How could they take such pleasure in violence? I began to wonder about our own investments in violence and the pleasure we get from watching it, especially at the movies. The deeper I went into this project, the more I saw that as a culture it is not just fictional violence at the movies that we enjoy, but real violence. We are obsessed with real violence, with reality television that shows us in gory details the physical and emotional violence that people inflict on one another. I recently discovered that some people even search the Internet for images of attacks on U.S. soldiers in Iraq because they "like to watch stuff blow up" (Wyatt 2006). And that the Abu Ghraib images have become icons on some pornography Web sites. How is it that violent spectacles have become innocent entertainment?

How could the girls at Abu Ghraib happily abuse men? That is the other strange part of this equation—*girls* were abusing *men*. I was used to hearing about men abusing women, but now the tables seemed turned. Here was a complex of racial and sexual violence directed toward men— Iraqi "detainees" treated like dogs. The image of a man on a leash like a dog, and reading about how the guards were instructed to treat prisoners like dogs, made me wonder, "Who treats dogs like that?" (I was writing a book on metaphors of animals and animality at the time—a book that I set aside to write this one.) Also, the sexual nature of the photographs made them strangely pornographic. And again I was confused: women raping and sexually abusing men? Wasn't it usually the other way around? I became suspicious of my own interest in the photographs. What was I looking for when thumbing through the pages of the *New Yorker* or special editions of *Time* magazine? Why did I find these images so mesmerizing? But I wasn't the only one fixed on these images. They captured public attention and made headline news throughout the mainstream media. The repercussions of the images are still being felt in debates over the powers of the president and the definition of appropriate interrogation techniques versus torture.

The image of a man wearing a black cape and hood, standing on a box with arms outstretched, was so well framed and striking that it made me think of an art photograph. I began to wonder about the difference between these photographs, these representations of violence, and artistic representations of violence. Even the photographs without the smiling girls seemed somehow familiar to me—not from yearbooks or picture postcards, but from contemporary art. In fact I've heard recently that some of the photos have been incorporated into artworks to protest the war. I had to keep reminding myself that these were photographs of real life, photographs of war. That was part of my problem: they didn't look like other war photographs I had seen. They were photographs of war, but with smiling women, men in sexual poses, girls giving thumbs-up. These images had a certain familiarity from other contexts, but not from the context of war. I began to wonder about the nature of this war, which made the Abu Ghraib photographs the latest in war photography. And the connections between women, sex, and war conjured by these images made me wonder about the connection between sex and violence more generally.

At about the time I started thinking about the women involved in abuse at Abu Ghraib, I began noticing special reports on Palestinian women suicide bombers. Again the glossy covers of popular news magazines grabbed my attention. Again I was fascinated by these violent young women. Quickly, however, I became even more intrigued by the media coverage of them. Why were these women showing up on the covers of magazines? Why were they making headlines? Would the abuses at Abu Ghraib have been so "shocking" if the guards had all been men? We don't see all of the male suicide bombers on the covers of magazines looking out at us with sad brown eyes. I began to suspect that within the public imaginary, women's violence was more interesting, more spectacular, more unexpected, than men's. Men have been waging war forever... but women warriors, is this something new? Soon I found a recurring pattern in media descriptions of these women warriors. They were repeatedly and consistently referred to as *weapons*—not soldiers *with* weapons or extremists *with* bombs. Rather, the female body itself, its presence, its very being, was being referred to as a weapon.

As I started to write the first chapter of this book on women figured as weapons in the media, again I was drawn to a news report that baffled me: an eight-year-old boy had died while playing what the report called the "hanging game." I was surprised to learn that suffocation was a form of entertainment among young kids and teenagers. I started noticing other articles on youngsters dying while playing the "choking game" or the "hanging game," which apparently has become more popular than ever due to the Internet. Then articles on "cutting" and other forms of self-injury popular among teenagers started popping out at me from the pages of the newspaper. I wondered why so many kids were hurting themselves, reportedly in order to feel "release," to feel "alive."... They were cutting themselves to feel free; they were killing themselves to feel alive. Again I began to ask what kind of culture produces young people who inflict violence on themselves or others in the name of freedom or life... or "just for fun." These are the kids we meet every day. They are my students, the children of friends, perhaps even family.

I wrote this book in order to try to figure out why "normal" American kids engage in deadly violence. Here I have focused on violence in war, particularly representations of women's violence, as it relates to stereotypes of the connection between sex and violence more generally. This analysis also speaks to "cutting," the "hanging game," and other forms of self-violence, along with school shootings, hazing, and other forms of violence toward others, as symptoms of a culture of violence, which is the result of having limited options for articulating emotions, especially violent ones.

Kelly Oliver
Nashville, Tennessee

Acknowledgments

I would like to thank Wendy Lochner, my editor at Columbia University Press, whose enthusiasm sustained me through substantial revisions of this project. Thanks to Eduardo Mendieta and Cynthia Willett, along with an anonymous reviewer for Columbia University Press, for extremely helpful comments and suggestions on an earlier version of this book. Thanks also to the audience at DePaul University in Chicago, where I presented a very different version of the last chapter. I am grateful to my colleagues at Vanderbilt University for their comments and questions after I presented an earlier version of chapter 1; special thanks to Colin (Joan) Dayan, Kathryn Gines, and David Wood for their suggestions.

As always I am indebted to my family for their support and encouragement. My deepest gratitude goes to Benigno Trigo for continued conversations that nourished this project, as well as my immense appreciation for his company on this winding, rocky road of life.

Women as Weapons of War

Introduction

Sex, Drugs, and Rock 'n' Roll

Because this war is unlike others in that there is no front line, women
are engaged in combat along with men. Women soldiers, not technically
allowed on the front lines, continue to see action, to kill and be killed. A
shortage of military personnel leads to stretching of the rules regarding
women in ground combat forces. But reportedly the American public is
no longer shocked at the idea of women dying in war; there is no more
attention paid to fallen women than to fallen men.[1] Women's participation in integrated units for the most part goes unnoticed. The women in
these units find ways to adapt their bodies to male standards of war—by
taking newer forms of birth control to make their periods less frequent
or to eliminate them altogether, and by using a portable urination device
disbursed by the military for long road trips (which women soldiers call
a "weenus"). Women are serving and dying, but, in the words of retired
Navy captain Lory Manning, "A lot of social conservatives have powerful
feelings about training mothers to kill."[2] And some military policy-makers
foresee reopening debates about women's participation in combat once
the war is over.

It is telling that although women's deaths in Iraq get little attention in
the media or from the American public, women's involvement in abusive
treatment of "detainees" at Abu Ghraib prison in Iraq and at Guantánamo

Bay prison in Cuba continues to haunt debates over acceptable interrogation techniques and American sentiments toward the war. In addition, the sexual nature of the abuse is used by some to argue that women shouldn't be in the military, that their very presence unleashed sexual violence. Although the deaths of women soldiers receive little attention, the reports of women soldiers' violence and abuse captured the public imagination. Why? Why did the images of women abusers from Abu Ghraib generate so much press and media speculation?

This book is an attempt to answer this question by analyzing both the media coverage and the events themselves within the context of a pornographic way of looking at sex and violence that is normalized through popular media. The pornographic way of looking or seeing takes the object of its gaze for its own pleasure or as a spectacle for its own enjoyment without regard for the subjectivity or subject position of those looked at. The pornographic way of looking reinforces the power and agency of the looker while erasing or debasing the power and agency of the looked-at.[3] This way of looking operates on both the literal and the figural level: sex and violence literally have become spectacles to be looked at; and sex and violence figuratively have become linked within our cultural imaginary, as evidenced by the fact that the phrase "sex and violence" has become part of our everyday vocabulary—in terms of Hollywood films, it is difficult to think of one without the other.

In a general sense, then, this book is about the connection between sex and violence in contemporary culture. More specifically, it is about how this imagined connection plays itself out in the theatre of war currently staged in the Middle East. Furthermore, it is about how this pornographic way of looking plays an essential role in waging war; and how historically it has been used, even developed, within the context of colonial and imperialist violence. In this regard, as we will see, the American occupation of Iraq follows in a long line of colonial and imperialist ventures executed by the "West" in the "East."

Placing the events at Abu Ghraib and their media coverage within the historical context of Western colonial violence allows us to see how they are a continuation of military practices that normalize violence, particularly in relation to women and sex. When the photographs first became public, there was a flurry of outrage and accusation. The photographs were considered "shocking" and mind-boggling; some considered the photographs themselves to be the real problem. Yet at the same time there was something strangely familiar about these photos. It is that combination of shock and familiarity that I seek to understand in this book. The faces of the perpetrators suggest that they could be the subjects of photographs in a high school yearbook. Judged by the gestures and facial expressions, they are photographs of triumph and victory, all smiles and thumbs-up. In this regard, the photographs are trophies that suggest that within the war of us versus them, we are winning. The trophy-viewing or trophy-seeing inherent in these photographs is just one aspect of pornographic looking. The objects of the photographs are abused, debased, humiliated, naked; and when these trembling and vulnerable bodies are photographed next to triumphant American military personnel, the clear message is that we can do whatever we want to these foreigners, these enemy combatants. We are in the driver's seat, while they are just along for the ride, in this case apparently a joy-ride at their expense.

In this book I argue that these "shocking" images are familiar to us not only from a history of colonial violence associated with sex, but also from a history of associations involving women, sex, and violence. Indeed, the association between sex and violence trades on stereotypical images and myths of dangerous or threatening women upon which our culture was, and continues to be, built. Women have been associated with the downfall of man since Eve supposedly tempted Adam with forbidden fruit. In this regard, I analyze literal and conceptual images of women from war in the Middle East, including Afghanistan, Iraq, and Palestine, in terms of both the legacy of colonial imperialism and the legacy of patriarchal associations of women, sex, and death.

In the chapters that follow I peel away layers of visual and rhetorical meaning in an attempt to understand the deeper significance of various aspects of this "war on terror"—the use of women by the military to "soften up" prisoners, images of burka-clad women shopping in Afghanistan, the defense that the Abu Ghraib perpetrators were just "having fun," techniques of war reporting such as embedded journalism—along with the connection between sex and violence in recent Hollywood films. By interpreting these events and images as they function within the larger context of a culture whose primary forms of entertainment revolve around sex and violence, we learn more about the function of women in this economy of violence. Moreover, by interpreting these events and images within the context of a cultural imaginary captivated by sex and violence, we can begin to understand our own investments in violence. My hope is that by understanding our own investments in violence we can short-circuit violent urges and stop making our violent fantasies into reality.

My multifaceted approach is intended to address some of the interrelationships between our fantasies, desires, fears, and phobias, on the one hand, and media rhetoric (visual and narrative), along with public policies, on the other. In other words, one of the questions motivating this analysis is: What is the relationship between our psychic, or emotional, lives and our actions, or public lives? I intentionally avoid the language of private and public because my working hypothesis is that these two realms are thoroughly and intimately related to a degree that makes any such distinction deceptive. In fact, in some ways the oppositions between private and public, between emotions and politics, between bodies and society, between nature and culture, feed into and off of the rhetoric of war. The oppositional thinking of us versus them, which erases any ambiguities between the two, also operates in these other areas. And, as we will see, it is the disavowal of ambiguities—those gray areas where one pole cannot be easily separated from the other—that contributes to a culture of violence.

In the chapters that follow I attempt to identify a deeper meaning in the visual and narrative rhetoric of the war against terror. The main focus of my analysis is how the war is perceived and represented; another operative hypothesis is that working to interpret representations of events in the popular media can tell us something about how we see ourselves and how we see others; critically reading the media can teach us about the deep-seated fears and desires that motivate our thinking and our behavior. We may not be aware of the fears and desires that lie behind our conceptions of ourselves and others and our actions toward ourselves and them. Using theoretical tools from philosophy, psychoanalysis, and sociology, I attempt to tease out the psychic and political stakes in our war on terror by combing through media representations of women involved in violence; by comparing discussions of women's liberation here and elsewhere; by examining the role of visual recording technologies in the enterprise of war; and by identifying the ways in which we justify our own (high-tech) violence and condemn the (low-tech) violence of others, including imagining that women's involvement somehow "softens the blow."

In the case of Abu Ghraib, the fact that women seemingly forced men into sexual postures confused even human rights organizations as they tried to classify, or simply identify, these actions as abuse. The sexual nature of the photos makes us uneasy. On the one hand, the "perky grins" and "cheerleaders' smiles" on the faces of these teenage girls seem out of place in the theatre of war. But, as I argue in chapter 1, the very idea that women can be interrogation tools plays on age-old fears of women and the fantasy of female sexuality as a threatening weapon. The familiarity of this connection between women, sex, and weapon makes the images uncanny—as strange as they are mundane. If in the past women were figured as "bombshells" and their sex imagined as a deadly weapon, the literal explosion of women onto the scene of war now should not be a surprise. From the women involved in Abu Ghraib and Guantánamo Bay prisons, to rescued Pfc. Jessica Lynch, to Palestinian women suicide bombers, recent media coverage has turned them into "weapons" of war. As we will see, in each of these cases metaphors of "weapons" are used repeatedly to describe women and female sexuality. In chapter 1, I analyze our fascination with what we imagine as the deadly power of these women.

In the first two chapters I also examine the rhetoric surrounding "feminism" and women's "liberation" as it has been used in relation to war in the Middle East. On the one hand, feminism has been blamed for women's violence against men; it has supposedly given women equal access to killing and abusing. On the other hand, feminism's concern for the liberation of women has been used to justify military action in the Middle East, Afghanistan in particular.

In chapter 2 I show how the Bush administration's rhetoric of liberating "women of cover" elsewhere shores up images of freedom and privilege for women here. Furthermore, it obscures the fact that this freedom brings with it new forms of discipline both here and abroad. One example of the new disciplinary constraints placed on women in the United States is the increasingly high standards of "professional motherhood": mothers are expected to have it all, family and careers, even if this means medicating themselves with Prozac, caffeine, or sleeping pills to maintain their busy schedules. In this chapter I link the recent rhetoric of liberating women in the Middle East with similar rhetoric used in earlier imperialist colonial enterprises to justify military action abroad even while denying women rights at home. Moreover, I show how the freedom that we are bringing to these women is figured as the freedom to shop, which suggests that the notion of American freedom offered to the rest of the world through war can be reduced to the freedom of the market. Within this rhetoric, women's right to shop and dress as they please becomes the watermark for global freedom. Women's right to *bare* arms is taken as a sign of freedom and progress.

women's actions

expectation of American women

women's freedom

Throughout this book I investigate the associations of the word "freedom" as it appears in popular media, in presidential speeches, and in scholarly articles. Questions of women's freedom have been central to feminism and women's liberation movements. Within the history of colonialism, women's freedom has become a cause for war. It has also been blamed for women's violence in the United States military and for women's violent participation in suicide bombings. The president has maintained that he intends to bring freedom and democracy to the entire world, and that the terror attacks of September 11 were an act of war against the entire free world. If freedom is at stake in the war on terror, it is crucial to ask what we mean by "freedom."

In chapter 3 I analyze the rhetoric of freedom as it has been used by the Bush administration to justify war. In examining presidential speeches, we discover an essential link between freedom and property, between freedom and ownership. We are fighting to protect our property and our right to ownership. Again, freedom is reduced to the free market. In these speeches, the rhetoric of freedom works in tandem with the rhetoric of good and evil. Once more, protecting the Good is reduced to protecting our goods. Thereby, the meanings of freedom, justice, and goodness become fungible, exchanged on the market of politics used to justify military action to gain and secure American wealth. Freedom and goodness become the rallying cries of global capitalism, where opening new markets and guaranteeing contracts for American companies become trademarks of success in the war against terror.

But, as we will see, the fear of losing our wealth, and the determination to protect it at all costs, leads to a paranoid patriotism wherein we feel our wealth threatened on all sides. The flip side of paranoia is delusion of grandeur, which is also evidenced in talk of "the entire free world" and "bringing democracy to the globe." The ideas that we are the center of the universe and that the entire world is at our disposal go hand in hand with the notion that we are surrounded by forces of evil out to destroy us. In psychoanalytic terms, these are classic symptoms of paranoia. Our sense of ourselves as a nation is strengthened by finding a common enemy, by seeing ourselves fighting the good fight against the forces of evil all around us. Our sense of ourselves as free is emboldened by comparing ourselves to people, especially women, elsewhere whom we imagine as enslaved.

The inflated rhetoric of good versus evil, of us versus them, feeds a paranoid patriotism that acts without thinking. Perhaps more worrisome are the ways in which, in presidential speeches, this rhetoric is linked to eternity and God: we are fighting a war for eternity because God is on our side. Bush concluded his 2006 9/11 memorial speech as follows: "We go forward with trust in that spirit [the spirit of the American people], confidence in our purpose, and faith in a loving God who made us to be free." If we are fighting for eternity, then we are fighting a war without end, *[our]* perpetual war without the possibility of peace. Another dangerous aspect *[endless war]* of this rhetoric of eternity is that it takes the war out of its sociohistorical context. The war is therefore not about oil, or nuclear weapons, or dictators, or maintaining America's position as a superpower, or rebuilding Iraq, or even free elections in Iraq, but about eternal goodness and our faith in God. The danger of removing events from their sociohistorical context is that we are not given the information needed to interpret and understand these events. We are given hyperbolic images that stir feeling, *[violence]* often violent feelings of hatred and revenge, but we are discouraged from *[is accepted]* thinking introspectively about those feelings. We are encouraged to feel violent, to want violence, without thinking about our own investments in that violence or about its consequences.

It is not just the administration, however, that undermines our ability to think critically about public policy and the war. The media, particularly in its coverage of 9/11 and the war in Iraq, contributes to the confusion. In chapter 3, I analyze the ways in which embedded reporting, rolling newsbars, and simulated events in newscasts not only decontextualize events but also blur the distinction between fantasy and reality. These simulations and imagined scenarios foment fear and paranoid patriotism. At best, embedded reporting gives a peek into the lives of soldiers or civilians in wartime and thereby evokes empathy; but because these slice-of-life reports are presented out of context and interspersed with simulations, commercial advertisements, and entertainment, this empathy is hollow and does not help us to understand the situation or to act on our feelings or knowledge. At worst, visual images from Afghanistan and Iraq continue a long history of the use of visual technologies in colonial pursuits.

In this chapter I examine the desire for live coverage and embedded reporting in terms of its effect on our sense of time and our sense of reality as they play into this colonial enterprise. I argue that live embedded reporting creates a perpetual present that decontextualizes and naturalizes events and thereby closes off the possibility of critical interpretation that is necessary to reflect on the meaning of those events. The perpetual present of broadcast and Internet media contributes to the breakdown of borders between fantasy and reality. I describe how feelings of vulnerability and lack of security result in a defensive form of paranoid patriotism. When fantasy replaces reality and when reality becomes marketable, violence becomes more extreme.

Given that immediately following the terrorist attacks of September 11, one of the most frequently used words was "vulnerable," it is important to reflect on the meaning and effects of vulnerability in relation to violence, particularly since the word most closely following on its heels was "war." In the final chapter I explore the connection between vulnerability and violence to understand why a sense of vulnerability quickly gives way to desire for war. Recently philosophers have embraced vulnerability as constitutive of our humanity. For example, Judith Butler and Julia Kristeva have in different ways taken up the notion of vulnerability to suggest that we need to accept our own vulnerability rather than try to deny it, because disavowing vulnerability is what leads to war. Certainly fantasies that we are invincible and not vulnerable can lead to war. As we will see, however, the notion of vulnerability already includes within it violence: vulnerable means both wounding and wounded. Here I question the notion that violence is constitutive of humanity and suggest instead that it is the ability to overcome violence by moving beyond it that is definitive of humanity.

My meditation on vulnerability begins with an analysis of innocence prompted by Abu Ghraib defendants saying at their trials that they were "just joking" or "just having fun." Apart from their orders and their place in the theatre of war, at another level these young soldiers abused prisoners to amuse themselves. They claimed to be ignorant of Muslim religious practices and to be morally innocent even if they were legally guilty. In chapter 4 I examine this split between moral and legal innocence in terms of a deeper split between bodily sensations and law or meaning in our culture. I analyze some of the ways in which the "black sheep" or "few bad apples" at Abu Ghraib are symptomatic of a part of our culture that valorizes innocence, ignorance, and violence.

My analysis is motivated by the question: What aspects of culture could give rise to young soldiers who abuse, even torture, others for "fun"? I answer this question by focusing on ways in which our society's civil and moral laws cannot give meaning to our emotional lives and embodied existence. Law—taken in the broadest possible sense as that which provides social structure to life—is being reduced to regulations and disciplinary codes that do not give robust meaning to life. They regulate, discipline, and, at the extreme, punish our bodies, but they do not give adequate meaning to bodily pleasures and pains. One outcome of this is the creation of what I call "abysmal individuals," people for whom emotional life is cut off from meaningful articulation; or, in psychoanalytic terms, whose bodily pleasures and pains are cut off from meaningful sublimation. This split *not complete in their senses.* between body and meaning or between emotion and law also plays a role in our attitudes toward legitimate and illegitimate force, and particularly our view of suicide bombers, or "body bombers," as philosopher Adriana Cavarero calls them.

The final chapter is a meditation on what forms of cultural meaning, or lack of meaning, result in the guiltless glee of sexual abuse at Abu Ghraib, on the one hand, and the profound commitment to death on the part of suicide bombers on the other. What cultural contexts make it possible for young men and women to "innocently" abuse prisoners "just for fun"? What cultural contexts make it possible for young women suicide bombers to dedicate their lives to killing themselves and others? And, moreover, why do images of women abusing and killing captivate us so? Moving from an analysis of the rhetoric used to describe these women involved in acts of war to their cultural roles and significance, I examine the pleasure in violence and the passion for death exhibited by these women and their companions in the context of the cultures and technologies that spawn them.

While suicide bombers are different from the Abu Ghraib abusers in many ways, they both participate in and rely on pornographic ways of seeing and trophy-viewing to perpetuate violence. Suicide terrorists rely on media to terrorize. They rely on a pornographic viewing to shock their enemies. They distribute videotaped testimonies of their willingness to "martyr" themselves as trophies of war. Terrorists videotape beheadings for viewing on television and the Internet, again as trophies of their violence. They use television and the Internet to circulate images that seemingly attest to their victory in a war of good against evil, of the godly against the infidel. On both sides violence and war have become media spectacles and media scandals in addition to political practices within a global economy or world history. They are taken out of their context and exploited for their marketability on broadcast and Internet media.

To this extent, the media participates in a pornographic looking that easily leads to trophy-viewing. We make ourselves the heroes of our own story by rendering the vanquished mere objects for our gaze, and they do the same. I suggest an alternative to pornographic looking, what I call "witnessing." Following my development of this notion in an earlier book entitled *Witnessing*, here again I elaborate how the double sense of the word can help us enrich our understanding of what we can see by taking care to attend to the ambiguities of life rather than disavowing them. Witnessing has the double sense of seeing with your own eyes, as in eyewitness, on the one hand, and being witness to something that you cannot see, to something that you can only experience, as in witnessing to the atrocities of war, on the other. The ambiguity of witnessing helps us to bring back the ambiguities of our experience, a kind of transfusion of living back into seeing. Most basically, I emphasize the importance of considering the sociohistorical context of the individuals seen along with their subjective agency, we could even say their spirit. Witnessing, then, requires seeing the sociohistorical situation that leaves the individual where she is, as well as seeing her spirit or agency that might allow her to change that situation. In this regard, witnessing involves attending to the past and to the future as they are related to present circumstances, rather than collapsing both into the perpetual present of most television broadcasts and Internet images.

In conclusion I suggest that witnessing can enrich our conception of freedom. Freedom as reduced to the free market is not complete. Even freedom reduced to the absence of prohibitions is not complete. Without the freedom to create the meaning of one's own life, most especially of one's own body, freedom is empty. Perhaps this is why so many citizens of the "free world" are taking prescription drugs—Prozac, sleeping pills, pain pills—to try to fill a void left by the evacuation of meaning from our lives. Perhaps this is why so many middle-class young people living in the land of the free resort to cutting themselves or playing the "hanging game" in order to feel alive, or, at the other extreme, go on shooting rampages at their local schools. The prevalence of depression, the use of various pharmaceutical drugs, self-injury, and violence among young people all signal the presence of strong emotions lying beneath the surface of our wealth and prosperity, emotions that become destructive when they don't have healthy outlets or alternatives.

The pressures of the free market create fears and desires that remain unarticulated and subterranean precisely because in a significant sense interpretation is antithetical to this flattened notion of freedom. The freedom of the market allows for interpretation only so long as it sells; and within our wealthy democracy the meaning of life is reduced to material wealth rather than wealth of the psyche or soul. Freedom of the psyche, of the soul, thrives on meaning. It is fed by the process of interpretation, which nourishes meaning. To be sure, a hungry body has difficulty feeding a hungry soul, and war is waged in the physical world on bodies, but it is also waged in the symbolic world of meaning. To understand the stakes of the war on terror, we need to interpret its meaning. We need to decipher the meaning of our own investments in violence. To be free, we need to interpret our fears and desires before acting on them. In addition to the political and economic stakes of violence toward ourselves and others are the ethical stakes of creating meaningful life.

The stakes of this book, then, take us beyond the war in Iraq or images of women warriors to considerations of ethics and politics more generally. In a sense, the media presentation of the war in Iraq is a case study through which we may illuminate the ethical and political stakes of particular ideas about our relationships with ourselves and others. The ways that we characterize ourselves and the ways that we characterize our enemies can determine how we respond to real-world political situations. The word "ethics" comes from the Greek word "ethos," which means character or way of life. Our ethos—our character, our way of life—is what we have been told is under attack by terrorists. Yet, what is this ethos? What is our way of life? particularly as it is related to ethics? Today we hear a lot about the "moral majority" and the moral conservatism of Americans. This notion of morality, however, works through ideals of good versus evil that divide people and actions into proper/improper, pure/contaminated, good/evil, etc. As I have argued elsewhere, colonization, oppression, and war justify themselves using morality—but a morality that fills our ethos with aggression and violence. Indeed, we use morality to justify the most extreme forms of violence and to absolve ourselves of responsibility for our actions: we believe that we have a divine right to our way of life and that Providence ordains the elimination of all who may challenge it. How can there be so much killing in the name of moral righteousness—on both sides?

Here, as an outgrowth of analyzing media images of war and determining our own investments in violence, I propose that we think of ethics outside of or beyond moralities of good and evil in order to conceive an ethics based on our fundamental dependence on others and our environment for our very survival and moreover for the possibility of a meaningful life. We must think about ourselves and others as being coinhabitants of one planet, as being part of the same ecosystem, and, more than that, as being first and foremost connected by various dependency relations that sustain us and give life meaning. We are dependent on others and the earth not just for our survival, for our biological life, but also for our quality of life, for our psychic life, for the lives of our souls. Unless we were to reduce our conception of the "good life" to mere goods and services, we must go beyond moral distinctions motivated by politics. Ethics, as conceived here, beyond morality, is not a set of codes that divide people into good and evil, dominant and subordinate, friend and enemy. Ethics is the acknowledgment that we live and flourish only by virtue of our relations with others, many of whom we have never met (the farmers who grow our vegetables, the factory workers who make our shoes, the dock workers who unload our electronics, etc.). And that it is our relationships, both intimate and distant, that give life meaning. In this important sense, how we imagine our relationships with others near and far is a central aspect of global politics.

Winning the "War on Terror"

What would it mean to win the "war on terror"? Would it mean that Americans would never feel threatened or vulnerable again? The Oxford English Dictionary defines terror as "intense fear or dread." Are we then fighting a war on fear? Would winning this war mean that we would never feel intense fear or dread again? Would winning the war against terror thereby eliminate fear and dread from our existence?

If these are the terms by which victory is defined, then the war on terror is impossible to win; and of course there is no winning this war. If not, then the war on terror is actually a war on something else, now wrapped up in the rhetoric of terror. What does the circulation of the phrase "war on terror" suggest? What kind of war are we fighting? And what would it mean to lose the war on terror? Would it, as President Bush suggests, mean that we are enslaved by evil dictators armed with nuclear weapons? The rhetoric of "Winning OR Losing," like the rhetoric of Good OR Evil, suggests that we live in a black-and-white world with no shades of gray: that we are either winner or losers, good or evil; that you are either with us or against us, you are either Us OR Them.

Since Hurricane Katrina, government officials have often spoken of preparations for natural disasters in the same vein as terrorist attacks; in one breath they talk about government agencies' abilities to respond to events like both 9/11 and Katrina. And the Department of Homeland Security has issued guidelines on preparedness for disasters of all kinds; after Katrina, the "Under Secretary for Preparedness" even issued an emergency preparedness brochure for pets. Does this mean that the war on terror extends to natural disasters? After all, how will Americans feel safe and secure in the face of deadly forces of nature such as hurricanes, tornadoes, and floods, which terrorize with the threat of death and destruction?

President Bush is waging a "war on terror." And wouldn't it be great if he could win the war against terror, against fear and dread... Imagine if people throughout the globe were free from terror, from the terror of starvation and disease, from the terror of natural disasters, from the terror of war itself. Obviously this is not the kind of war on terror we are fighting. As much as we hope that our government can take care of us in a natural disaster, it seems absurd to think that it can prevent such an event from happening. And this war is not a war to end starvation, disease, and the terrors of poverty across the globe. We are not really fighting to end terror wherever it exists. So the "war on terror," as it is called, is perhaps a more modest war on terrorists. But the leap from terror or even terrorism to terrorists is huge. In the face of terrorism, even terrorists seem to shrink.

So if our enemy is not actually terror, but terrorists, then this is not a war on terror per se, but rather a war on people who terrorize others by using deadly force. In this case winning the war on terror might mean capturing or killing all people who use deadly force against others. But this conception of terror or terrorism doesn't really get at what we mean by the "war on terror" either, particularly since our own government, military, and civilian prison guards have used and continue to use deadly force, which must in all likelihood terrorize the people affected by it, including innocent civilians. It must be, then, that our enemies in the war on terror use deadly force in certain ways against certain people and that this is what distinguishes their use of force from ours. The administration makes a distinction between legitimate force and illegitimate force; ours is legitimate and theirs is not. Since the word "legitimate" is defined as legal, this is to say that ours is legal but theirs is not. But "legal" according to whom? We say their violence is illegitimate, but they say it is justice.

We say we're right, they're wrong.

In this kind of dispute we might think that the legality of war should be governed by international law, which certainly would condemn terrorism and the brutal attacks of 9/11. For the last several years, however, our government has been engaged in court battles and congressional debates over the applicability of the Geneva Convention and of international law to the war on terror. Attorney General Alberto Gonzales called the Geneva Convention "quaint," suggesting that it is outdated and that its rules don't apply to our current situation. Since we are fighting a war "unlike any we have fought before," the rules that we have used before—even international·law—no longer apply. In addition, the release of pictures of abuse of "detainees" at Abu Ghraib prison in Iraq, along with revelations concerning bizarre interrogation techniques at Guantánamo Bay—including the use of rock music and fake menstrual blood—raised questions about whether the United States military was following international law. There were, and continue to be, debates over what counts as torture and about how to define it. Likewise, there were, and continue to be, debates over what counts as terrorism and about how to define it. Who are terrorists? Are we using legitimate or illegitimate force? The definition of "legitimate force" seems up for grabs.

If we cannot distinguish ourselves from our enemies in terms of deadly force, or even legitimate force, how do we see ourselves in relation to this enemy? On the fifth anniversary of the terrorist attacks of September 11, 2001, President Bush said that "nineteen men attacked us with a *barbarity unequaled in our history*. They murdered people of all colors, creeds and nationalities, and made war upon *the entire free world*. Since that day, America and her allies have taken the offensive in *a war unlike any* we have fought before… On 9/11, our nation saw *the face of evil*" (my emphases). Our enemy, then, is evil itself. In the words of President Bush, our enemies "are evil and kill without mercy"; they "hate freedom" and plan to attack "civilized nations," thereby waging "war upon the entire free world." He describes the war on terror as "a struggle for civilization" itself. The war against terror, then, seems to be a war against barbarians who oppose civilization. It is the fight of Good against Evil, of freedom against tyranny, of mercy against hatred.

Leaving aside the fact that for those entering this realm of ideology, one man's poison is another man's nourishment, what would it mean to win the fight of good against evil, the fight for civilization? President Bush lays out the stakes as all or nothing: either we emerge victorious "or the extremists emerge victorious," "you are [either] with us or against us." Does that mean that either we win and thereby rule the world, and as Bush says bring democracy to the globe; or we lose, and are then enslaved or killed by terrorists who will rule the world and bring what the administration has called "Islamic fascism" to us all? Can we even imagine a triumph or defeat as grand as this, except perhaps in a James Bond movie?[4] Could the United States ever control terrorists across the globe to such an extent that no one would ever be threatened by them again? Could extremists really take over America and make us slaves to what Bush calls "a perverted vision of Islam"?

If the war on terror is a war against the forces of evil that kill without mercy, then what would it mean to win this war? Either it means eliminating terror from human existence, or at least from the lives of Americans, or else the war on terror is really not a war on terror at all, but something else. If the war on terror truly aims to eliminate fear and dread from our lives then it is impossible to win this war. Even if the aim of the war is restricted to eliminating the fear or dread of terrorist attacks, how can we wage war against a mental state? This war is not like any other because it is a war that we cannot even imagine winning. What would it mean to defeat evil itself?

Part of the difficulty in imagining winning this war is that the stakes have been raised so high: civilization itself is supposedly in danger. The hyperbolic rhetoric of good versus evil, freedom versus tyranny, is not new to this conflict. And it is used by both sides. The above exercise in imagination, however, has made it apparent that whatever else the war on terror is about, it is also an ideological war over beliefs and values, over what counts as freedom, justice, good, evil, torture, and terrorism. Even the idea that we are "at war" seems peculiar given the nature of our enemy and the ways in which we have gone about "hunting them down." The military campaign includes a massive public relations mission to drop pamphlets over Iraq and Afghanistan that urge people not to resist but to embrace democracy—a clear indication that part of this war is being fought through media; but pamphlets are on the low end of the technologies involved in the media campaign. On our side, the government and military have tried to control what images of war we see; the administration and the Pentagon even control images of coffins and combat.

Moreover, according to U.S. intelligence agencies, our means of waging this war on terror have actually increased the threat of terrorism by causing a rise in "global Islamic radicalism" that has "metastasized and spread across the globe."[5] We talk as if terrorism is a disease out of control,

The idea is being blown up creating a bigger problem for everyone

a disease that we can fight with our surgical strikes, but a disease that we can never conquer, because in our war on terror we are in fact creating terrorists. The cure is spreading the disease. But not only are we creating our own enemy by fueling the "Global Jihadist" movement, we are creating an image of our enemy as bigger than life, a menacing image that possibly exaggerates their power—a move that they endorse. In addition, we are moving the theatre of war from Iraq to the entire globe. War everywhere at once. War without any foreseeable end. As President Bush says, "We are now in the early hours of this struggle between tyranny and freedom." If these are the early hours, when will dawn break? When can we expect the much-touted victory of freedom over tyranny? How can the terror of war defeat the terror of terrorism? How can more violence beget peace?

The all-encompassing rhetoric of "forces of evil wherever they lurk" should make us wonder what this war is really about. The 9/11 terrorists are dead. We are hunting down their accomplices. But there must be more to this endless war than revenge for 9/11. Even President Bush now admits that Saddam Hussein and Iraq had nothing to do with the attacks on the Twin Towers. Still, Bush repeatedly says that this is a war to maintain our lifestyle and to secure our prosperity. This suggests that there are economic motives for war. Certainly war can be profitable not only for military contractors but also for government contractors who rebuild the infrastructures we destroy. The strong rhetoric on both sides clouds material and economic issues with self-righteous attributions of good and evil, the Faithful and the Infidels, the Godly and the Damned. Both sides talk as if they see the world in simple black-and-white without any of shades of gray. The rhetoric of war is absolute; it is extreme; it admits no ambiguity. It is all or nothing; us or them; we are winners or losers. And yet this type of hyperbolic rhetoric is both overly simplistic and dangerous. It is a worldview that pits one side against another in a deadly battle without end, particularly since it is a battle for mental as much as for physical territory. How do we measure the conquest of minds, or souls, in the war against terror? What constitutes a triumph in the battle for civilization?

financial motives to the war

The rhetoric of extremes—good or evil, freedom or tyranny, civilized or barbaric, winners or losers—obscures the ambiguities inherent in life itself. There is no absolute good or freedom in a war where violent means necessarily contaminate even the most idealistic ends. Moreover, seeing the world in terms of winners and losers is a deadly game that perpetuates the violence of some against others indefinitely. That kind of game needs an enemy and even creates one if necessary. Within the logic of good versus evil we are bound to an eternal war, a holy war, a war without end. The space and time of this war become infinite because our enemy is infinite. And in a world divided into us versus them, our notion of ourselves as a nation, as a people, as free and good, becomes dependent upon finding a "them" against whom we can fight. The war against terror imagined as a war of good against evil creates enemies everywhere; the very ambiguities of life raise the specter of the enemy.

This book is a reflection on the deeper cultural significance of rhetoric and metaphors that continue to circulate through the media around the war on terror, especially as it involves women and sex. It is also a meditation on techniques used in current television broadcasts and Internet postings that affect our ability to critically interpret the meaning of this rhetoric and of events themselves. Although the facts of war are relevant to this discussion, my focus is on the way in which those facts appear within the media and the ways in which they circulate through the popular imaginary. How are facts represented and interpreted? This book is a meditation on the meaning of representations of violence in the war on terror. Media images do not give us direct access to the events as they are in themselves. Rather, the media is, as its name implies, a medium through which events are re-presented in particular ways. The meaning of an event or an image is not something that lies behind its appearance, waiting and eager to be revealed. Rather, meaning is produced and reproduced in our relationships with events and images. By interpreting the meaning of narrative and visual images of war, we can learn something about our relationship to this war, and to war and violence more generally. Surprisingly perhaps, in the case of this war we also learn something about our relationship to women and sex.

By working to interpret images from Iraq and Afghanistan, we can begin to understand how we imagine ourselves and others. What initially seemed to be isolated incidents of violence can be seen as symptomatic of a culture of violence and death connected with sex. In a war about conquering and securing the symbolic landscape as much as the physical landscape, it is important to examine the war on terror in terms of both its symbolism and its material impact. Life is never black-and-white, but full color. On "our side," across the country, debates in courts and congressional houses, mournful tears for fallen soldiers in small-town funeral parlors, and shouts of peace protesters continue to bring out shades of gray. The ambiguities of experience continue to needle the extreme rhetoric of war. The terror of war itself is becoming one of the greatest obstacles to the war on terror. Maybe the Good war is not so good—think of the tens of thousands of Iraqi civilians killed; maybe the good guys also behave badly—think of the misconduct by soldiers who have reportedly raped and killed civilians in cold blood and abused, even tortured, prisoners of war. And maybe these good guys aren't even *guys*, but girls ...

Women—The Secret Weapon of Modern Warfare?

The figures and faces from wars in the Middle East that continue to haunt us at the beginning of the twenty-first century are those of women: think of the Palestinian women suicide bombers, starting with Wafa Idris in January 2002; or the capture and rescue of Pfc. Jessica Lynch early in the U.S. invasion of Iraq just over a year later; or the shocking images of Pfc. Lynndie England and Army Spc. Sabrina Harman at the Abu Ghraib prison the following spring. These images and stories horrify yet fascinate us because they show young women killing and torturing. Their stories as they have circulated through the U.S. media create a sense of shock and confusion evidenced by various conflicting accounts of what it means for women to wage war. They have both galvanized and confounded debates over feminism and women's equality. And, as reported in the media, tellings of their stories share, perhaps more subliminally, an ambivalence toward women, who are figured once again as dangerous; and now they are represented as both offensive and defensive weapons of war, a notion that is symptomatic of age-old fears of the "mysterious" powers of women, maternity, and female sexuality. Even as the presence of women in the military seems to signal their "liberation" from patriarchal traditions, the rhetoric surrounding their involvement betrays the lingering association between women, sexuality, and death. We might think that we have moved beyond these questionable images of women, but media representations of women's recent role in warfare tell us otherwise.

In the past, American women served behind the front lines as nurses in Korea and Vietnam, and women even ferried warplanes in World War II. But the idea of women soldiers working in combat zones is new to the American public. Technically, these women are assigned to supply carriers and military support troops. But given the absence of well-defined "enemy lines" in Iraq, however, women regularly confront combat situations. Women have been active warriors in other countries. For example, some Nazi women became infamous for their torture and abuses of Jewish concentration camp prisoners; Ilse Koch, called the "Bitch of Buchenwald," was known for riding the camps on horseback looking for interesting tattoos on prisoners that she could turn into lamp-shades made from human skin.[1] Women also served in the Soviet army in World War II. Reportedly, memoirs of German soldiers suggest that they feared the Russian women more than the men, and that they refused to surrender to them for fear of the consequences. And during Pinochet's regime in Chile some detainees reported that "among the torturers 'the women were the worst.'"[2] Recounting such tales, Scott Johnson concludes that "such stories rekindle images of Amazons, and the myth of women even more savage than the most savage men."[3] While women are obviously capable of the most heinous abuse and torture, this myth of women more savage than men continues today with the stories of women torturers and women interrogators in Iraq.[4]

The most uncanny images from the U.S. occupation of Iraq are those of women engaging in abuse. Although these images of teenage women who smile while abusing prisoners at Abu Ghraib are shocking, they are also somewhat familiar to us as the result of centuries of literature, philosophy, history, religion, and, more recently, film and television in which women have been imagined as dangerous, particularly in terms of their sexuality. By now the virgin-whore dichotomy setup within cultures that historically have excluded female bodies from the properly social or political realm is well known. Women have been figured as either innocent virgins or dirty whores; and in fantasies one easily morphs into the other... the virgin uses her innocence to trap and betray, the whore with the heart of gold saves the jaded man from his humdrum life.

In the case of Abu Ghraib, we see seemingly innocent girls gleefully torturing men. The images are uncanny precisely because they conjure both the strange and the familiar, or perhaps here we could say the familiar within the strange. In his essay "The Uncanny," Sigmund Freud describes the uncanny as *unheimlich,* which means both at home and not at home. Things that are uncanny have a double nature: a familiar face that hides a mysterious danger, or the evil villain who is somehow familiar. The double, or doppelganger, both is and is not what s/he seems. It is this ambiguity between good and evil that makes us uneasy. To Freud, the most uncanny figure is that of the mother because she is associated with both life and death, with both plenitude or nourishment and threats of withholding nourishment.[5] For Freud, the life-giving power of the mother is the uncanny double of her death threat.

Significantly, Freud's analysis of one of his own dreams in *The Interpretation of Dreams* makes this connection. In the "Three Fates," after going to bed tired and hungry, Freud dreams of a woman in a kitchen. She is making dumplings and tells him that he will have to wait; he is impatient and tries to put on his overcoat to leave, but the coat is too long, with strange fur trim and embroidery, and seems to belong to another man. In his analysis of the dream, Freud identifies the woman making dumplings with his mother. His dream appears to him as the wish fulfillment of the basic need for food and love, which he claims come together in the mother's breast. In his analysis, however, no sooner is the maternal figure in his dream associated with love and nourishment than she becomes a messenger of death. Freud associates the dumpling-making hand motion with an experience from his childhood when his mother taught him that everyone dies and returns to the earth by rubbing her hands together as if making dumplings to show him the "blackish scales of *epidermis* produced by the friction as a proof that we are made of earth."[6] Not only in Freud's dream, but also within patriarchal culture more generally, the mother is the symbol of life-giving nourishment (dumplings), but also of the inevitability of death and returning to the (mother) earth.

The woman in Freud's dream might be interpreted using another one of his works, "The Theme of the Three Caskets," in which Freud talks about the appearance of three beautiful women connected to choice and death in literature and myth, as the three faces of woman—birth, sex, and death—that ultimately belong to the mother: "We might argue that what is represented here are the three inevitable relations that a man has with a woman—the woman who bears him, the woman who is his mate and the woman who destroys him; or that they are the three forms taken by the figure of the mother in the course of a man's life—the mother herself, the beloved one who is chosen after her pattern, and lastly the Mother Earth who receives him once more. But it is in vain that an old man yearns for the love of woman as he had it first from his mother; the third of the Fates alone, the silent Goddess of Death, will take him into her arms."[7] Birth, sex, and death are condensed into the figure of woman, specifically the Mother as a triple and ultimate threat. In important ways, Freud's views of women are symptomatic of his culture's views of women more generally.

Today, Freud's theories about women seem outdated, even sexist. But recent representations of women as weapons of war suggests that the associations between women, sex, and death are as powerful as ever. In this chapter I will examine the ways in which women are figured as both offensive and defensive weapons of war. In the case of the Abu Ghraib and Guantánamo Bay prisons in particular, women have been identified with sex and their sexuality has not only been figured as a weapon in the media but also explicitly used as a weapon by the military. According to some commentators, just the presence of women in the army naturally turns the scene into a sexual orgy. And the supposed power of that so-called dangerous natural sexuality can be harnessed by the military to "break" and "soften up" recalcitrant prisoners. The use of fake menstrual blood in the interrogation of prisoners at Guantánamo Bay is especially telling. Patriarchal cultures have traditionally regarded menstrual blood as unclean and disgusting. Now the imagined abject power of menstrual blood is being used as a weapon of war. It is not just that we suppose that our Muslim prisoners will think that they are unclean by exposure to menstrual blood, but also that within our own culture and the rhetoric of the soldiers and media reporting these incidents, menstrual blood is seen as unclean and grotesque. Freud's analysis of the uncanny effects of the mother and the female genitals or sex in may help explain our ambivalence toward menstrual blood, linked as it is both to life and life-giving powers and to fear, perhaps even fear of death. And it may help diagnose why and how female sexuality and the presence of women could be conceived of and used by the military as an interrogation tactic.

In this chapter I will examine various ways in which women involved in war in the Middle East have been imagined as dangerous weapons linked with death. Insofar as for centuries women and female sex and sexuality have been figured as dangerous and deadly, it should not surprise us now that women are associated with some of the most outrageous horrors of war. What makes women's involvement in war—from Abu Ghraib and

Guantánamo Bay to Palestinian suicide bombings—uncanny is a continued ambivalence toward women and female sexuality. The difficulty that
we have in comprehending that these girls-next-door can be so violent has
everything to do with stereotypes of femininity and female sexuality. Along
with the ambivalence toward women manifest in metaphors of women
as weapons comes an ambivalence toward feminism, which is simultaneously blamed for unleashing these man-hating aggressive harpies and put
forward as a justification for invading and occupying Muslim countries
to liberate women. Like the associations between women and death, this
selective appropriation of feminism and women's liberation and equality
also has a long history, and has been part and parcel of colonial enterprises for centuries.

Feminism Is Torture

Syndicated columnist Kathleen Parker suggests that the prison abuses at
Abu Ghraib are the result of what she calls the "myth of gender equality."[8]
Indeed, the photographs of women's involvement in torture and sexual
abuse at Abu Ghraib rekindled debates over whether women should be in
the military and debates over gender equality. They also prompted a debate
over the role of *feminism* not only in response to the photos, but also in the
abuses themselves. Writers on both sides of the feminist divide implicate
feminism in women's criminal behavior at Abu Ghraib. For example, on
the antifeminist side, *MensNewsDaily.com* suggests that women's sadism is
not only responsible for Abu Ghraib but also the norm: "all of the females
implicated at Abu Ghraib will have little trouble finding jobs in the mul-
tibillion-dollar VAWA (Violence Against Women Act) domestic violence
industry, just as soon as 'American, gender feminist justice' rationalizes
away all their misbehavior."[9] A columnist for the *American Spectator* argues
that the abuse at Abu Ghraib "is a cultural outgrowth of a feminist culture
which encourages female barbarians."[10] Some conservative journalists have
blamed the torture on the women's feminist sensibilities, arguing that the
abusers resented the Islamic attitude of men toward women and therefore
enjoyed what they took to be their feminist revenge on the prisoners.[11]

While conservatives blame feminism for the brutality at Abu Ghraib, even
some feminists associate advances made by the women's movement with
the abuse. For example, columnist Joanne Black concludes: "Throughout

[handwritten margin note: women being equal to men has created more confidence of violence]

history, when they have had the chance, women have shown themselves as capable as men of misusing power and inflicting brutality. They have, till now, merely lacked the opportunity. Feminism has remedied that. Sadly for those of us who thought we were better, women have proved themselves men's equal."[12] Brooke Warner blames a postfeminism world in which "young American women" have "a certain I-deserve-it attitude." She claims that "brashness, confidence, and selfishness are norms" and that "American military culture promotes these values as much as the university system, though it manifests itself as physical rather than intellectual prowess."[13] Feminism, then, is implicated in the abuse by both sides for having given women opportunities equal to men's and for making them more confident— to the point that feminism has created violent women.

Some feminist scholars and journalists explain the abuse by pointing to women's marginal place in the male-dominated military, which not only makes it more likely that they will follow orders and try to fit in, but also that they will be scapegoated and held up as representatives of all of their sex, which seems to be true of the three women indicted as portrayed in the press. Conservatives, on the other hand, argue that coed basic training is responsible for what one commentator calls the "whorehouse behavior" at Abu Ghraib.[14] The same commentator asks if police soldiers at Abu Ghraib were weak in basic operational skills "because 10 years ago, for political reasons, politicians and feminist activists within the ranks established coed basic training to promote the fiction that men and women are the same and putting young women in close quarters with young men would some-how not trigger *natural* biological urges?" [my emphasis].[15]

[handwritten margin note: Photos are similar to porn — confused on how to classify]

Much of the conservative commentary surrounding the Abu Ghraib abuse has explicitly or implicitly associated women and sex. Explicitly, we see comments on women triggering men's sexual urges and the presence of women leading to "whorehouse behavior." But, as Susan Sontag points out, these images of women smiling while engaging in sexual abuse and sadistic torture are subliminally familiar from the S&M porn industry, which is booming on the Internet and popular with soldiers, and which tra-ditionally puts women in the role of dominatrix.[16] Feminists have argued for decades that the prevalence of pornography promotes violent images of sex and desensitizes us to sexual violence. Perhaps desensitization to this type of sexual violence is part of why at first human rights groups were not sure how to categorize the abuse.

Gender stereotypes also play a role in the confusion regarding these images: not just because women are the abusers but also because men are the ones being sexually abused. It is important to note that the men in question are racialized men being abused by white women. Of course, we know that female Iraqi prisoners are also sexually abused and raped, but that is so much business as usual that it does not capture our imaginations in the way that images of women sexually abusing men does. It makes us wonder: How can a man be raped by a woman? How can a man be forced to perform, and thereby seemingly be an agent of, sex acts? These questions point to our assumptions about desire, sex, and gender. And it is these gender stereotypes that make the smiling faces of Lynndie England and Sabrina Harman so "abject"—both terrifying and repulsive and at the same time fascinating and captivating. Psychoanalyst Julia Kristeva characterizes the abject as something that calls into question borders; it threatens by means of an ambiguity that cannot be categorized. Yet it is precisely this ominous ambiguity that draws us to the abject. Like noticing road kill on the side of the highway while driving, we look at it in spite of ourselves. This is our reaction to the photographs from Abu Ghraib: We are repulsed by them, but we can't help but look. We are appalled, but we want to see more. And the photographs that are the most uncanny, the most difficult to categorize, are those of women engaging in abuse while smiling for the camera.

Female Sexuality as Tactic

Reportedly gender also plays a role in the abuse itself. Some journalists claim that women were used as "lethal weapons" against Iraqi male prisoners. In the words of a *Baltimore Sun* reporter, "forcing men in a fundamentalist Muslim culture to parade naked (let alone feign sex acts) in the presence of women was conceived as an especially lethal brand of humiliation."[17] This report suggests that the presence of women in the Abu Ghraib prison allowed for even more humiliating forms of abuse supposedly used to "soften up" prisoners before interrogation. Because of their "sex" and its seemingly "natural" effect on men, women become the means to compound not only sexual and physical abuse but also abuse of religious and cultural beliefs.

The presence of women also has the effect of "softening up" torture itself and making it more palatable to the American public. Just as the rhetoric of liberating Afghan women made the invasion more palatable to the American public, so too highlighting women's involvement in at Abu Ghraib and Guantánamo helps redefine torture as abuse, misconduct, perversion, "whorehouse behavior," or "pranks" and "letting off steam," as Rush Limbaugh called it. Crime outlawed by Geneva Convention regulations against torture was redefined as "legitimate force" in the war against terrorism. Secretary of Defense Donald Rumsfeld said of the abuses at Abu Ghraib: "I'm not a lawyer, but I know it's not torture—probably abuse." And White House and Defense Department lawyers "redefined the meaning of torture and extended the limits of permissible pain."[18] One effect of women's involvement in abuse designed to "soften up" the prisoners is to "soften up" public perceptions of torture. Late-night television and the Internet showed a popular response to reports of women disrobing to interrogate prisoners at Guantánamo: men wished that women would abuse them like that!

Playing on traditional associations between women and poison, but now in the context of war, *New York Times* columnist Maureen Dowd calls this a "toxic combination of sex and religion."[19] This "toxic combination" actually seems to be part of the military's interrogation strategy in Guantánamo Bay, where hundreds of prisoners from Afghanistan and elsewhere have been held for over four years now. In his book *Inside the Wire* (written with Viveca Novak), army sergeant Erik Saar, who worked as a translator at Guantánamo Bay prison, describes various "interrogation" techniques used there that he says compromised the Geneva Convention. But one session in particular caught the public's attention: a midnight session in which a female army interrogator unbuttoned her uniform "almost like a stripper," rubbed "her breasts against" the prisoner's back, and then later "placed her hands in her pants" and wiped fake menstrual blood on the prisoner's face.[20] Saar remarks that "had someone come to me before I left for Gitmo and told me that we would use women to sexually torment detainees in interrogations to try to sever their relationships with God, I probably would have thought that sounded fine.... But I hated myself when I walked out of that room, even though I was pretty sure we were talking to a piece of shit in there."[21] What does it mean when the "enemy" is characterized as shit and menstrual blood is used as a weapon of war?

In January 2005, before the publication of the book, nine pages of Saar's manuscript held by the Pentagon were leaked to the press. The pages describe female interrogators using "sexual touching," "provocative clothing" (including miniskirts, bras, and thong underwear), and "fake menstrual blood" to "break" Muslim prisoners by making them unclean and therefore "unworthy to pray." The pages were accompanied by a letter from Guantánamo officials, in which they marked for deletion a section describing a Saudi prisoner whose face was smeared with red ink pulled from the pants of his female interrogator, who told him it was menstrual blood. The officials marked the section SECRET, advising the Pentagon that it revealed "interrogation methods and techniques that were classified."[22]

Can we conclude from this then that menstrual blood has acquired a role in war, as part of a top-secret interrogation technique? As bizarre as this seems, in a way it should be no surprise, since within patriarchal cultures of all varieties menstrual blood represents the abject and unclean. Perhaps menstrual blood is imagined as threatening because it provokes fears of women's procreative powers, the power of life that can never be completely controlled by men (or women). Kristeva suggests that within Western culture menstrual blood conjures the maternal body as an uncanny border and ultimate threat to individual autonomy. As she describes it, the maternal body is the ultimate abject because of the infant's ambiguous connection to it and difficulty separating from it; the infant, particularly the male, finds the maternal body both threatening and fascinating, which is why he imagines both possessing it and destroying it.[23] Even within Western cultures that consider themselves "liberated," menstrual blood is not commonly considered an appropriate topic for art or conversation. Menstrual blood is shocking, and popular culture typically avoids it altogether. The "South Park" movie, in which one male character says to another, "There is something wrong with an animal that bleeds for five days and doesn't die," is a telling exception.

In an interview, philosopher Angela Davis challenged the notion that these forms of abuse are specifically designed to violate cultural taboos of Muslim men: "I am always suspicious when culture is deployed as a strategy or an answer, because culture is so much more complicated. The apparent cultured explanation of these forms of abuse reveals a very trivial notion of culture. Why is it assumed that a non-Muslim man approached by a female interrogator dressed as a dominatrix, attempting to smear menstrual blood on him, would react any differently from a Muslim man? These assumptions about culture are themselves racist."[24] Even Erik Saar's somewhat self-congratulatory account of his disapproval of army interrogation

[handwritten margin note: Menstrual blood is uncontrollable. Part of nature, nothing more]

techniques suggests that the invocation of menstrual blood—more than any other "technique" he describes—made him feel "unclean." He describes taking a shower after the session: "There wasn't enough hot water in all of Cuba to make me feel clean.... I sat down in our filthy tub and let the hot water hit my head and the steam thicken the air as I cried. I sat there for half an hour. When I finally lay down in bed, I just stared at the ceiling. Sleep kept being chased away by shame."[25] In his account of his participation in various abuses at Guantánamo, this is the only time that Saar mentions feeling unclean and crying. Saar took the shower that the female interrogator threatened would be denied the prisoner. Even as he reports his horror at the use of fake menstrual blood as an interrogation tactic, Saar's account makes manifest his own disgust not just at the military but also at the specter of menstrual blood.

Although late-night television had a heyday with jokes about thong-clad women interrogators "torturing" male prisoners, the fake menstrual blood didn't quite fit with the S&M fantasy of the dominatrix. For example, on his Web site, Nkrumah Shabazz Steward says in "I'm Juxtaposing," "Ok, I was getting into it before we got to the menstrual blood. Up until that point it was sounding like a damn lap dance.... I can't help it. I am a guy... I guess I have to admit to myself that I am sorta into that whole 'women with power thing' because this thing sounds like fun to me."[26] Although in the popular imaginary menstrual blood is not alone in the category of "gross" bodily fluids, you still don't see it showing up in Hollywood films that are filled with vomit, semen jokes, and toilet scenes (if it did, imagine the transformation in *Something About Mary*'s special "hair-gel"). The military's use of pretend menstrual blood in interrogation makes apparent the imagined threat of menstruation in patriarchal cultures, most particularly ours. The imagined threat is made explicit when menstrual blood becomes part of the arsenal of "sexual tactics" used by the military.

Saar describes the U.S. military "us[ing] women as part of tougher physical and psychological interrogation tactics to get terrorist suspects to talk."[27] One of the officers in charge of the prison, Lt. Col. James Marshall, refused to say whether the U.S. military intentionally used women as part of their tactical strategy. But according to a document classified as secret and obtained by the Associated Press, the military uses "an all-female team as one of the Immediate Reaction Force units that subdue troublesome male prisoners in their cells."[28] The FBI also has complained about the "sexual tactics" used by female interrogators. Reportedly, "some

Guantánamo prisoners who have been released say they were tormented by 'prostitutes.' "[29]

When this story first broke, and until months later, little media attention was given to the sexual and religious abuse in Guantánamo, aside from the Associated Press release by Paisley Dodds. What there was, however, is instructive, with its characterization of the abuse as "women us[ing] sex to get detainees to talk," "women us[ing] lechery as an interrogating tactic," "sexually loaded torment by female interrogators," and " the use of female sexuality as a tactic."[30] The head-note of an article in *Time* magazine reads: "New reports of detainee abuse at Gitmo suggest interrogators used female sexuality as a weapon."[31] The rhetoric of women as weapons is even more explicit in reports of Guantánamo than in the reports of Abu Ghraib. It is telling that the media continues to associate women and sex, going so far as to say that female sexuality itself is a weapon. Here, sexualized interrogation tactics become metonymical substitutes for all of female sexuality. And female sexuality is reduced to a tactic or strategy to "break" men, a threatening weapon that can be used against even the most resistant men.

This condensation between interrogation tactic, weapon of war, using sex, and female sexuality reveals a long-standing fear of women and female sexuality that has been evidenced in literary, scientific, and popular discourses of Western culture for centuries. Indeed, it is the familiarity of the association of women and their sex with torment and deadly threats that makes these reports so uncanny. The association of female sexuality and danger recalls Freud's account of the fear of castration supposedly evoked in males by the sight of female genitals. For Freud, female genitalia not only make visible and concrete the threat of castration but also the threat of death; maternal sex in particular is imagined as both life-giving and devouring, and therefore uncanny; that is to say, both shocking and yet familiar.[32]

The photographs from Abu Ghraib and the reports from Guantánamo of women torturing men with sex are shocking and yet familiar to us from Hollywood images of the femme fatale seducing men and driving them to their deaths. They are familiar from pornographic images of the sadistic dominatrix wielding a whip or leash, and her Hollywood counterparts Cat-woman, Electra, and Charlie's Angels, pseudo-feminist avengers who use sex and violence to entrap and kill men. Although the image of the feminist superhero getting revenge against the men who dominated her may be relatively recent, the image of female sexuality as potent and deadly as the black widow spider's has been part of our cultural imaginary for centuries—think of mythological characters such as Medusa and Jocasta or biblical figures such as Salome, Delilah, and Judith.

In the rhetoric surrounding Abu Ghraib and Guantánamo, it seems that what the media describes as a "toxic cocktail" is two parts female sexuality and one part the feminism that unleashed it, with a religious twist that makes it particularly uncanny. Female sexuality can be used to contaminate and make impure because it is seen as impure, not just within conservative Islam (as represented in Western media) but also within the U.S. military and the American cultural imaginary more generally. Within popular cultural representations from Hollywood to commercial advertising, female sexuality is represented as abject, both terrifying and fascinating at the same time; like the Abu Ghraib photographs, it is uncanny, shocking, yet we can't take our eyes off of it.

Susan Sontag argues at the same time that they make us ashamed, there is a shameless quality to the photographs: "Soldiers now pose, thumbs up, before the atrocities they commit, and send off the pictures to their buddies. Secrets of private life that, formerly, you would have given nearly anything to conceal, you now clamor to be invited on a television show to reveal. What is illustrated by these photographs is as much the culture of shamelessness as the reigning admiration for unapologetic brutality."[33] As we will see, this shamelessness and the seemingly innocent, even gleeful, way that young soldiers engaged in abuse is part and parcel of a culture that valorizes naiveté. Presumably there has been all kinds of abuse performed by male guards on both male and female prisoners at Abu Ghraib and other U.S. prisons, but the photos that have captured our imagination are those of women engaging in sexualized abuse. The one exception is the photograph of the hooded Abu Ghraib prisoner standing on a box, arms out, attached to electrical wires, which conjures the image of Christ's crucifixion. In contrast, Dana Cloud suggests that "the image of a hooded Iraqi standing on a crate, holding wires he was told would electrocute him if he fell, seem to mimic images of veiled women in Afghanistan."[34]

As Sontag insists, "The photographs are us." Not primarily, as she would have it, because we are shameless and admire brutality, but rather because women, and particularly female sexuality, are represented as abject and threatening. It is the association between women, sex, and violence that make these images an uncanny reflection of our culture. In addition, if the photographs "are us," as Sontag maintains, it is not just because they are images of "the girl next door" engaging in abuse; and it is not primarily, as she suggests, because these young people are constantly exposed to the violence and sadomasochistic pornography prevalent on the Internet. Rather, it is because these young soldiers are part of a history with deep roots in racism and sexism that at once eroticize and abject female, black, and brown bodies. In the words of Hazel Carby:

> The young soldiers in the Abu Ghraib photos resemble high-school kids on their first trip abroad, smiling self-consciously while announcing to the natives that they have arrived, assuring themselves of their superiority and their right to dominate while saying "hi" to mom back home. They could be American tourists in a fantasyland where eroticized bodies become the conduit for expressing and acting upon racist desires that can be fully realized only in the contact zones of the other. But to assume such apparent innocence would be a mistake, for the invaders have created, and reinforced time and again in popular texts, the image of peoples they expected to find.[35]

While Carby insightfully addresses the racism inherent in the actions and images from Abu Ghraib, she does not acknowledge the sexism that informs the role and images of women in these photographs. As we have seen, stereotypes of women as inherently sexual and dangerous play into and set up both the events themselves and how we interpret them. As for the "apparent innocence" of these young soldiers, this too is complicated by the meaning and valuation of innocence in contemporary American culture, a topic to which I return in the last chapter.

Equal Opportunity Killers, "More Deadly Than the Male"

In reports of women's involvement in abuse, there is a telling ambiguity between the rhetoric of tactic, technique, and weaponry and the rhetoric of natural biological urges and female sexuality. Implicit in this discourse is the notion that women's sex is an especially lethal weapon because it is *natural*. Within popular discourse, women's bodies, menstrual blood, and female sexuality can be used as tactics of war because of the potency of their association with the danger of nature, of mother-nature, if you will. Akin to a natural toxin or intoxicant, women's sex makes a powerful weapon because, within our cultural imaginary, it is *by nature* dangerous. Yet it becomes more threatening because we imagine that it can be wielded by women to manipulate men; it can become the art of seduction through which women beguile and intoxicate to control and even destroy men— think again of Hollywood's femme fatale.

The condensation between the rhetoric of technology and of nature in the construction of woman as weapon is even more dramatic in the British and American media reports of Palestinian women suicide bombers. A news story in the London *Sunday Times* describing the frequency of suicide bombings by Palestinian women begins: "They are anonymous in veils, but when they go out to kill they may be disguised with a ponytail and a pretty smile.... Israel's new nightmare: female suicide-bombers more deadly than the male"; the reporter goes on to call them Palestine's "secret weapon," and says that their trainers describe them as the new "Palestinian human precision bombs."[36] One Islamic Jihad commander reportedly explains, "We discovered that our women could be an advantage and one that could be utilized.... [women's bodies have] become our most potent weapon."[37] In this report, women's bodies are described as "secret weapons," "potent weapons," "human precision bombs," and the means to fight a war machine. The image of the human precision bomb again combines the rhetoric of technology and of nature to produce what the *Times* calls "female suicide-bombers more deadly than the male." This tension between technology and nature, bombs and bodies, is explosive. These women suicide bombers make manifest this tension insofar as they bring the repressed female and maternal body back into politics. Their bodies appear as the uncanny double: body and weapon.

Like the women involved in Abu Ghraib, the *shahidas*, or female martyrs, not only unsettle assumptions about gender but also make manifest age-old associations between women and death. Images of pretty young nineteen- and twenty-year-old women torturing or killing themselves transfix us with their juxtaposition of life and death, beauty and the grotesque. Compare what the *Times* calls their "ponytails" and "pretty smiles" to descriptions of Sabrina Harman's "cheerleader's smile" or Lynndie England's "perky grin" and "pixy" haircut.[38] If the images of these American women conjure fun-loving girls—"America's sweetheart" or "cheerleaders"— the images of Palestinian *shahidas* portray them as tragic rather than comic, more masochistic than sadistic, sadly beautiful rather than perky. Within Palestinian communities the *shahidas* are reportedly described as beautiful, pure, and self-sacrificing; their images are printed on posters and pocket-sized icons to be idolized. While the American interrogators are portrayed as prostitutes or whores, the Palestinian *shahidas* are portrayed as virgins. Again, we see the age-old dichotomy: women portrayed as virgins or as whores, but in either case dangerous.

Like the women abusers, these women killers leave us with the stinging question of how our ideals of youth and femininity, or girls and women, can be reconciled with such brutality. Yet our bewilderment, confusion, and indignation, as evidenced in the rhetoric of popular media, are symptoms of the "return of the repressed." For centuries women have been associated with both beauty and the grotesque; within the history of our literature, philosophy, and medicine they have occupied both the position of virgin and of whore. They have been portrayed as using sex as a weapon of seduction that is figured as all the more deadly because of its connection to nature. In a sense we have always imaged girls' ponytails, haircuts, and smiles as dangerous lures.

Speaking perhaps to a deep-seated stereotype or a biological fact that has repercussions for our emotional lives, in her book *Army of Roses: Inside the World of Palestinian Women Suicide Bombers*, Barbara Victor laments that "the most mysterious aspect of the cult of death that has permeated Palestinian society, especially when it comes to shahida, is the transition that each woman makes from bearer of life to killing machine."[39] Victor's rhetoric of transformation from "bearer of life to killing machine" repeats the slide from nature to technology that makes images of these women so uncanny. She is mystified at how bearers of life become killing machines; yet the association between the mother and death seems central to a patriarchal imaginary within which the life-bearing power of women is precisely what makes them so dangerous, not to mention so mysterious. According to Victor's account, most of these women, caught between two cultures, belonging to neither, have few options for gaining recognition and acceptance.

Reportedly the actions of women suicide bombers has lead several Islamic clerics to proclaim that women, like men, can reach paradise as martyrs despite earlier beliefs that women could not be holy martyrs. Training women from conservative religious groups, however, requires loosening restrictions on their freedom of movement and contact with men outside of their families. It also means changing regulations on what they wear and on showing their bodies, which are not permitted to be seen by men even in death.[40] After nineteen-year-old Hiba Darahmeh blew herself up on behalf of Islamic Jihad in May 2003, one influential cleric said that she didn't need a chaperone on her way to the attack and she could take off her veil because "she is going to die in the cause of Allah, and not to show off her beauty."[41] The conservative patriarchal religious restrictions on women's movements and bodies become fluid as leaders begin to imagine the strategic value of women as weapons of war. On the morning of January 27, 2002, just hours before Wafa Idris, the first woman suicide bomber, blew herself up, Yasser Arafat spoke to women in his compound at Ramallah and told them that "women and men are equal.... You are my army of roses that will crush Israeli tanks."[42]

Like the metaphors used to describe the American women prison guards, the metaphor of women as an "army of roses" that will crush tanks renders an uncanny split between women's bodies imagined as natural and the technology of war—Israeli tanks—that they have the power to crush. Women are on the dangerous frontier between the cultural and the biological, an army of roses. They become beautiful flowers but flowers with thorns, flowers armed with bombs that can crush modern technologies of war; they represent the threatening power of nature against modern technology. Consistent with the stereotype of female bodies in most patriarchal cultures, women's bodies represent nature while men are associated with culture: men wield culture while women can only wield their bodies, and when they do, they are dangerous. In the history of philosophy women are associated with the body, and both are excluded from properly philosophical discussions of truth, justice, or politics.[43] Bodies, traditionally associated with women, are opposed to reason, order, and the state. So it should not be surprising that the phenomenon of women using their bodies as weapons conjures this uncanny association that is both revealed and concealed within contemporary culture.

Women's Bodies Are Dangerous?

Italian philosopher Adriana Cavarero argues that in the West technology has become a criterion for distinguishing legitimate and sanctioned violence from illegitimate and horrifying violence. The use of Western technology on both literal and figural levels works to conceal the role of bodies in warfare; high-tech weaponry allows armies to engage in mass destruction with few real causalities on their side and so-called surgical strikes supposedly allow precision targeting to minimize enemy and civilian casualties as well—although, as we know, these strikes frequently either miss their targets or are aimed at civilian sites. Cavarero claims that

> The body as such, the mere body transformed into a mortal weapon appears instead as totally irregular and, so to speak, disloyal, illegitimate, treacherous. This...depends on the scandal of lethal weapons that consist of bare and non-technological bodies. As matter of fact, a homemade explosive belt doesn't evoke technology. As suicidal Rim Salah al Riyachi claims, her body is the weapon, it is *her* body that explodes in a thousand killing splinters. She doesn't think of her body as an instrument that carries and utilizes weapons, like in the case of a trooper carrying a rifle or a warrior carrying a sword. She thinks of her body as the weapon. This is totally anomalous in the Western tradition concerning war. And it is particularly upsetting for a type of war in which technology aims at replacing, covering, and neutralizing the traditional role of fighting bodies.

Cavarero concludes that within the Western political cannon, "only technology is allowed to claim the correct and legitimate status of weapon."[44]

Cavarero's analysis suggests that, unlike technology, the body, particularly the female body, and more especially the maternal body, is horrifying when it becomes a weapon. Her work shows how the Western metaphor of the *body politic* has traditionally excluded the female body, which is associated with "flesh, contingency and becoming," while simultaneously idealizing the male body, which is "constructed on an abstract image of proportionality, perfect balance and timeless stability." Because warriors are traditionally male, Cavarero argues that "female bodies performing as weapons make the old, notorious connection between politics and war looking extraordinarily anomalous, not only from a feminist perspective, but especially from the perspective of traditional political thought."[45] Yet, given the traditional association between bodies and women, and the further association between women's bodies (perhaps especially maternal bodies) and danger, contra Cavarero, the uncanny effect of women suicide bombers is not anomalous but in fact, in a sense exemplary of the greatest imaginable danger—mothers/women who have power over life and death.

If, as Cavarero argues, "bare, non-technological, so to speak, *natural* bodies... appear illegitimate and politically incorrect" when they become weapons of war against technological weapons that conceal the role of the

Suicide bombing is more than using a person

body in war, then the bodies of suicide bombers are bound to evoke, at least within the Western imaginary, our fear of "natural bodies." Given the well-documented historical associations between the body, nature, and women, the fear of natural bodies usually evokes fear of female or maternal bodies. Moreover, the bodies of suicide bombers make manifest the tension between bodies and technology in the modern imaginary; that is to say, these bodies do not stay within the realm of nature, but their political meaning explodes onto the scene of Western politics. The horror of these bodies is not just that bodies are associated with nature—as Cavarero argues—but also and moreover that these bodies explode that stereotype by making the body and life itself into political actions. In later chapters, I will return to a discussion of the complex role of the body and our attitudes toward it in violence toward ourselves and others.

Because we think of war as a masculine pursuit, it seems especially strange that women engage in war and brutal violence. At the same time, however, we continue to imagine women's bodies as inherently dangerous (as my analysis of the media rhetoric around women warriors demonstrates). It is this latent association between women and danger that makes the recruitment of women into what Ghassan Hage describes as a "highly masculine and competitive" culture of suicide bombers so powerful and shocking.[46] Women suicide bombers and our bewilderment in the face of such violence make manifest the powerful and age-old myth of the dangers inherent in the female/maternal body, a danger associated more with their ambiguous status between nature and culture than with their association with nature.

There are practical reasons why women might be recruited for such activities. In his history of suicide bombing, German journalist Christoph Reuter discusses the high rates of women suicide bombers amongst the Tamil Tigers in Sri Lanka, whom he says comprise close to sixty percent of suicide commandos. He attributes the high rate of participation by women to "the modern emancipation of Tamil women" and to "their being accorded the same rights and military duties as men"—to women's liberation—and to the practical effectiveness of women bombers. At the same time that he invokes women's liberation, he distances this from Western feminism: "It is highly doubtful that this high rate of women's participation in bombing missions has had much to do with a commitment to a Western form of feminism. More likely, it is because of the LTTE [Liberation Tigers of Tamil Eelam] leadership's constant need for *new blood*. Many Tamil men of fighting age have died or emigrated. The few still available have been needed for combat duty against the government troops. Men are deemed more suitable for combat, being able to march greater distances while carrying heavier weapons, but women more easily conceal bombs under their clothes by, for example, passing themselves off as pregnant. It's a division of labor by gender: the exploding belt worn by suicide assassins, which the LTTE had managed to perfect over the years, was even originally developed specially for the female body."[47]

This passage from Reuter's book on suicide bombers is instructive for analyzing the complex and paradoxical ways that the female body, particularly the maternal body, functions in the Western imaginary. First, it is noteworthy that Reuter speculates without giving any examples that women more easily conceal bombs under their clothes because they can pass themselves off as pregnant. Without presenting any evidence for his supposition (which is especially odd in the context of his otherwise detailed account), Reuters imagines the seemingly pregnant body as the most effective suicide bomber. This image of pregnant bodies become lethal weapons conjures the specter of the dangerous and mysterious power of the maternal body over life… and death. Given that Reuter points out that the exploding belt was originally designed for the female body, enlisted as "new blood," can we be far off the mark to think of other types of feminine belts associated with new blood, sanitary belts? And, given the metaphor of blood, could it be the supposed fluidity of women's bodies that makes them more useful as what Adriana Cavarero calls "body bombers"? Reuter's discussion of the greater elasticity of women's bodies, which can change their shape in pregnancy, allowing the use of flowing clothes that can conceal weapons, further substantiates the imagined fluidity of the female body.

In the context of the Algerian revolution against French occupation, psychiatrist Frantz Fanon also describes that changing nature of women's bodies and clothes as they become useful to warfare and violence. In "Algeria Unveiled," Fanon analyzes how the veil is both removed and donned to enable women to effectively pass through check points with weapons.[48] He describes how the changing dress of Algerian women affects their conceptions of their bodies, the movements of their muscles, what he calls their "bodily schema." This is to say that these women's lived experience and their sense of their embodiment changes with their changing wardrobe. Like Reuter's account of women suicide bombers, Fanon's analysis also suggests that there is something inherent in women's bodies that makes them malleable and fluid, what he problematically calls the "instincts" of Algerian women.

My point in bringing Fanon's description of armed women's bodies together with Reuter's is to show that women's bodies are figured as fluid and changing in ways that overdetermine their use as weapons. At the extreme, women are imagined as chameleon-type animals who (instinctively) change their bodies in order to camouflage and conceal the danger that lies beneath their clothes. Their entire bodies are reduced to bodily fluids, especially blood; bodily fluids come to represent female bodies themselves. As Cavarero and other feminist philosophers have demonstrated, "the body expelled from politics is a female body" imagined as fluid, inconsistent, and irrational, while the male body is imagined as solid, permanent, and rational.[49] But again this imagined fluidity of women's bodies makes us uneasy not just because it is associated with nature, but moreover because it cannot be contained. Fluids connote a slipperiness, messiness, and shapelessness that overflow any attempt to contain them within a neat category like nature or culture. The female body imagined as fluid spills over from nature into culture, and it is this slippage that unsettles and makes it appear dangerous and improper; fluid bodies don't properly belong to nature or to culture. Indeed, it is their challenge to this distinction that makes them uncanny.

Selective Feminism

Reuter also claims that the increase in women suicide commandos among the Tamil Tigers is the result of the emancipation of Tamil women but not the result of a commitment to Western feminism. Perhaps he is distinguishing between forms of feminism unique to Tamil women and Western forms of feminism. In any case, his conclusions about the role of women's emancipation and feminism are unclear. Feminism seems to occupy an ambiguous place in his account of women suicide bombers, even while women's equality—the same rights and duties as men—is in his account clearly responsible for the increasing participation of women.

As we have seen, Yasser Arafat explicitly invokes the rhetoric of women's equality to encourage women to participate in violence. Like the so-called equal opportunity abusers at Abu Ghraib, the women suicide bombers have sparked a feminist debate among Palestinians over the question of whether women should, as one reporter put it, "hop over conservative societal barriers to join the almost exclusively male ranks of suicide bombers."[50] Like the feminist debates, or debates over feminism, ignited by the photos at Abu Ghraib, the appropriation of the rhetoric of equality in order to justify women's participation in violence and warfare, especially suicidal forms, not only points to the fluidity of discourse but also to problems inherent in the rhetoric of equality as it has been employed by both feminists and conservative patriarchs waging war.

Just as metaphors of women and female sexuality as dangerous, or the uncanny and lethal condensation of artifice and nature is nothing new, the appropriation of the rhetoric of equality has been used for centuries to justify military action and imperialist occupation. And it is still used by Western governments when it is convenient to justify sending in "freedom fighters" to "liberate" societies branded as backward because of their treatment of women. We can simultaneously blame feminism for the abusive women at Abu Ghraib and use it to justify invading Afghanistan to liberate women. U.S. justifications for the invasions in Iraq and especially in Afghanistan revolve around what literary scholar Gayatri Spivak calls the Western imperialist discourse of "saving brown women from brown men."[51]

Selective appropriation of feminism and concern for women have become essential to imperialist discourses. For example, at the turn of the nineteenth century Lord Cromer, British consul general in Egypt, founded the Men's League for Opposing Women's Suffrage in England at the same time that he used arguments about women's oppression to justify the occupation of Egypt.[52] And in the 1950s much of the rhetoric used to justify French colonial rule in Algeria focused on the plight of Algerian women, whose oppression was seen as epitomized by the veil.[53] We have seen a similar concern with the veil in recent media, when it was used to justify military action in Afghanistan, where the burka and veil became the most emblematic signs of women's oppression. The media was full of articles referring to the U.S. invasion as liberating Afghan women by "unveiling" them, and President Bush talked about freeing "women of cover."[54] I will say more about the obsession with "unveiling" Muslim women in the next chapter[55].

In her radio address just after the military campaign, First Lady Laura Bush used Afghan women to justify the invasion, saying that, "Because of our recent military gains in much of Afghanistan, women are no longer imprisoned in their homes.... The fight against terrorism is also a fight for the rights and dignity of women."[56] President Bush echoed this sentiment in his 2002 State of the Union address: "Last time we met in this chamber, the mothers and daughters of Afghanistan were captives in their own homes, forbidden from working or going to school. Today women are free." (Note that Bush refers to the mothers and daughters of Afghanistan, not only appealing to family but also to an association between Afghanistan itself and women or girls).[57] An article in the *San Francisco Chronicle* also associates Afghanistan itself with women, "As women emerge from the shadows, so will Afghanistan."[58]

In sum, the assimilation of the rhetoric of women's rights and equality in the name of violence—by conservative Christians as exemplified by the Bushes and by conservative Muslims as exemplified by Islamic Jihadist clerics embracing *shahidas*—demonstrates that the struggle for women's rights and equality is as much a discursive struggle as a material one. And it suggests, as many feminists have argued, that the discursive constellation of rights and equality alone cannot account for sociohistorical or material differences that govern, if not determine, our lives and, perhaps more important, the meaning of those lives. As we will see in the final chapter, it is crucial for women to be able to create new meanings for their lives outside of patriarchal conventions that continue to link women, sex, and death. Otherwise, women's freedom is reduced to the freedom to kill themselves.

Beauty Subdues the Beast

While we were fascinated by images of teenage women suicide bombers and women abusers at Abu Ghraib, the teenage woman warrior who most captured American hearts is Jessica Lynch. Hers is not a story of attack but of self-defense and ultimately of suffering and survival. Originally media reports heralded Lynch as a "female teenage Rambo" who fought off the enemy by firing her rifle until she ran out of ammo and in spite of bullet wounds engaged in a knife fight before she was captured by Iraqi forces. Her story has now been altered to the point that we know instead that her life was saved by Iraqi doctors who treated her with kindness and not as a POW after she sustained injuries in a Humvee crash; she neither fired her gun, stabbed any Iraqis, nor received any gunshot wounds or abuse at the hands of Iraqis.

In spite of the changing story, Jessica Lynch is celebrated as a hero seemingly because she represents the best of American womanhood, whatever you take that to be; she has become a Rorschach test for our ideals of both femininity and girl-power: she is a "princess," a "damsel in distress," a teenage "female Rambo" gunning down any men that get in her way, the naïve "country girl" who grew up in a hollow in West Virginia whose pen pals are a group of kindergarten kids, "Miss Congeniality," the "scrappy tomboy" who learned the ways of the woods and survival from her "sexist" brother and father. All in all, she is "a strong girl bred from good American stock" and a "pretty blonde warrior" who suffered for us and just wants us to acknowledge that she is a "soldier, too." [59]

"There's a funny shift," says military historian John A. Lynn, "We want to fight wars but we don't want any of our people to die and we don't really want to hurt anybody else. So Pvt. Lynch, who suffers, is a hero even though she doesn't do much. She suffered for us." [60] In other words, she is the ideal hero because she is a woman who suffers, the ideal of feminine self-sacrifice and suffering, akin to that of the Virgin Mary, who suffers for us. She is a symbol of our pain, and it is no accident that the power of this image of suffering has everything to do with her being a woman. More particularly she is venerated for her eight days in an Iraqi hospital because she is a seemingly innocent, young, pretty white girl, the girl next door; while Shoshana Johnson, an African American woman captured in the same skirmish and held for twenty-one days in various prisons and the victim of abuse, remains in the shadows. Jessica Lynch's response to her rescuers from under her bedsheets—"I'm an American soldier, too"—when they tell her that they are American soldiers who have come to protect her and take her home, operates as a contrast to the confusion during Shoshana Johnson's rescue, when American soldiers at first did not believe that she was one of them and ordered her down on the floor with her Iraqi captors.

Jessica Lynch, and to a lesser extent Shoshana Johnson, became part of the military's media campaign; Lynch's story was wielded by the press and the Pentagon alike not only to shore up public support for the war but also to rally the troops on the ground. According to Rick Bragg, Lynch's biographer, rumors of Jessica's capture and torture made American soldiers "want to kill" and "proud" to do so. [61] In the words of one *New York Times* reporter: "When American forces were bogged down in the war's early days, she was the happy harbinger of an imminent military turnaround: a 19 year old female Rambo who tried to blast her way out of the enemy's clutches,

[margin handwritten note: media blew up story to give motivation & gain support]

taking out any man who got in her way."[62] These reports turned out to be false and again metaphors of weapons, human shields, and propaganda wars turned up in the press: journalists began to figure Lynch and her dramatic rescue as "weapons" in the Pentagon's "propaganda war" to bolster American confidence in the military.

Historian Melani McAlister argues that Private Lynch was used by news media in a way that a man "never could have been," as both victim and hero; she was both characterized as fighting to the death and figured as young, pretty, and therefore vulnerable.[63] McAlister points out that even descriptions of her courage feminize her; for example, Senator Pat Roberts remarked, "Talk about spunk!"—a term that would not be used to describe a male soldier. McAlister concludes that "accounts of the Lynch rescue have depicted it, implicitly or explicitly, as the classic happy ending of a classic American captivity story. If the war's first weeks didn't give us many pictures of Iraqis welcoming their own rescue by American liberators as we expected, the image of a blonde American woman being saved may be the next best thing."[64] She also describes her as a defensive weapon for both Saddam and the Pentagon.

[margin handwritten note: Held onto her for protection]

Rick Bragg speculates that she was kept alive because she had "propaganda" value for Saddam Hussein: "She was a pretty, blond American soldier and would look good on television, if Saddam held on to power long enough to use her as propaganda."[65] Bragg claims that Saddam Hussein's federal militia used Lynch as a "human shield" and used the hospital where Lynch was being held as a safe haven, knowing that "the Americans would certainly not bomb a hospital with a female U.S. soldier lying helpless in her bed.... She was more than a prisoner of war. She was a human shield."[66]

Bragg is not the only one to describe the use of women as defensive tools of war; Journalist Nicholas Kristof also describes women as defensive weapons, human shields, that were used strategically in Iraqi. He says, "In the Muslim world, notions of chivalry make even the most bloodthirsty fighters squeamish about shooting female soldiers or blowing them up at checkpoints. For just that reason, I asked a woman to sit beside me in the front seat while I drove on a dicey highway in Iraq on the theory that befuddled snipers would hesitate to fire." In this same article, in addition to their use as human shields, Kristof details several ways in which women are useful in Muslim countries like Iraq as part of military strategy.[67] Here we see that in addition to being depicted as offensive weapons of war in the cases of Abu Ghraib, Guantánamo, and the *shahidas*, women also can be figured as defensive weapons of war used to protect men. We are told that even so-called bloodthirsty fighters will be "befuddled" by the mere presence of women.

The Lynch story evolved from the story of a teenage Rambo to the story of a wounded helpless girl saved by Iraqis because she was blonde and pretty. One reporter put it like this: "An Iraqi doctor felt so sorry for Jessica Lynch that he risked his life to help rescue her, and that probably wouldn't have happened if she'd been a big, hairy, smelly Marine."[68] Or, in the words of her brother, "Look at that face. Who isn't going to fall in love with that face?"[69] We could say that the Jessica Lynch story became part of what, in another context, Rey Chow calls the "King Kong Syndrome," in which beauty tames the beast and even the most bloodthirsty fall for a *suffering* sweet-faced white woman.[70] As Chow says, "Herself a victim of patriar- *b/c female* chal oppression . . . the white woman becomes the hinge of the narrative of progress, between enlightened instrumental reason and barbarism" associated with the Third World; "The white woman is what the white man 'produces' and what the monster falls for."[71] Given the fact that she now has status as a hero, with TV documentaries and books written about her, we see that the "monstrous enemy insurgents" and their doctors were not the only ones to fall for the helpless white woman; the American public has greedily swallowed her bittersweet story, perhaps a tonic for war wounds and imperialist guilt.

McAlister connects a historical trope similar to the "King Kong syndrome" to the Lynch rescue story. She argues that the media hype around the Lynch rescue is part and parcel of hundreds of years of tales about the capture and rescue of women: "In these stories, the captive (an ordinary, innocent individual, often a woman) embodied a people threatened from outside. The captive confronted dangers and upheld her faith; in so doing, she became a symbol, representing the nation's virtuous identity to itself."[72] This is an apt description of the role that the Lynch rescue story played in the imaginary of the nation. Americans identified with both her innocence and her toughness, traits that crystallized and coalesced after September 11, when Americans simultaneously adopted the persona of innocent victim and righteous avenger (we will return to this combination of innocence and militarism in chapter 4). McAlister describes how centuries of rescue narratives turn on innocent virtuous women exhibiting courage in the face of barbaric heathen captors. She concludes that "ultimately, the narratives suggested, God would protect a worthy nation as he saved his innocent daughters."[73] The innocence and vulnerability combined with spunk and grit associated with young Jessica Lynch became emblematic of the courage-in-the-face-of-danger of the post–9/11 American mentality. In addition, this virtuous combination of innocence and courage became a justification for the war itself—she is worth fighting for. As Bragg points out, stories of Lynch inspired soldiers to risk their lives. The story of Lynch's rescue captured the imagination of a nation again at war because, in the words of McAlister, "Americans were primed to expect a story of rescue—not just because our president told us that we would save Iraq and ourselves, but because for more than two centuries our culture has made the liberation of captives into a trope of American righteousness."[74]

"The Most Astounding Modern Weapon in the Western Arsenal"

Whether as individuals supposedly representing all American women or all Muslim women, as heroes or as scapegoats, as victims or as torturers, as oppressed or as feminist avengers, women have been a central element in the discursive constellations revolving around recent military action in the Middle East. In all of these cases that I have touched on briefly in this chapter, women have been figured as either offensive or defensive weapons of war—and not just as any weapons of war, but as the most dangerous and threatening ones. Within this rhetoric, a woman can break the most devout with just the threat of her sex; her ponytail and pretty smile can be used as deadly weapons; and with the charms of her vulnerability and sweet face, she can subdue even the most bloodthirsty villains and win over the hearts of friend and enemy alike.

The words of *New York Times* columnist Nicholas Kristof crystallize the rhetoric of women as weapon: "The only time I saw Iraqi men entirely intimidated by the American-British forces was in Basra, when a cluster of men gaped, awestruck, around an example of the most astoundingly modern weapon in the Western arsenal. Her name was Claire, and she had a machine gun in her arms and a flower in her helmet."[75] Traditionally, bombs and airplane bombers have been given the names of women: the plane that dropped the atom bomb that ended World War II was named after the pilot's mother; and the bomb itself was named after Hollywood "bombshell" Rita Hayworth's most famous femme fatale character, Gilda. Now the most astounding modern weapon in the Western arsenal is named

Claire. The secret weapon of modern warfare turns out to be a woman wielding a gun and a flower. She occupies a place in our imaginary not so different from Hollywood's femme fatale, who, with a flower in her hair and a gun in her purse, lures men to their deaths. She herself is a deadly flower... perhaps part of an army of roses. It should come as no surprise that women continue to occupy the position that we have built for them discursively, only in more explicit forms. At the extreme, women become weapons, literally blowing up, the bombshell become the bomb.

[2]

Sexual Freedom as Global Freedom?

From the rhetoric of liberating "women of cover" and debates in the United States Congress over women in the military, to sexual abuses at the Abu Ghraib and Guantánamo Bay prisons, gender, sexual difference, and sexuality are coming to play a major role in the construction of the Western notion of "global freedom."[1] In this chapter I argue that global freedom is being defined in terms of sexual freedom, imagined as the freedom to expose the female body, to wear any clothing, and to shop for that clothing. Women's freedom in the West has been reduced to the freedom to dress (especially in revealing clothes for the eyes of others), governed by market forces of fashion and consumerism. This view of women's freedom is used to justify military action elsewhere, and to reassure Western women of their own freedom at home. The rhetoric of liberating women elsewhere conceals women's oppression here at home while at the same time reassuring us that we are liberated. In this chapter I analyze the ways in which talk of liberating "women of cover" from "backward traditions" shores up images of freedom and privilege at home.

Moreover, I show how these forms of emancipation—whether here or in the Middle East—bring with them new disciplinary practices and structures. In the United States, for example, the professionalization of motherhood has produced new disciplinary norms that are internalized by women to the point that many of these women must resort to the use of pharmaceutical drugs—sleeping pills and Prozac, for example—and lots of caffeine to keep their stressful schedules in tact. In this context, what does it mean to talk about women's freedom or consent? If freedom is reduced to the freedom to shop or the freedom to reproduce and raise the next generation of good consumers, then is it any wonder that so many women suffer from depression and feelings of meaninglessness or worthlessness?[2] I conclude the chapter by introducing an alternative conception of freedom that moves beyond the free market and toward the freedom to create meaningful lives.

Exporting Feminism

In other contexts and historical periods (e.g., British colonialism in Egypt and India, French occupation of Algeria, and republican reformers in the Ottoman Empire) feminist scholars have persuasively argued and forcefully demonstrated that gender, sexual difference, and sexuality are essential elements of nationalism and imperialism. For centuries, liberating women and women's rights have been used as justifications for imperialist and colonial missions that shore up notions of nation and homeland or patriotism. These missions also have been associated with the normalization of sexuality against the sexual deviance associated with those colonized from the perspective of the colonizers or associated with the colonizers from the perspective of the colonized (especially in Western imperialistic enterprises in countries identified with the East—the West views the East as sexually repressive while the East views the West as sexually promiscuous).

Notions of nation and homeland have been developed, propagated, and justified through gender, including gendered metaphors of motherland and fatherland, or metaphors that feminized or masculinized countries or territories, and gendered notions of citizens or citizen-soldiers as masculine along with the feminization of those colonized. Within the U.S. media most recently Afghanistan and Burma have been figured as feminine, as countries in need of liberation or as fledgling democracies in need of protection.[3] For example, as we have seen in the last chapter, in his 2002 State of the Union address, President Bush refers to the mothers and daughters of Afghanistan, not only appealing to family but also to an association between the country itself and femininity.

Recent rhetoric in the United States through which notions of nation, patriotism, and homeland are formed continue to revolve around the "question of woman." Specifically, the force of the discourses of freedom, democracy, and security relies on the use of gender, sexual difference, and sexuality—defined in terms of women's dress—to construct a free, democratic and secure West against an enslaved, theocratic and infirm Islamic Middle East. The current discussion continues the oppositional logic of imperialist discourses that pits "West" against "East," "civilized" against "barbaric," "backward" against "progress," measuring these qualities in terms of women and sexuality. For example, in his 9/11 anniversary speech in 2006, President Bush said that we are fighting a war against "a radical Islamic empire where women are prisoners in their homes" and that this war is "a struggle for civilization" against "evil" Islamic extremists.

The United States' interest in liberating women elsewhere from oppressive religious traditions that are seen as backward works to reassure us about women's sexual freedom in the West, one the one hand, and to legitimate constraints on women's sexual agency on the other. This is to say that the focus on "freedom" elsewhere as it is articulated in relation to women and sexuality thinly veils an anxiety about women's sexual freedom in the United States. The recent controversy over giving the HPV (human papilloma virus) vaccine to young women is a telling example of how conservative forces here work to limit women's freedom. Medical trials suggest that the vaccine is effective in preventing this widespread sexually transmitted disease and the cervical cancer that often results from it.[4] Christian conservatives oppose giving the vaccine to girls because they argue it will encourage premarital sex, as if young women have heard of HPV, let alone abstain from sex in order to prevent getting it.

Are Christian conservatives less concerned with the lives of girls and women than they are with keeping women in restrictive domestic roles? By limiting access to birth control, abortion, and vaccinations against sexually transmitted diseases, they essentially limit women's sexual freedom. Katha Pollitt argues that "right-wing Christians increasingly reveal their condescending view of women as moral children who need to be kept in line sexually by fear. That's why antichoicers will not answer the call of prochoicers to join them in reducing abortions by making birth control more widely available: They want it to be less available. Their real interest goes way beyond protecting fetuses—it's in keeping sex tied to reproduction to keep women in their place."[5] It is noteworthy, then, that people on both sides of this controversial issue have come together in condemning restrictions on women in Muslim countries, promoting American values of women's liberation without reflecting on the ways in which women's freedoms are in fact curtailed here at home. We should be reminded of the nineteenth-century Lord Cromer, who fought against women's suffrage at home in England and at the same time justified British occupation of Egypt by using the rhetoric of women's liberation. This selective use of feminism when it is convenient to justify military action creates the illusion of a society primarily concerned with women and women's rights.

In addition, the association of the lack of democracy in theocratic Islamic states with religious restrictions on women normalizes Christianity and renders its conservative factions' circumscription of women and sexuality invisible. In other words, our focus on conservative Islamic traditions as they influence politics, particularly the politics of gender, sexual difference, and sexuality, operates to project "backward" religious traditions outward in the name of another religious tradition, Christianity, that becomes invisible in the process. If Islamic fundamentalism is associated with violence and oppression, Christian fundamentalism becomes like the air we breath, the familiar backdrop to normal political and social relations, particularly the role of women and sexual relations; its violence is pure and good while the other violence is impure and evil.

There is a vast literature on the role of women, gender, and sexuality in Western colonial and imperialistic incursions in the East, and on the role of gender in nation building through these incursions. From Gayatri Spivak's seminal essay "Can the Subaltern Speak?" (where she analyzes ways in which Indian women are silenced in colonialist discourse about India that relies on the rhetoric of white men saving brown women from brown men), to recent discussions of how this same rhetoric was used by the United States to justify the invasion of Afghanistan to save Afghan women from the Taliban, feminist scholars have demonstrated that women's interests have been made central to so-called civilizing or democratizing missions.[6] Partha Chatterjee has made an exemplary analysis of how the British used women's rights in India to undermine Indian men in their power struggle to control their colonies.[7] Feminist scholars have also illustrated the ways in which both conservative and reformist movements within the Middle East have engaged the oppositional rhetoric of East versus West focusing - on women, their place in domestic and public spheres, and most especially their clothing, as crystallized in debates over veiling.[8] For example, Leila

Ahmed argues that from the beginning of the twentieth century the veil becomes a symbol of Muslim resistance and tradition in the face of a European concern with unveiling Muslim women.[9]

Women's Right to Bare Arms

The veil (*hijab*, along with the burka and various forms of *chador*) continues to be a contested symbol within Western imperialistic discourses and within discourses of resistance to westernization. Reminiscent of the French occupation of Algeria in the 1950s, the U.S. invasion of Afghanistan focused on the plight of Afghan women, whose oppression was seen as epitomized by the veil and the burka. Several articles praised the military campaign for "unveiling" Afghan women, and President Bush talked about helping "women of cover." Current efforts to re-veil women in Iraq seem to be a reaction against U.S. occupation wherein westernization becomes associated with women's sexual freedom as evidenced by their dress and the amount of body covered or revealed. As in the nineteenth and twentieth centuries, the veil has become a symbol of resistance to Western imperialist forces; and the circumscription of women's movement and dress comes to stand for "traditional" or "authentic" values against modernization, democratization, and westernization, whose "evil" is epitomized by women's sexual freedom. The association between the West and women's sexual freedom has its correlate in Western notions of liberation and freedom that revolve around freeing "women of cover," who are seen as most oppressed by having to remain under cover.

In Western discourses women uncovering their bodies is a sign of their sexual freedom. Women's dress and the amount of body bared become signs of their freedom. Women's freedom is reduced to women's sexual freedom, which in turn is reduced to the freedom to reveal their bodies in public. Whether women's right to bare arms merely makes them more sexually available to men or allows them to celebrate their own bodies, their agency is circumscribed by social forces that discipline even as they liberate. The "modern" woman is the subject of the free market. Hers is the freedom to shop. It is noteworthy that President Bush introduced the phrase "women of cover"—an analog to women of color—in relation to the freedom to shop. In a speech before the State Department shortly after September 11, 2001, Bush told "stories of Christian and Jewish women alike helping women of cover, Arab-American women, go shop because they were afraid to leave their home" and in a news conference a week later he again invoked the religious unity of America epitomized in women getting together to shop: "In many cities when Christian and Jewish women learned that Muslim women, women of cover, were afraid of going out of their homes alone … they went shopping with them … an act that shows the world the true nature of America," suggesting that true nature of America is the freedom to shop for women of all faiths.[10]

Even if she has a platinum credit card with the maximum credit limit, however, a woman's freedom to shop is still subject to dress codes governed by class, race, age, ability, profession, etc. You don't see Laura Bush or Condoleezza Rice wearing belly-shirts, navel studs, and skintight low-riding jeans. And while you don't see George wearing low-slung baggy pants that reveal his boxers, not only are women the target consumers of clothes but they are also defined in terms of them. Clothes may not make the man, but they do make the woman. For example, you don't see articles mentioning Alberto Gonzales's wardrobe, even if they do mention that he is the first Latino attorney general (maybe his role in finding loopholes to the Geneva Convention regulations on torture detracted from his attire), but a *New York Times* article on the promotion of Frances Fragos Townsend to homeland security advisor remarks that "she has become the model of decorum with coiffed hair, well-cut suits and toned down public demeanor."[11] Her new job means new clothes, and her new persona is described in terms of those clothes—clothes that in this case suggest upward class mobility. And when Secretary of State Condoleezza Rice wore black boots, the media was abuzz with talk of her "foxy 'Matrix'-dominatrix black leather stiletto boots."[12] Even *Washington Post* staff writer Robin Givhan could not resist imagining Rice as dominatrix because she wore an all black outfit and boots: "Rice's coat and boots speak of sex and power—such a volatile combination, and one that in political circles rarely leads to anything but scandal. When looking at the image of Rice in Wiesbaden [Germany], the mind searches for ways to put it all into context. It turns to fiction, to caricature. To shadowy daydreams, Dominatrix! It is as though sex and power can only co-exist in a fantasy. When a woman combines them in the real world, stubborn stereotypes have her power devolving into a form that is purely sexual."[13] Although Givhan remarks on how the combination of sex and power is reduced to sexual power, she does not comment on why women are associated with sex in the first place. This focus on women's clothes (and not men's) not only demonstrates one of the ways that women are identified with their bodies and sex but also subtly identifies their agency with the choice of clothes they wear.

Free to Shop

In various cultures and in various ways, clothes are important markers of class (and race, gender, sexuality), but Western clothes are also associated with modernization and civilization. For example, in discussing twentieth-century unveiling and re-veiling campaigns in Iran, Afsaneh Najmabadi concludes that "it is highly indicative of the stakes played out on women's dress code that official government memoranda of the 1930s repeatedly referred to the new dress code as *libas-i tajaddud-i nisvan* (clothes of modernity of women) and that women's rights issues were discussed in terms of 'clothes of modernity' and 'clothes of civilization' associated with westernization and western notions of freedom."[14] Conversely, Western notions of freedom are essentially linked to women and specifically to women's freedom to uncover their bodies and their right to shop for clothes and makeup. As we have seen in media coverage of the fall of the Taliban in Afghanistan, women's freedom becomes the freedom to choose what to wear; and the liberated woman exercises her freedom of choice by shopping. As important as her right to vote is her right to shop.

For example, a *Time* photo-essay entitled "Kabul Unveiled" begins, "A woman in a traditional burka walks through the ruined urban sections of Kabul, near the main market. The freedoms denied Afghani women under Taliban rule have been instantly restored by the city's fall—now it is up to them to make their way ..."[15] The photo-essay goes on to show burka-clad women shopping for burkas, all of which look alike, and for makeup and hair-care items, and men shopping for postcards of women and entranced by a hula dancing doll. Half of the photos are of feminist meetings and of women in a maternity hospital, and half are of shopping, suggesting that Afghan women's liberation is the freedom to shop. In her forceful analysis of the way that these images were used to justify the U.S. invasion, Dana Cloud concludes that the photo-essay "Kabul Unveiled" oscillates between showing women in burkas and women "unveiled," women in traditional clothes and feminists and one woman news anchor, to visually suggest that women were liberated by U.S. troops. Through its juxtaposition of images, this photo-essay suggests that liberation, democracy, and modernity are defined in terms of the freedom to shop.[16]

The vice president of the Afghan Women's Mission, Sonali Kolhatkar, remarks that "while Oprah Winfrey provides touching vignettes of Afghan women finally able to don high heels and lace dresses, politically Afghan women have been marginalized and promised more Sharia law."[17] As Kolhatkar and other feminists, including the Revolutionary Association of Women of Afghanistan (RAWA), have argued, Afghan women's freedom of wardrobe and right to shop trade on other freedoms and bring with them different disciplinary restrictions.[18] It is noteworthy that Kolhatkar also criticizes the leader of the Feminist Majority for being concerned only with forced female genital mutilation in Afghanistan (a practice that does not in fact occur) and thereby suggesting that Afghan women's "oppression stems from not being able to have an orgasm."[19] Even the leader of the Feminist Majority seems to conflate women's freedom and sexual freedom. It is significant, however, that to her sexual freedom is not reduced to baring one's body for others, but involves sexual satisfaction and pleasure, which suggest sexual agency rather than sexual objectification.

Feminist anthropologist Lila Abu-Lughod has documented the ways in which the current rhetoric of liberating Muslim women echoes earlier colonial and missionary discourses that not only were used to justify imperialistic ventures but also resulted in domestic and educational practices and policies that were simultaneously emancipatory and disciplinary.[20] She shows how women and gender have become the contested symbols of modernity, westernization, and democracy; moreover, she articulates some of the ways in which they demonstrate that so-called modern or Western forms of dress, marriage, and domestic organization bring with them new disciplinary regimes in the everyday lives of women.[21] For example, in Iran and Turkey unveiling and entrance into public spheres required that women find new ways to present their bodies as disciplined, chaste, and modest.[22] And, in the words of Abu-Lughod, "young Bedouin women in Egypt try to resist their elders and the kin-based forms of domination they represent by embracing aspects of a commodified sexuality—buying makeup and negligees—that carry with them both new forms of control and new freedoms."[23] They become subject to new standards of beauty and femininity. In recent reports even the so-called tank girl army of Iranian expatriates is described in terms of their dress—"khaki headscarves, combat trousersuits and boots"; according to the conclusion of one article, they seem to be fighting for the right to wear lipstick.[24] Once again freedom is associated with sexual freedom that not only reduces freedom to the free market but also commodifies women's bodies and sexuality and makes them available in the form of postcards of women now sold in Kabul and familiar images of scantily clad women from Hollywood and Bollywood.

If the liberation of "women of cover" from "backward traditions" results for them in new forms of discipline and the commodification of sexuality, we might ask what function this rhetoric performs in terms of shoring up images of freedom and privilege for Western women. In what ways do images of oppressed women elsewhere reassure Western women of their own freedom? Indeed, how do these images participate in the construction of Western notions of women's freedom as sexual freedom that re-inscribes women within disciplinary and restrictive economies of gender and sexuality? Certainly images from other countries where women appear completely covered, relegated to the domestic sphere, and denied freedom of expression make women in the West glad to live in a society that appears to value women's freedom. These images do seem to highlight the value placed on women's freedom in the West. Moreover, they appear as reminders of a time seemingly now long past when Western women's freedom was not valued, when women did not have the right to vote or to hold public office, when women were relegated to the domestic sphere and were considered the property of their fathers or husbands. But it was not so long ago (a matter of decades) that laws were still on the books in several states indicating that women were not persons, that strict dress codes were enforced in all public schools, and women were (and still are) barred from certain jobs, sports, and public positions. Seeing Muslim women as victims of "backward" traditions helps to construct women's oppression as a thing of the past for the West and cover over the ways in which women continue to be disadvantaged within the United States and other so-called Western cultures.

The Bush administration's use of the rhetoric of "bringing democracy" to "whole regions of the world" that "simmer in resentment and tyranny" and freedom to "women of cover" continues a colonial legacy that treats other civilizations as "contemporary ancestors" who need to be modernized by Western technologies and ideologies—thereby justifying occupation and warfare.[25] Several scholars working in Middle Eastern studies have discussed the ways in which notions of the modern and modernity, along with notions of the civilized and civilization, play off the supposed backwardness and barbarity of the East, already overcome in the West.[26] In the words of Lila Abu-Lughod, "Notions of modernity have been produced and reproduced through being opposed to the nonmodern in dichotomies ranging from the modern/primitive of philosophy and anthropology to the modern/traditional of Western social theory and modernization theory, not to mention the West/non-West that is implied in most of these dichotomies."[27]

Western democracies can reassure themselves that they are free and that slavery and women's oppression are in their past by projecting that past onto others who are seen as underdeveloped, primitive, backward, or barbaric, all suggesting that they represent a past stage in the evolutionary development of the West. We see this logic at work today, for example, when President Bush, in response to questions about the effect on the Muslim world of the photographs of Saddam Hussein in his underwear, said, "I don't think a photo inspires murderers. I think they're inspired by an ideology that's so barbaric and backwards that it's hard for many in the Western world to comprehend how they think." Bush's rhetoric suggests that the Western world is distanced from not only barbarity and backwardness but also from ideology. And, in response to the Amnesty International report that U.S. torture practices have turned the prison in Guantánamo Bay into a "gulag," one conservative spokesman called the report "immoral" and not "adult," and suggested that a "civilized" person would morally approve of using rough tactics in this situation.[28] Vice President Dick Cheney said that "the important thing to understand is that the people that are in Guantánamo are bad people."[29] Note his use of "bad people" rather than "potential criminals." These remarks imply that people in the United States are good, moral, adult, and civilized while people elsewhere, especially those places identified with terrorists, are bad, immoral, childish, and uncivilized.

As we have seen, as they gained independence in the Western world, women became symbols of oppression—bad, immoral, childish, or uncivilized cultures—elsewhere. In the United States, conservative women have been put in prominent positions to speak out against the oppression of women and racism elsewhere. Have they become apologists for the wealthy white men who still dominate politics? For example, First Lady Laura Bush and Prime Minister Tony Blair's wife Cherie Blair were enlisted in 2001 after the invasion of Afghanistan to give speeches that spoke of the liberation of Afghan women, and, in the words of Laura Bush, how "the fight against terrorism is also a fight for the rights and dignity of women" and "civilized people throughout the world." And the first black U.S. Secretary of State,

Condoleezza Rice, reminded Egypt that the United States has "its own history of slavery and racism," suggesting not only that racism is in the past of the United States but also that Egypt exemplifies a past stage in U.S. development. (It is noteworthy that Rice defines freedom and liberty in terms of economy, asking how the entire region of twenty-two countries only has a collective economy the size of Spain: "How can that be the case? It certainly isn't anything about the intelligence of the Arab people. It certainly isn't anything about their aspirations. It's about the absence of freedom and the absence of liberty.")[30]

The role of the veiled Muslim woman in the construction and consolidation of the free Western woman continues the ways in which Western notions of emancipation and citizenship for women played off images of Eastern women as slaves to tradition. Anthropologist Jane Collier speculates that the Western notions of consent, particularly women's consent, and freedom were defined against the image of Islamic women's lack of consent in arranged marriages and harems at the turn of the century in Europe:

> Images of veiled Islamic women and harems must also have play a role in constructing understandings of Western women's liberties.... . Consent emerges as a key difference between "oppressed" Islamic women and "free" Western ones during the nineteenth century, when industrialization was transforming adult women from productive members of family enterprises into economic dependents of wage-earning husbands.... . Images of oppressed Islamic women, who could neither marry for love nor develop intimate relations with polygamous husbands, must have played a crucial role in constructing images of Western women as consenting to their disempowerment within increasingly privatized and confining homes.[31]

Notions of freedom and consent continue to be defined against images of Islamic women's supposed lack of freedom and consent. Western women, specifically U.S. women, become the ideal for freedom. But, freedom for what? What counts as consent?

Managerial Motherhood; or, Soccer Mom as C.E.O.

Today in the United States we are witnessing not only a backlash against feminism in conservative movements such as the Promise Keepers' Christian men's rallies and in the politics of family values, but also, thanks to the Internet, an increase in middle-class and professional women working at home in order to raise their children.[32]

The image of the modern middle-class woman is of a "soccer mom" who is expected to manage the family like a C.E.O. With ever fewer public social services to help support child-care and child-rearing, there are greater expectations put on middle-class women to get their children into the right schools and to shuttle them from one activity to the next on tight schedules. This combination of fewer public supports and increased professionalization of the domestic sphere makes for more pressure on mothers. For example, a recent article in the *New York Times* series on class features a middle-class white family who regularly relocate for the husband's career. Kathy Link, the wife, keeps a color-coded itinerary to chart the daily activities of her three daughters and her husband: "Her youngest daughter, Kaleigh, 8, is coded red. With school over this afternoon, she has already been dropped off at her soccer practice blocks from home. Kristina, 11, is dark green, and Kelsey, 13, is yellow. Kristina must get to her soccer practice four miles to the north, and Kelsey to her practice 14 miles to the south... . After dropping Kelsey and Kristina, Kathy Link had to double back, pick up Kaleigh and take her to golf. She will wait for Kelsey to finish soccer before picking up Kristina and taking her to cheerleader practice. Another mother will have to retrieve Kristina so that Kathy Link can be home when Kaleigh's math tutor comes."

These "relos," as the article calls them, segregate themselves in suburban developments according to class, their choices governed by the houses that they can afford: "These families are cut of from the single, the gay and the gray, and except for those tending them, anyone from lower classes."[33] Within these planned and segregated communities, the white middle class literally protects and polices its "proper" borders with security guards, fences, and gates. Behind the gates of these exclusive communities are women who statistically are suffering from ever increasing rates of depression treated with ever new forms of pharmaceutical drugs. Running on caffeine and nervous energy, these women are an exhausted group, shuttling from one child's event to another. The situation of these career mothers raises the question of what it means to consent to one's situation, what it means to be free.

Once again, we can learn a lesson from history. In the nineteenth century, with the onset of industrialization, there was a move to make women leave behind the public sphere and workplace to take charge of the domestic sphere. Middle-class women were expected to stay at home and raise their families; and popular literature was full of guidelines for ordering and disciplining the household. Running the home became a science and women were expected to create the most hygienic and productive environments possible for their children. In a 1833 essay in the *Edinburgh Review*, middle-class women were called "ministers of the interior" who were expected to operate in the household like politicians operate in the public sphere. Literary scholar Judith Newton points out that the metaphor of politics in the domestic sphere replaced any real political power that women were allowed in the public sphere.[34]

The nineteenth-century professionalization of housewifery and scientizing of child rearing that made women "ministers of the interior" has given way to a business model in which women manage the household to produce future leaders in the global economy. Disciplinary discourses of science and medicine that governed child rearing have been replaced with new disciplinary practices modeled on business.[35] They may not be C.E.O.s in the public sphere, but they are in the domestic sphere. Again real corporate and economic power is displaced onto domestic responsibilities traditionally assigned to women, only now taken to a new professional level. As women take their work back home and move their work out of public spaces and back into domestic space, they also are expected to run their households like a business; their public interactions center around their children and building the best public environment in the community or at school for them. Home-based workers are mostly white women who are attracted to this type of labor, made more available via computers and telecommunications, because of family and children (in addition to the increase in women working at home, "the labor force participation rate for mothers with children under 18 has been declining since 2000").[36]

While this new era of middle-class motherhood seemingly allows women to have it all—family and career—they occupy an increasingly busy space full of expectations that require constant work of one kind or another. We need to ask whether these new possibilities for women, especially the freedom to work from home engendered by the Internet, also produce new coercive norms and new forms of discipline, most especially self-imposed forms, that govern middle-class women's lives, and perhaps lead to their high rates of depression, which are controlled and regulated by the pharmaceutical industry.[37] The professionalization of motherhood and the household that valorizes the domestic sphere in one sense and seemingly empowers women at home brings with it new disciplinary practices that restrain women's choices. Moreover, women's supposed power at home continues to displace their political and economic power in the public sphere.

The focus on coercive and disciplinary practices to which women are subjected elsewhere overshadows new forms of coercion and discipline in the United States. Imagining those practices in other places as being primitive or backward, and therefore already in our own past, reassures us that we have moved beyond patriarchal oppression of women, which exists there but not here. The projection of oppression outward shores up our sense of ourselves as free from constraints. The constraints of sexism and patriarchy are associated with those other women so that Western women are constructed as free and as the beneficiaries of a democracy that grants equality to all people regardless of sex, race, or religion.

Dressed to Kill

As we saw in the last chapter, in the "war on terrorism" anxiety over women's sexual agency is manifest not only in the Western concern to unveil "women of cover" but also in associations of female sexuality with a weapon of war. The most striking example of this is the use of women interrogators in Guantánamo Bay prison, where reportedly miniskirts, thong underwear, sexual touching, and fake menstrual blood have been used to "break" recalcitrant Muslim male prisoners. It seems that women's sexual freedom and agency have been used as a torture technique by the United States military. As we have seen, the media coverage of sexual abuse at Guantánamo associates women and sex, going so far as to say that female sexuality is a weapon. Recall the head-note of an article in *Time* magazine: "New reports of detainee abuse at Gitmo suggest interrogators used female sexuality as a weapon."[38]

As discussed in chapter 1, sexualized interrogation tactics become metonymical substitutes for all of female sexuality and women represent sex itself. Female sexuality is reduced to a tactic or strategy (again associated with clothing—or lack thereof), a threatening weapon that can be used against even the most resistant men. Now this "threatening power" has been harnessed by the United States military to be used in counterterrorism efforts, efforts that have been associated with liberating "women of cover." Liberated women become "free" to use their barely covered bodies in the service of their country; the freedom to bare arms takes on a new meaning. Recall that in the case of prison abuses at Abu Ghraib, the fact that women were involved and some of the abuse was sexual and religious made it difficult at first even for human rights groups to classify; and some reactions to reports of the use of miniskirts and sexual touching at Guantánamo prison conjured images of free lap-dances.[39] In a piece entitled "Torture Chicks Gone Wild," columnist Maureen Dowd says, "It's like a bad porn movie. 'The Geneva Monologues'. All S and no M."[40] While some prisoners reported being tormented by "prostitutes," conservative media fueled a corner of popular sentiment that these women interrogators, along with the women involved in abuse at Abu Ghraib, must be man-hating lesbians ... or feminists, which may amount to the same thing within the public imaginary.[41]

"Dykes or Whores"

The idea that women in the military are either dykes or whores is not new. A standard welcome for women entering the Navy in the 1990s was "Welcome to the fleet. In the Navy's eyes, you're either dykes or whores—get used to it."[42] Indeed, the military command at Camp Delta appears to be trading on stereotypes that date back to World War II, when the Women's Army Corp (WAC) was accused of being "a prostitution cadre designed to fulfill the sexual needs of male soldiers."[43] In "'Dykes' or 'Whores': Sexuality and the Women's Army Corps in the United States During World War II," Michaela Hampf points out that gender and sexuality in the WAC were closely associated with dress. In fact, cross-dressing rather than behavior was taken to be the major sign of lesbianism in women, which was not the case with male homosexuals: "Discursive categories for lesbianism in the 1940s were not sodomy but gender disguise and cross-dressing."[44] The military uniform supposedly made women appear mannish and therefore women wearing it were suspected of being "mannish women" or lesbians. The WAC leadership worked hard to counteract the image of mannish and/or promiscuous women by presenting a desexualized image "that resembled a boarding school for white middle-class daughters."[45]

"Birth-Control Glasses"

In Rick Bragg's biography of Pfc. Jessica Lynch—the "beauty" rescued from the "beast" in the first month of fighting in Iraq—we see a similar desexualization (even infantilization at the same time as "prissification") when he paints a portrait of her in soft hair ribbons and sweet pastel pinks. She is the good girl, the poster girl whose "Miss Congeniality" smile somehow goes bad on the faces of the girls of Abu Ghraib.

In a chapter entitled "Princess," Bragg describes in detail Lynch's concern for fashion and her "preoccupation with matching" and makeup. He quotes Lynch as saying, "I would have done more in high school, but I didn't want to mess up my clothes."[46] As Bragg tells the story, the transition from pleated skirts, princess gowns, and painted nails to army fatigues in camouflage green was the most difficult part of Lynch's move from Miss Congeniality at the Wirt County Fair to basic training: "It started with a fashion nightmare. A soldier took her sizes and gave her four uniforms. 'Well,' she thought, 'this is disgusting. At least they match.'"[47] According to Bragg, Lynch "was a perfect solider, until the hair-bow incident" when the drill sergeant made her do ten push-ups for supposedly wearing the wrong hair-bow, which he says "was perfect" because she wouldn't mess up on a hair bow; the suggestion is that if she knew anything it was about how to dress and wear her hair. The crowning glory of her army wardrobe was military issue eyeglasses, a huge black-rimmed model that Bragg says made her look like a cartoon character. Bragg quotes Lynch: "They called 'em birth control glasses—and they really were. A method of birth control. Ain't no guy gonna come anywhere near you as long as you are wearing a pair of those glasses"; "'I am a four-eyed, birth control glasses-wearing geek,' she thought."[48] Bragg claims that she didn't want to see badly enough to wear those glasses.

Bragg's biography tells the story of a sweet, shy little girl more concerned about matching her pinks than fighting; she is portrayed as a little girl who keeps her girlish innocence through it all and takes her teddy bear into surgery with her after she is rescued. Through basic training this innocent girl becomes a cartoon character whose fatigues "swallowed her like a big frog" and whose birth-control glasses kept the guys away. No longer the girl in pink, she is protected by her army fatigues from the men around her and from her own sexuality.

Her image as an all-American girl made her story an effective part of the military's media campaign; the dramatic rescue, complete with night-vision camera footage, was wielded by the press and the Pentagon alike not only to shore up public support for the war but also to rally the troops on the ground.[49] Recall that according to Bragg, rumors of Jessica's capture and torture made American soldiers "want to kill" and "proud" to do so.[50] Lynch's story justified the war. On the book jacket, her biography is touted as "a uniquely American story," through which we "learn the importance of what its means to be an American." Pfc. Jessica Lynch comes to stand for what it means to be an American in the context of a nationalism built on war. The American story is the story of beauty against the beast.

Women Soften the Blow

Gayatri Spivak's analysis of the role of subaltern women in both the discourse of colonization and resistance to it takes a new twist with the re-definitions of abuse at Abu Ghraib and Guantánamo Bay prisons, where media attention focused on women's participation. Spivak argues that "the protection of woman (today the 'third-world woman') becomes a signifier for the establishment of a *good* society which must, at such inaugurative moments, transgress mere legality, or equity of legal policy."[51] In the case of *sati*, what was a ritual was redefined as a crime. In the case of Abu Ghraib and Guantánamo Bay prisons, crime outlawed by Geneva Convention regulations against torture was redefined as "legitimate force" in the war against terrorism. Just as the language of liberating Afghan women made the invasion more palatable to the American public, so too highlighting women's involvement in at Abu Ghraib and Guantánamo helps redefine torture as abuse, misconduct, perversion, or "pranks" and "letting off steam."[52] Women's participation in interrogations to "soften up" detainees results in lessening the impact of finding loopholes in the Geneva Convention regulations on torture.

Even as President Bush in his 2004 inaugural address proclaimed that "America will not pretend that jailed dissidents prefer their chains, or that women welcome humiliation and servitude," women were being made sexualized tools of military interrogations of jailed "detainees" held without the protections of the Geneva Convention. Perhaps it is telling that this speech, which repeats the rhetoric of women's freedom, appeared on

CNN.com side-by-side with a Victoria's Secret advertisement with a provocative photo on a beach of a bikini-clad model with pursed lips looking seductively at the camera; the ad reads, "Create your perfect bikini.... Suit yourself, any way you like." Freedom becomes women's freedom, which becomes women's sexual freedom, which becomes the commoditization of women's sexuality reduced to the right to choose any bikini.

We might again ask Gayatri Spivak's question about the rhetoric of bringing free choice to so-called third-world women. She wonders: "Imperialism's image as the establisher of the good society is marked by the espousal of the woman as *object* of protection from her own kind. How should one examine the dissimulation of patriarchal strategy, which apparently grants the woman free choice as *subject*?" [53] Within this imperialist discourse woman is made an object so that she might become a free subject. But, in the words of Lila Abu-Lughod (describing women in the Middle East), this freedom ushers "in new forms of gendered subjection (in the double sense of subject-positions for women and forms of domination) as well as new experiences and possibilities."[54] As Spivak's analysis suggests, Western notions of freedom are tied to imperialistic enterprises that are motivated now by the forces of global capital. These forces interpret women as both objects to be saved and subjects with free choice as defined by the free market: freedom to shop.

As we have seen, images of oppressed women elsewhere work to construct the image of women's freedom and consent to their own circumscription by sexual commoditization and management of their agency, particularly their sexual agency, by Western institutions, from advertising, entertainment, and pornography to the military. Women's sexual freedom is managed, circumscribed, commoditized, and then secured as *free* in relation to apparent enslavement of other women, epitomized by their dress and supposed lack of sexual agency.

The "F" Word

Does the popular American version of freedom reduce freedom to the free market? In her discussions of freedom and peace in *Hate and Forgiveness*, Julia Kristeva argues that global capitalism has appropriated one version of freedom from the Enlightenment and has mistakenly taken its legacy to be abstract universalism. Following Enlightenment philosopher Immanuel

Kant, this prominent version of freedom is not negatively conceived as the absence of constraint but as the possibility of self-beginning that opens the way for the enterprising individual and self-initiative. This is the freedom of the free market, which, Kristeva says, "culminates in the logic of globalization and of the unrestrained free-market. The Supreme Cause (God) and the Technical Cause (the Dollar) are its two co-existing variants which guarantee the functioning of our freedom within this logic of instrumentalism."[55]

This entrepreneurial form of freedom may be the foundation for human rights through which we conceive of individuals as autonomous, self-motivating, self-caused agents; yet it also effaces the singularity of each individual and reduces human life to an equation. This version of freedom, in which every individual is equal to every other, leads to something like the free-market exchange of people in a calculus that offers only Formal Freedom and Empty Equality. Freedom becomes defined in terms of economies and markets; and governments liberate through occupation in order to open up new markets and free new consumers with little regard for cultural differences that might undermine the universalization of this fungible freedom. Technology becomes the great equalizer through which all individuals are reduced to this lowest common denominator; its brokers are paying lip-service to respect for cultural differences even as they exchange some freedoms for others in the name of the "F" word, Freedom with a capital F.

Kristeva reminds us, however, that there is a second version of freedom that reemerges from the Western tradition as a counterbalance to universalized individualism, one that is "is very different from the kind of calculating logic that leads to unbridled consumerism."[56] This type of freedom comes through language and meaning as they support the singularity of each individual. Singularity is at odds with individualism insofar as it cannot be reduced to a common denominator in the name of equality. Indeed, neither meaning nor singularity can be fixed within an economy of calculation; they are fluid processes that make possible the products and individuals of the free market. In a sense, those products and individuals are leftovers from a process that they efface. Both meaning and the singularity of individuals are imbued with unconscious dynamics that may be manipulated by the market but that always exceed it.

This second kind of freedom is not concerned with maximizing relations through efficient technologies of marketing, management, and surveillance, but rather with meaningful relationships. Freedom as the quest for meaning is an ongoing project. Kristeva calls it an "aspiration ... driven by a real concern for singularity and fragility of each and every human life, including those of the poor, the disabled, the retired, and those who rely on social benefits. It also requires special attention to sexual and ethnic differences, to men and women considered in their unique intimacy rather than as simple groups of consumers."[57]

We need to move from conceiving of freedom as the absence of prohibition to conceiving of freedom as the absence of sacrifice. Freedom is not anything goes but everyone stays (because of their differences and singularity and not in spite of it), not no-thing is excluded but no one is excluded. In *Visions capitales*, Kristeva suggests that artistic representation expresses a freedom that resides "not in the effacement of prohibitions, but in the renouncement of the chain/gear of sacrifices (l'engrenage des sacrifices)," which moves us beyond loss to "a joy that loses sacrificial complacency itself."[58]

Transcending a sacrificial economy requires moving beyond identities based on the exclusion of others toward inclusion and interaction enabled by questioning and representing what it means to be an "individual," an "American," a "Muslim," a "human," etc. This reversal of fear and loathing of other people who are different from ourselves requires overcoming an Us-versus-Them, you-are-either-with-us-or-against-us, mentality by interpreting and articulating our desires and fears in relations to others. Instead of representing, articulating or interpreting their violent impulses or hatred and fears, fundamentalists act out their violent fantasies in the real world, which, as contemporary politics teaches us all too well, leads the members of one religion to sacrifice the members of another, along with themselves. Moving beyond the real-world abjection and exclusion of others, representations of hatred and fear can translate violent impulses into creative life force. As we will see in the last chapter, the hope is that meaning can replace violence toward self and others; representations of violence and vulnerability can replace literal violence and wounding.

[3]

Perpetual War, Real Live Coverage!

All this is the work of powers who make endless ado about their piety, and who wish to be considered as chosen believers while they live on the fruits of iniquity.

—Immanuel Kant, *Perpetual Peace* (1795)

Ever since cameras were invented in 1839, photography has kept company with death.

—Susan Sontag, *Regarding the Pain of Others* (2003)

In this chapter I identify some of the ways in which both visual and narrative images reproduce and justify violence. Specifically, I examine media representations of the United States occupation of Iraq and images sent back home from Iraq by U.S. soldiers. I argue that these images are evidence of the latest forms of colonialism and imperialism, in which racism and oppression are not only still present but enlivened by new technologies; they are part and parcel of the history of imaging technologies as used in colonial enterprises. I discuss how visual technologies—such as digital cameras, cell phones, wireless Internet, and video—affect our sense of space and time in relation to global politics. Like feminism and the latest ideologies, the latest technologies are being manipulated in the service of war. In addition to visual images, I investigate the language used by the government in order to justify military action, war, and violence. In particular, I interpret how notions of security and freedom have been used to frame war as liberation. Finally, I suggest that what I call *witnessing* might provide an alternative to visual and narrative images that undermine our ability take a critical position from which to interpret what we see ... and what we do not see.

Postcards from Occupied Iraq

The infamous photos of young soldiers gleefully torturing Iraqi prisoners
are only a few of the thousands of digital snapshots taken by guards at Abu
Ghraib, photos of abuse, sex scenes between soldiers, camels, the daily life
of Iraqis, landscapes, and soldiers' adventures in Iraq. Reportedly, these images from the daily lives of American soldiers were routinely sent home to
friends and family via the Internet. Perhaps this helps to explain why some
of the abuse photos show military personnel giving thumbs up for the
camera ... and for the viewer back home; these photos seem to have been
taken as part of the visual record kept by soldiers for personal exchange
and correspondence. With their smile-for-the-camera faces and "we're having fun (and winning)" gestures, the images barely require the addition of
the familiar "wish you were here" to become postcards from Iraq. It may
sound strange that photos of naked stacked prisoners, along with soldiers
on camels and pictures of barracks, could have been sent home to loved
ones as so many "postcards" with the typical messages that betoken intimacy. But as various accounts of other colonial enterprises make clear,
the images from Iraq are just the latest in a long history of images of oppression and occupation used to record the experiences of the occupiers as
news for the people back home.

For example, already in the nineteenth century the latest technology,
namely the camera, was used by British military to document everyday life
in colonial India for family back home. Photographs of violence and war
were taken along with pictures of family and British high tea. As Zahid
Chaudhary argues in an insightful analysis of the role of the camera in
British-occupied India, the proximity of war and everyday life in these photographs served to normalize violence for those participating in it and for
those back home; violence appears as a part of everyday life along with
having tea or playing with children.[1] Chaudhary shows how these photographs not only record but also reproduce colonial domination through
both the normalization and the justification of violence. The photographs
justify violence by constructing or framing the colonial world in such a way
that the occupier is in the position of the subject while the occupied are in
the position of objects.

In addition, Chaudhary claims that violence is "mystified" through photographs in that in the images it becomes diffused into the manners and
customs of the everyday life of colonizers. The photographs present only a

particular view of the colonial relation—that of the occupier. The camera extracts a particular scene from a particular perspective from the landscape and thereby renders invisible the context or background against which its slice-of-life is taken. Furthermore, according to Chaudhary, the photographs taken by the British military depict the Indian "natives" as violent or barbaric in nature. Violence, then, becomes a normal part of the landscape rather than something that is imposed on it by the occupying army (with its image-making technologies along with its weapons of war).

In the United States, at around the same time as this, postcards of lynching were used in a similar way to both record and reproduce dominance. These gruesome postcards of black bodies hanging from trees were used to send good wishes to friends and family. With this history in mind, the photographs of female soldiers next to naked male prisoners who have the word "rapist"—misspelled as "rapest"—written on their buttocks are especially eerie, as they suggest an anxiety on the part of white male guards (the photographers choreographing the scenes) about brown men raping white women that harkens back to the rhetoric surrounding the lynching of African-American men in the United States. Lynching had become a gristly spectator sport among white Christian southerners, and they sent photographic records in the form of postcards to relatives. Indeed, Susan Sontag compares the photographs of abuse at Abu Ghraib to lynching photographs in their function as posed documents intended to "show" the superiority of one race over another; the images serve not only as justification for domination but also as "trophies" distributed around the world by digital technology.[2]

Hazel Carby criticizes Sontag's conclusion that the Abu Ghraib photographs differ from lynching photographs in that they are not so much "trophies" to be collected as messages to be disseminated; in her view, Sontag attributes the inspiration for lynching postcards to racism and the images from Abu Ghraib to Internet pornography.[3] Carby, however, sees both as deriving from the same source, and maintains that "the importance of spectacles of abuse, the taking of photographs and videos, the preservation and the circulation of the visual image of the tortured/lynched body, the erotic sexual exploitation which produced pleasure in the torturers—all these practices are continuities in the history of American racism."[4] While I agree with Carby that historically sex and sexual humiliation have been part and parcel of racist oppression and violence, it is also true that technological advances and changes in the ways that images are produced and disseminated have transformed the practices of racism and abuse. Carby concludes that "the digital form in which the Abu Ghraib images circulated is new, but the message they are designed to convey is as old as racism itself: this is material evidence of the wielding of power, of the performance of conquest over an enemy."[5]

Like postcards of lynching, the images from Abu Ghraib function in complex ways as trophies of war that reinforce American/white supremacy, warn other Iraqi prisoners and insurgents of the consequences they could suffer, and compound the torture and abuse itself through the dissemination of images of humiliation and subordination. We should not, however—like Carby—discount the importance of the "newness" of the digital form of these images, which allows for much quicker and wider dissemination in ways that, as we shall see, change both the time and the space of colonialism. New technologies not only perpetuate pornographic ways of looking that lead to trophy-viewing but also facilitate them. Moreover, as we will see, in important ways technological developments add new dimensions to ways of looking that contribute to and support colonization and imperialist occupation.

It might be helpful to interpret recent images of women in the Middle East in the light of French postcards of Algerian women in the early twentieth century. Postcards of Algerian women were taken by French occupiers and sent home to friends and family. In *The Colonial Harem*, writer and poet Malek Alloula interprets some of the ways in which these postcards reproduce colonial domination, again by putting the occupier and the viewer in the position of subject looking at Algerian women as objects—posing them, framing them, and creating thereby a certain image of them. Alloula analyzes the ways in which these images produce and reproduce stereotypes of Arab women. He argues that the postcards of Algerian women operate through the ruse of a triple agency: ethnography that claims to represent the truth; colonial ideology that leaves unsaid the relation of oppression between the French and Algerians; and phantasm revealing the repressed fantasies harbored by Frenchmen about Algerian women.[6]

The postcards not only create the fantasy of an Oriental or Middle Eastern woman, *but also establish the space and time of domination and oppression.* The French photographer is the active agent gazing at the Muslim woman; she appears as his object, to be looked at by him. Moreover, many of the photographs taken inside the harem suggest that the photographer has somehow gained access to the women's private space, that he has had intimate contact with them. The photographs are thus violent intrusions into the private lives of Muslim women. And it is precisely that invasion of privacy that makes them so seductive to their French audience. Through the assumption of the place of an active subject in relation to women represented as passive objects to look at, the French colonizer further establishes his right to see and oversee the "natives."[7] Alloula argues that the picture postcards were "an imaginary revenge upon what had been inaccessible until then: the world of Algerian women."[8]

We see a similar phenomenon in Afghanistan with the American longing to unveil Muslim women. Instead of postcards, however, we have newspaper photos, photos in glossy magazines, and photo-essays on the Internet. Recall the photo-journalism essay "Kabul Unveiled," in which women are shown shopping. The live-action effect of digital technologies increases the sense of intimacy and gives the viewer the feeling of being there. The viewer is not merely put in the place of the photographer as subject looking at the "native" other as object; the moving images and real-time Internet and television broadcasts give to the viewer the dynamic agency of the looking subject, along with his apparent right to look at and even manipulate the bodies of "native" others.

Just as British photographs from India, American photographs of lynching, and French postcards of Algerian women not only record but also reproduce relations of domination, so too do the images coming from Afghanistan and Iraq. Just as these pictures from the past serve a colonial and/or oppressive enterprise, so do the more recent pictures coming from the Middle East. And just as these other images function in ways that create the reality that they supposedly merely record, so do the recent images.

Visual Technologies and Imperialist Power

In the American occupation of Iraq reality is constructed and manipulated through images that are part of a complex web of torture and tourism that can be traced back to the first uses of the camera in the nineteenth century. At that time, the camera was used to document "exotic" locales visited by professional explorers looking for new resources on behalf of their governments, by occupying armies, and by business men (or merchants, as they used to be called). The camera has again become a weapon of colonialism used to objectify and dehumanize in order to justify imperialist economic ventures through the rhetoric of civilizing and liberating missions: historically it has been used to "prove" that brown people are backward and uncivilized, and live like animals, thereby justifying their imprisonment or enslavement both for the protection of the civilized world and for their own good.

The idea now is that we are *liberating* the people of Iraq; once we can *make them understand* this and teach them about our democratic ways, they will stop resisting the American occupation. The discourse becomes more complicated in that the Iraqi people are represented as victims, first of Saddam Hussein and now of "terrorist groups" and "radical insurgents" or "Islamic-Fascists"; Arabs—at least those in Iraq, Afghanistan, and Lebanon—are figured as either helpless victims in need of rescue or forces of evil trying to thwart our good deeds.

What is at stake here in both the visual and the narrative images is what is visible and what remains invisible, what can be seen and what cannot be seen. I am not just talking about government-imposed restrictions on media access or media self-censorship—although decisions not to show photographs of war dead or soldiers' coffins determine in the most basic way what can and cannot be seen. More significant because more deceptive are the ways in which what we are shown, what we do see, involves concealing and not seeing. This happens in at least two ways: first, images focus on something while excluding everything else—they are from just one particular perspective; and second, visual images even more than narrative images conjure an immediate reality seemingly "as it actually is." It is this second illusion that makes visual media so powerful and so resistant to critical interpretation. We have not yet learned to adequately evaluate and interpret visual media, to see what is hidden; or more profoundly, we have not learned to see that seeing always involves not seeing, and that *really seeing* means acknowledging that we have blind spots ... and that our blindness is political. We see what we want to see, what we have come to expect, what we are told to see.

What do we see when looking at the photographs from Abu Ghraib? Do we see torture or pranks? Do we see atrocities of war or a few bad apples behaving badly? Viewing the photographs from Abu Ghraib not only exposes these activities but also implicates the viewer in the colonial logic of seer and seen, subject and object, human and animal set up in the snapshots. The viewer is put in the position of the camera/photographer, the position of the subject looking at its object, naked brown male bodies being abused and playful young white women smiling and giving thumbs up. The photos "show" teenage girls having fun and pointing to naked bodies stacked, leashed, and treated as objects for the amusement of these girls. Upon further reflection, we realize that they also show the girls' glee and the humiliated naked men for the greater amusement of the photographer(s) and by implication the viewers. These posed "snapshots" show white women and brown men in sexual poses familiar from S&M pornographic images of the dominatrix. But, as Susan Sontag points out, they also show the girls' reaction to being photographed: "To live is to be photographed, to have a record of one's life ... to live is also to pose.... The events are in part designed to be photographed. The grin is a grin for the camera. There would be something missing if, after stacking the naked men, you couldn't take a picture of them."[9] The camera affects comportment; we have been trained to smile and pose.

Digital technology feeds, if not produces, the compulsion to record life as a sort of proof that it has been lived. Think of the hundreds or thousands of digital images of loved ones, especially babies or pets, that eat up megabytes on personal computers. The photograph, which used to be the souvenir that could defy death, in the digital age has become a race against death that leads to a glut of images. This compulsion to record, fueled by the seemingly infinite capacity for digital records, turns the archive into an indiscriminant jumble of images and texts that are difficult to discern or interpret. On the one hand, this may open up possibilities for alternative histories or what French philosopher Michel Foucault calls "subjugated knowledge"; but on the other hand, it can level differences as it takes things out of their contexts and throws them into an infinite but already saturated electronic space. The photographs of abuse from Abu Ghraib do both: they reveal heretofore hidden activities of military guards and testify to the abuses endured by prisoners there; at the same time, however, the jumble of images, especially as they stream back home via the Internet, normalizes these activities; which is to say, they make violence part of the normal everyday lives of soldiers. Moreover, even as they reveal abusive practices they also frame them and package them in ways that produce and reproduce colonial attitudes. As Foucault's work so persuasively demonstrates, technologies are part and parcel of the politics of vision that determines what can and cannot be seen at any given time.

Technologies of vision such as the camera, video camera, digital camera, and cell phone camera literally affect and determine how and what we see ... and what we do not or cannot see. Documentary photography began with photographs of colonial occupation and violence that, in the words of Chaudhary, "at once record and reproduce the brutality of history, as mediated through shifting registers of visibility."[10] Documentary photography continues to "bring images of carnage into the security of our domestic spaces."[11] And it does so in particular ways that produce our conceptions of ourselves and others. In the case of colonial photography, as many scholars have argued, the photographer both records and reproduces his dominance over those colonized. Chaudhary says, "Colonial photography produces a visibility that legitimates and records the 'value' of the colonial effort in the same frame as it measures the colonial subject by fixing it. It aids in the production of regularities, showing us ghostly series of racial forms, sublime vistas of foreign lands, or history distilled into picturesque ruins." [12] Although Chaudhary here is analyzing British colonial photography in India in the nineteenth century, his description resonates in the images from U.S.-occupied Iraq, which legitimate the values of American occupation by showing us chaos and destroyed infrastructure along with racial forms, foreign lands, and ancient ruins; most of the images we see of war zones are images of ruins now occupied by U.S. military, who are figured both visually and in narrative commentary as the heroes bringing order to disorder.

In the case of Abu Ghraib the digitalized compulsion to record fraternizes with the pornographic not only as voyeurism but also as sex-aid (reportedly, pictures were exchanged between soldiers as part of their own sexual activity). Surveillance technologies produced to serve regulatory and disciplinary power, as Foucault might say, also produce desires for more voyeuristic and exhibitionist sexual practices using cameras, video-recorders, telephones, and the Internet. And military technologies designed to facilitate surveillance and containment are now used to disseminate images of "real live bodies in action" that cannot be contained. Moreover, the compulsion to record commingles (as it often has) with the colonial impulse to document and thereby to justify military occupation, imprisonment, and torture.

Insofar as the colonial impulse involves making colonized people and locales into exotic or barbaric objects-to-be-looked-at, it engages in a pornographic way of viewing. The colonial pornographic mode of viewing frames and figures colonial subjects as objects; their bodies are at the mercy of the colonizers, who can either save or kill them at will. Abused and disfigured bodies become trophies to be photographed as evidence of dominance and victory. They are shown like dogs on leashes being lead by young American soldiers. The pornographic view denies both the subjective agency and the subject position of the colonized.[13] The agency and individual and social identity of the "objects" of the colonial pornographic gaze are rendered invisible. Sexualization of colonial subjects, then, is just one aspect of the pornographic gaze. Sexualization compounds the objectification of people living under occupation and both records and reproduces the occupiers' control over them. By depicting prisoners as sex objects under the control of military guards who can command even their sexual performance, the management of their bodies is both justified and repeated. In the first reports from Abu Ghraib, guards maintained that the prisoners behaved "like animals" and cited sexual activity as evidence; of course it turned out that the prisoners were forced by the military to simulate sexual activities as part of abusive rituals of domination and objectification.

Still, the colonial mentality was not invented with the camera or digital technologies. The injustice that eighteenth-century German philosopher Immanuel Kant describes as eaten like fruit in Europe is the "the *inhospitable* conduct of the civilized states of our continent, especially the commercial states of part of the world." His description of eighteenth-century European interests in the Caribbean echoes today's U.S. interests in Iraq:

> The injustice which they display in *visiting* foreign countries and peoples (which in their case is the same as *conquering* them) seems appallingly great.... The worst (or from the point of view of moral judgments, the best) thing about all this is that the commercial states do not benefit by their violence, for all their trading companies are on the point of collapse. The Sugar Islands, that stronghold of the cruelest and most calculated slavery, do not yield any real profit; they serve only the indirect (and not entirely laudable) purpose of training sailors for warships, thereby aiding the prosecution of wars in Europe. And all this is the work of powers who make endless ado about their piety.[14]

More than two hundred years later, Kant's description seems uncanny: an occupation equivalent to conquering for the sake of commercial gain that now stands on the verge of collapse and does not produce real revenue except insofar as it funds the military and its contractors—and all of this done in the name of piety and righteousness.

Technological advances in the last two hundred years—including the camera, especially its most recent forms, video and digital—however, bring "reality" to bear on the colonial enterprise in ways that can level time and space and that take colonial logic to an extreme. The camera documents reality in a way that transforms our relations to both *history* and *truth*. Paradoxically, the seeming reality of the camera, especially the video or television camera, turns all time into the present—this is particularly true of wireless digital images that can be broadcast "live." Collapsing all events and images into a perpetual present creates a truth-effect through which fantasy and reality flow into each other. This time-shifting operation turns history into myth and vice versa by dislodging events from their contexts and making them ever-present and thereby seemingly eternal or mythical (VCRs were originally called time-shifting machines because they allowed viewers to watch their favorite television shows at a time more convenient for them).

As Susan Sontag argues in her commentary on Abu Ghraib, the immediacy of digital technology makes impossible the censorship that could be imposed when soldiers were sending letters back home. Now soldiers are sending e-mail messages with digital attachments all over the world. This makes it possible for photographs and messages to evade military censorship but it also compresses the time and space between reality and representations of reality. Sontag comments that "the distinction between photograph and reality—as between spin and policy—can easily evaporate as government and military officials seem to identify the photographs and not the actions captured by them as the wrong-doing."[15] But contra Sontag, it is not just the fact that the military blames the photographer that blurs the distinction between reality and fantasy; it is not just the question of responsibility or blame that is twisted by the immediacy of digital technology and media spin: digital technology reproduces reality almost as fast as we are experiencing it and thereby collapses the time between reality and representation of that reality. As we will see, it is not just the fact that the photographs or visual images are distributed within the discourse of a particular political spin that mandates what we can and cannot see, but also that the images themselves already determine what we can and cannot see by presenting events in a specific way from a particular perspective and in media that create the illusion of immediate access to reality. While the seeming immediacy and constant flow of images and information make it impossible to censor them—which is why the military and government work even harder nowadays at censorship—simultaneously they compress the time and space available for the critical reflection and contextualization necessary to interpret the meaning of these images.

Cameras as Weapons of War

Since their invention, photography and other forms of imagery have been used in military intelligence. Soldiers now watch live reports of other soldiers to get information on the war. Quoting reporter Sarah Boxer, cultural critic Ann Kaplan comments on this phenomenon: "Boxer concludes that there is 'general confusion as to who is acting and who is watching. And at the crux of the confusion are the traditional eyewitnesses to war, the journalists, 'embedded' with the troops.' She perceptively asks: 'Are the television cameras witnesses to war, or are they part of the weaponry? Or both?' "[16] Not only do soldiers armed with digital cameras send images around the world via e-mail and the Internet, but the military itself is taking video equipment along on missions to document successes—the rescue of Jessica Lynch is the prime example of military operations that include the use of special night-vision video equipment to create the image of the heroic and successful rescue mission. The anonymous soldier behind the camera during the Lynch rescue records the event and participates in it—only (not unlike the prison guard behind the camera at Abu Ghraib) s/he wields a camera instead of a gun.

Several scholars have analyzed the connection between cameras and weapons of war, particularly in colonial situations where one country's military is occupying another country. As we have seen, Malek Alloula has examined the effects and politics of postcards of Algerian women taken by the French occupying Algeria. And Chaudhary has discussed the role of the camera in the British occupation of India; Chaudhary argues that "the newest technological apparatus for the articulation of this nexus of concern-investment-knowledge was the camera with which the army officers planned to 'shoot' their 'interesting subject' ... the camera could replace the gun, at least under certain circumstances.... The double shadow of fear and displaced violence [that] accompanied colonial photographic practice generally and specifically."[17] Chaudhary analyzes some of the ways in which colonial photography produced "knowledge" about the colonial subjects and purportedly showed the "truth" about them (that they both needed and were receptive to British culture). In addition, the camera recorded and thereby reproduced violence that could be circulated in its captured and virtual form in order to keep the colonial subjects in line. Cameras, then, were as effective as guns in some circumstances.

John Berger also suggests a rhetorical connection between a camera and a gun, which is telling in terms of the military's use of cameras in war. Discussing photographs from the Vietnam War, Berger comments on the double role of the camera, which not only captures violence on film and thereby participates in it, but also does violence to time itself: "The word trigger, applied to rifle and camera, reflects a correspondence which does not stop at the purely metaphysical. The image seized by the camera is doubly violent and both types of violence reinforce the same contrast: the contrast between the photographed moment and all others."[18] Chaudhary's analysis shows, however, that the connection between the camera and the gun is not just rhetorical; cameras have been used to threaten colonial subjects, as if to say, "Behave, or this is what will happen to you!" In this way cameras take the place of guns as weapons with which to manage individuals and populations. Think again of Abu Ghraib, where prisoners were shown photographs both as part of the operations of humiliation and as threats. Not only were they threatened that this could happen to them—that they could be stripped naked and put in sexual poses—but also that if this did happen, it would be photographed for all to see, thereby compounding the prisoners' degradation.

Berger concludes that war photographs do not stop violence unless those viewing the photographs have the political power to do something, a power that the ordinary viewer does not have: "In the political systems as they exist, we have no legal opportunity of effectively influencing the conduct of wars waged in our name. To realize this and to act accordingly is the only effective way of responding to what the photograph shows. Yet the double violence of the photographed moment actually works against this realization. That is why they can be published with impunity."[19] The double violence works against the realization of our lack of political power by depoliticizing moments of agony and war and making them "evidence of the general human condition."[20] Viewed as such, they can be published and viewed outside of any historical or political context and outside of any discourse of responsibility. The viewer can easily disavow the ways in which s/he is implicated by the images.

Insofar as photographs isolate moments and rip them from their historical context, they perform a second-order violence to time and history.

When a momentary event is extracted from its temporal and historical context, the photographic content or subject becomes both an abstract individual and an indeterminate representative of human suffering more generally. Decontextualizing depoliticizes because it results in what cultural critic Ann Kaplan calls "empty empathy." Analyzing the *New York Times* coverage of the beginning of the 2003 invasion of Iraq, Kaplan criticizes the media for sentimentalizing the war by presenting fragmented images out of context and by focusing on individuals rather than on the political context.[21] Interviews with individual soldiers and human-interest stories about their families back home personalize the war but also depoliticize it. This focus on individuals (think of Jessica Lynch) gives the sense of these people as both unique and as representative. They become exemplars of "The American Solider" or "Heroic Individuals," and thereby the scene is depoliticized. In the words of Kaplan, "One is encouraged to identify with specific people, to enter into their experiences rather than to think about what we are looking at, or to engage on any larger intellectual or analytical level."[22] Viewers and readers are left with sentiment and empty empathy that do not translate into political reflection, let alone action. The political becomes personal.

Embedded "Witnessing"

The politics of vision is complicated by the recent phenomenon called "embedded" reporting, which exacerbates the sense of the political as personal. With embedded reporting, the journalist becomes a participant in the action along with his/her military escorts. Both the effects on the journalist in this situation (where his/her life depends upon the soldiers with whom s/he travels) and the effects on the viewing audience (where we see the journalist hunkering down under attack or attacking along with the military) undermine the ability to get any critical distance from events as they unfold. Journalist Michael Massing gives an example of such an embedded report on MSNBC: "Dr. Bob Arnot—normally assigned to the health beat—excitedly followed his cameraman into an unlighted building where two captured Iraqi fighters were being held near the entrance while a group of women and children could be seen in back. 'They're fighting outside,' Arnot said with indignation. 'Here in the front are RPGs [rocket-propelled grenades] used to kill Marines, and in the back are these women

and children—civilian hostages. And they're terrified.' But terrified of
what? The captured men in the front room? The fighting outside? Were
they being held against their will? Arnot never asked."[23] Massing notes
that the embedded MSNBC reporters usually "recounted tales of American bravery and derring-do ... utterly intoxicated by the war."[24] Caught up
in the moment as eyewitnesses to war rather than war correspondents,
these embedded reporters focus on the emotions of war—their own and
those of the military personnel around them—rather than contextualizing
events as part of a narrative that might help viewers interpret them.

The embedded reporter, inserted as an integral part of the surround-
ings, is emblematic of the phenomenon of an individualized yet indeterminate location in time and space. The proximity to events allows the viewer
to "participate" in the war by identifying with the individuals involved—the
reporter and the soldiers s/he is interviewing or moving with—as protagonists of a drama unfolding as media spectacle. Massing explains that embedded reporting arose partially in response to the danger posed to wartime
reporters, who therefore choose to move with the military for protection.[25]
But it is also the result of government restrictions that give journalists access to the military campaign only on certain conditions outlined by the
military and the government. As Judith Butler points out, "Journalists agree
to report only from the perspective established by military and governmen-
tal authorities. They traveled only on certain trucks, looked at only certain
scenes, and relayed home only images and narratives of certain kinds of
action. Embedded reporting implies that this mandated perspective would
not itself become the topic of reporters who were offered access to the war
on the condition that their gaze remain restricted to the established param-
eters of designated action."[26]

The result of all this is limited access to events, which are seen only from
the vantage point of the physical position of troops and increasingly only
from the ideological perspective of the military. In the words of Massing,
"Often, American journalists seem embedded with the military not only
physically but also mentally."[27] Massing gives several examples of news reports from Iraq that present a one-sided account very much identified with
the military. One of his examples involves Los Angeles Times correspondent
Tony Perry, who had been embedded with Marines in Fallujah in a housing project on the outskirts of town. The Marines had forced the residents
of the apartment building to leave so that they could establish their base
there. Perry reports that the families were safe and better off out of harm's

way even though he could not know where they went since he stayed with the Marines:

> So, in Perry's telling, the Marines, in driving the family from their home, were actually doing it for their own good. And happily, the family was able to flee to rural areas and stay with tribal relatives [Perry reported that these were tribal people and so were used to moving] rather than be forced into a refugee camp. What's more, the Marines—"we," as Perry put it—were going to "make amends" by sprucing up the area and building a soccer field. Perry, unable to move about the city and talk with Iraqis, could only pass on optimistic, reassuring speculation that those displaced would "live and survive." Sharing quarters with the Marines, Perry seemed to share their outlook as well.[28]

Feeling guilty about displacing the family, Perry reports that he "put a few bucks" under a Mr. Potato Head doll for when they return.

The current popularity of embedded journalists also makes manifest a tension in television reporting inherent in photojournalism since its inception. Susan Sontag maintains that photographs seemingly provide a record of the real since a machine can't deceive, but they also bear witness to the real since there is a person framing the shot: "This sleight of hand allows photographs to be both objective record and personal testimony, both a faithful copy or transcription of an actual moment of reality and an interpretation of that reality."[29] It is interesting to note that Sontag concludes that photography accomplishes a feat to which literature hopelessly aspires—simultaneously providing a copy of reality and an interpretation of it—while using metaphors of textuality, interpretation, and transcription to describe photography. In other words, even while attributing a privilege to photography over literature, Sontag describes photography's relation to reality in literary terms.

Sontag's position on the immediacy of photography, however, is not as one-sided as Judith Butler makes it out in her critical essay "Photography, War, Outrage." Butler argues that for Sontag the photograph is beyond interpretation and so needs captions and narrative to accompany it. But, as is alluded to in the quotation above, this is because the photo performs a double function—it is precisely because the photo is an interpretation in disguise that it needs another narrative layer of interpretation to make visible what Butler calls the "frame of the photograph," which will remain invisible to the viewer without some critical analysis. As Butler so force-fully argues, "to learn to see the frame that blinds us to what we see is no easy matter ... our inability to see what we see is also of critical concern."[30] In part this is because we are not yet a visually literate culture—although we are surrounded by them, we have not yet learned how to critically assess images. In order to begin to account for our emotional reactions to photographs and what they mean to us as individuals and as a society, we need to recognize that the photograph or visual image is always created from one perspective that already interprets and creates reality; it is this framing operation, this embedded interpretation, that we must come to see. We must recognize the invisible in the visible; which is to say that we must learn to recognize that there is always something beyond our recognition in these images. What we see and what we do not or cannot see both require ongoing interpretation.

Photography occupies a place between recording reality and interpreting it that points to the paradox of witnessing an event as an eyewitness and bearing witness to it, a paradox that I explain elsewhere and to which I will return shortly. Embedded journalism brings to a head this tension between reporting and witnessing. The embedded journalist is both reporting on events and participating in them. Describing the media coverage of the collapse of the World Trade Center towers, media theorist Andrew Hoskins says that "the extended outside broadcasts placed its anchors as both part of and also as bearing witness to the spectacle.... This is indicative of an accelerating trend in correspondents constructing themselves as both reporting on and constituent of media events."[31] Occupying the place of the eyewitness, the reporter in this instance presents what s/he sees at the same time as bearing witness to its horror. But the reporter's testimonial to the horror is given without political or social commentary that could help the viewer interpret the situation. Rather, horror or terror is presented ripped out of time or context and thereby closed off from interpretation. The same is true of embedded war reporting.

Both the immediacy of embedded reporting and the reporters' identification with the soldiers protecting them make it difficult for viewers to get any critical distance on events. Embedded reporting thereby turns real events into media events and produces a confusing effect on the viewer, who is pulled into the action as if watching a war movie. The new wireless technology that allows soldiers and reporters to broadcast live from the front lines makes the coverage seem more like a war movie than a news report of a real one.[32] The combination of proximity in space and the real-time reporting work to isolate a particular space and time, extract it from its context, and present it as immediate, part of the eternal present of television, thereby evacuating its historical meaning. Embedded live reports are just the latest developments in media that displace history and time into a permanent "here and now," developments that are symptoms of media culture's obsession with, and anxiety over, the Real and the Live—an obsession that is not only a symptom of repressed anxiety over death but also a thin screen over a culture of death and violence.

Spectacles of Violence

In the 2005 Hollywood blockbuster *Mr. & Mrs. Smith*—which generated more off-screen heat in the tabloids than on—Brad Pitt and Angelina Jolie play a couple, John and Jane Smith, whose marriage has lost its spark after only "five or six" years and who rekindle their passion by beating, shooting, and cutting each other. The film begins with the couple in therapy reluctant to answer questions about their lackluster marriage, especially about their sex life. In the course of the film we learn that unbeknownst to each other, both are accomplished assassins working for competing companies. They sleepwalk through their marriage and everyday lives together like automatons, while their violent killing sprees are executed as manic moments in their otherwise empty lives. The few words they exchange are passionless—until they receive orders from their respective companies to kill each other. Unlike the failed couples' therapy mockingly shown at the beginning and end of the film, their brutality toward each other enflames their desires and reinitiates sex and conversation, both of which revolve around violence. Neither loses sleep over their killing sprees; Jane brags that she has lost feeling in three of her fingers, and it seems that—outside of their violent mania—neither of them feel much of anything, even for each other. They have become killing machines who abuse others as automatically as they brush their teeth or eat dinner. Their violence is so mechanical that when ordered they turn it on each other without a second thought. And it is their automatic violence that apparently saves them from their robotic marriage.

Unlike classic Hollywood remarriage films from the 1940s such as *His Girl Friday* (1940), *My Favorite Wife* (1940), or *The Philadelphia Story* (1940), where marriages are rekindled through fast-paced dialogue and physical comedy, in *Mr. & Mrs. Smith* the marriage is rekindled via fast-paced action with very little dialogue and lots of physical violence.[33] In the older movies the estranged couple is often brought into close physical contact through a comic turn of events, sometimes involving sight gags and slapstick choreography. In the later the close physical contact is the result of choreographed action and brutality in which the "battle between the sexes" is taken to a literal level. As in *His Girl Friday*, where newspaperman Walter Burns (Cary Grant) wins back reporter and ex-wife Hildy Johnson (Rosalind Russell) by giving her an irresistible news story, Jane and John find common ground in a passion for their work, though in this case their work happens to be killing people. Whereas in the classic films the couple's successful reunion is often measured in terms of a compromise that obviously only temporarily abates tensions in the relationship, in *Mr. & Mrs. Smith* the success of the relationship is reduced to the number of times the couple has sex. Just as literal violence has replaced the metaphorical battle of rapid-fire dialogue, literal sex has replaced the excitement of sexual tension built through dialogue and comic accidents of physical proximity.

Watching this glorification of sadomasochism and sexual violence might remind us of the young military personnel who used sexualized abuse to enhance their sex lives at Abu Ghraib (where one soldier gave another pictures of prisoners forced to simulate sex acts as a birthday present, and pictures of sex between soldiers were interspersed with abuse photographs). The idea that abusing others is a form of sexual arousal seems to move easily between the everyday fare of sexual violence and violent sex of Hollywood films and the shocking photographs from Abu Ghraib. Why is one banal and the other shocking? Is it that one is real and the other is fantasy? In the light of reality television and virtual "facts" and virtual personalities on the Internet, how can we tell the difference? In fact, don't our fantasies affect our perceptions of reality? And weren't the young soldiers at Abu Ghraib not only following orders to "soften up" the prisoners but also acting out their own fantasies?

The border between reality and fantasy is precisely the dangerous terrain of human habitation, filled as it is with hair-trigger land mines, images both virtual and real. In the face of these real and fictional images of sadomasochistic violence, it is as if the only way to give meaning to life has become destroying it, that we only embrace life by denying it to the point of murder and suicide. The events at Abu Ghraib display a sadistic pleasure in violence toward others to the point of murder.

Is the violence toward others "enjoyed" by teenagers and young soldiers at Abu Ghraib as a means to "let off steam" related at least in part to the wider phenomenon of ritualistic violence among teenagers and young people? The abuse at Abu Ghraib reminded many of fraternity hazing, which is known for its rituals of abuse and humiliation. Self-injury and abuse are also becoming popular among teenagers and young people, who cut themselves or choke themselves in order to feel extreme sensations. Increasingly, teenagers are engaging in the self-injuring practice of "cutting"; they ritualistically cut themselves in order to "feel something" or to prove they "exist." One study reports this message on a self-injury Internet board post: "How do I know I exist? At least I know I exist when I cut." Another reads: "I may try and quit but even if I succeed, I'll always dream of razorblades and blood."[34] And a psychotherapist in Lancaster, Pennsylvania, reports that her clients say, "I was numb. I needed to feel something" or "I feel so dead inside, that when I see the blood flowing, I feel alive."[35] This psychotherapist concludes that these kids (predominately girls) cut themselves because they have difficulty expressing emotions.

Another deadly "game" gaining popularity among teens and children as young as eight years is the "choking" or "hanging" game, where kids cut off their air supply to get a rush as they pass out. Some of these kids use ropes or even dog leashes; reportedly the "game" is "fueled by the Internet."[36] These attempts to feel something more intensely are dangerous masochistic practices that can and have led to death. At the same time, however, they are practices that make manifest the way in which raw sensation and spectacle are replacing other forms of meaning in popular culture. So too do films like *Mr. & Mrs. Smith* replace the dialogue of older Hollywood films with the spectacle of violence, including images of raw sensations—cutting, bruising, rough sex, etc.

These sadomasochistic forms of entertainment are symptomatic of a general sense of loss of purpose or of the meaning of life that, as we will see, in part results from a disconnect between emotions and socially proscribed expressions of those emotions. In a culture that values a "just do it" approach, reflecting on our actions and interpreting our experience are devalued. We are doers, not thinkers. And meditating on the meaning of our actions, desires, and values is seen as a waste of time, especially in the world of business, where "time is money." So, in the place of narratives in which we interpret our emotions and our lives and give them meaning, we move between acting with as little thought as possible and images on television and computer screens. Both our actions and these media images appear to us as immediate and real, without any need for interpretation—"they are what they are."

But there is nothing inherent in actions or images that makes them antithetical to interpretation and meaning. On the contrary, in a sense they call out for interpretation; they need to be analyzed and interpreted to become meaningful parts of our lives. In the absence of reflection such images have the power of an unquestioned unexamined reality that feeds on itself in ways that nourish violent acting out rather than thoughtful mediation, which in turn might prevent this acting on violent impulses. Critical interpretation of actions, desires, and values both requires and results in connecting the present to the past and the future, and putting those actions and desires into a context that can make sense of them. Critical interpretation is a process that slows reactions and modulates sensations in ways that help us integrate actions and sensations into systems of meaning and also help us to prevent a first and immediate aggressive response.

In that sensations and images appear especially immediate we seem to experience them as real in a way that defies interpretation—"it is what it is." For example, my undergraduate students are much more likely to resist interpreting images, especially Hollywood films, than, say, philosophy texts or novels. They insist that "it is just a movie" and has no meaning outside of its entertainment value; the movie is reduced to spectacle to be watched but not analyzed. A spectacle can produce a visceral reaction, a bodily response, but resists interpretation—any such introspection on the part of the viewer is deemed superfluous. Spectacles seem to resist contextualization, which requires the creation of narratives that explain or study them in relation to other images, actions, desires, or values. This seeming resistance is only in part an illusion produced by increasingly realistic forms of audio-visual representation, which create a sense of virtual reality.

In addition, the illusion of immediacy perpetuates visual illiteracy. In the whole of human history, visual images, especially moving images that look real, are relatively recent phenomena, and we have yet to develop a schema for how to "read" them. Most of us learn to read books and newspapers, and to some extent we even learn to interpret these texts; for example, we might "take with a grain of salt" an editorial in a newspaper that we know to be particularly conservative or radical. But we don't learn to interpret media, Internet, and film images in any such context. While in general or as a culture we know that the value that we place on interpreting texts could be enhanced to benefit our sense of a life full of meaning, we don't seem to place any value on interpreting images, particularly those that appear to directly mirror reality—or more accurately, those that seem to function as windows onto reality, such as news programs and photographs, including the photographs from Abu Ghraib.

Speaking about the photographs from Abu Ghraib in particular, Angela Davis points to the lack of visual literacy needed to interpret them in the context of the history and meaning of torture and violence:

> Images are very complicated and we haven't promoted, at least not in a mass sense, a visual literacy necessary to critically understand them. To think of the image as an unmediated representation is problematic and often has the effect of producing precisely the opposite of what was expected. I'm thinking of the Rodney King controversy. For example, we saw the police beating Rodney King on video, but the prosecutor was able to develop a particular interpretation of that image that bolstered his claim that Rodney King was the aggressor. So I think it is important not to assume that the image has a self-evident relationship to its object. And it is important to consider the particular economy within which images are produced and consumed.[37]

Davis's last point is especially important. We must consider the context within which the images are made and seen, particularly the political, social, and economic contexts. For example, going back to the photographs from Abu Ghraib, the photographs of young people smiling and giving thumbs-up behind a pyramid of naked hooded men was interpreted by some as kids having fun, akin to fraternity pranks (in fact, *Weekly Standard* editor Jonathan Last said, "Worse things happen in frat houses across America")[38]; this type of image seemed familiar to us from images of fraternity pranks, and so we might place it in that context. But this is all the more reason why it is crucial to interpret context—both the context in which we "see" or "read" the photo (as prank or as torture) and the context in which the photo was taken (in a fraternity or in a war prison), not to mention all of the complications of who is taking the picture and why and how the picture is used. Visual literacy requires learning to "read" and interpret media images in their historical contexts.

Popular media culture, however, feeds the sense of the immediacy and therefore uninterpretability of images by turning reality into a spectacle—extreme images and situations designed to provoke a visceral rather than thoughtful reaction. As a result, we desire more intense experiences, more real experiences. We oscillate between trying to shut off our emotional lives with pharmaceutical drugs—antidepressants, Ritalin, and sleeping pills—and channel or net-surfing to find alternative realities. Witness the fascination with reality television and live Internet web cams. The extreme emotions prepackaged and presented as spectacle—think of the outraged lovers and outrageous situations on talk shows and reality television—on the one hand desensitize us to extremes and on the other contribute to a sense of the meaninglessness of experience that in turn leads to feelings of emptiness and depression. Confronted by extreme yet empty emotions in the media, we turn off our own emotions with pharmaceuticals. As bodily sensations are ever more marketed and sold to us in artificial forms in reality shows and video games, we also crave real sensations. In a culture where emotions are modulated by drugs and images, we crave more intense sensations, as evidenced by the growing popularity of "cutting" and the choking or hanging "game" among teenagers.

As reality itself becomes commoditized, we crave more extreme forms of bodily experience. Reality has become a property that can be bought and sold; we place a premium on "real," "genuine," "authentic" at the same time that such qualities are marketed as spectacles to be watched. Both spectacles of reality in the media and making bodily sensations into spectacles through cutting, the hanging game, etc., leave us with seemingly immediate and therefore uninterpretable reality. How do we interpret a spectacle? Especially if it is intended to shock or arouse? These questions raise the deeper question of our conception of the body and bodily sensation as somehow outside of the realm of culture or interpretation, which is to say also outside of the realm of ethics and politics.[39] The body has the status of biological fact and not something in need of interpretation. In place of meaning, we crave spectacular media images and raw bodily sensations; yet because both appear to fall outside of the realm of interpretation, they leave us feeling empty, without meaningful lives. Reality is no longer something we live but something we crave. But, this craving for reality only thinly masks our deeper craving for meaning. We consume reality like the newest breakfast cereal, but because it is lacking in substance, we never feel satisfied ... so we take more antidepressants, more sleeping pills, and go to therapy.

Our fascination with the spectacle of reality enhances the power to terrify of the videotapes from Osama Bin Laden or of beheadings in Iraq. In fact, terrorism relies on the media for its effect. Without the media and the dissemination of images of violence there would be no mass terror. The beheadings in Iraq are ritualistically staged and recorded for maximum effect, for an audience. They are intended to shock, to threaten, and to exploit vulnerability. Decapitation is especially threatening because it is aimed at the head. The various philosophies of the significance of the face, particularly that of Emmanuel Levinas, conclude that the face and the head are the most vulnerable parts of the human body; or, at least insofar as they are associated with language, thought, and ethics, as well as kissing and looking, they signal what we take to be essential characteristics of humanity. And the head is associated with the mind, the soul, and individual sovereignty, to the point that our leaders are called heads of state.

Within Western culture the genitals, specifically the male genitals, are the only rival to the head in terms of their association with vulnerability. Freud's entire developmental psychology revolves around the threat of castration and the vulnerability of the male organ. Perhaps this is why so much of the torture at Abu Ghraib was aimed at the prisoners' genitals. Probably the most terrifying images from Abu Ghraib are the photographs of dogs threatening prisoners who are shown looking horrified and holding their hands over their genitals. In the abuse at Abu Ghraib and in the ritualistic beheadings performed by al Qaeda, the goal is not just to hurt or kill—given the way that bodies are used and abused, it is to terrify by exploiting feelings of vulnerability. In neither case do the perpetrators simply inflict pain or simply kill; the hurting and the killing are performed ceremoniously, and the photographs and videotapes of those debasing rituals are then used to intimidate others. The photos and videos are used to make others feel vulnerable by exploiting the vulnerability of the human body itself.

In *Visions capitales*, the book that accompanied the Louvre exhibit curated by Julia Kristeva in 1998 on severed heads in the history of art, Kristeva repeatedly suggests that artistic representations of decapitation are sublimated means of negotiating anxieties over castration and death, what, following her latest work, we might call "anxieties over vulnerability." The threat of decapitation has long been connected with the threat of castration. Kristeva suggests that artists paint and sculpt severed heads in order to mitigate anxieties over vulnerability as an alternative to projecting and abjecting it onto others. Here and throughout her work, she argues that representations of violence can prevent real violence; echoing psychoanalyst Jacques Lacan, she maintains that what is effaced in the imaginary and the symbolic risks returning at the level of the real. Analyzing images of beheadings from the French Revolution, she concludes that perhaps the figures of decapitation and severed heads can be seen as an intimate form of resistance to what she calls the "democracy" of the guillotine. She says that "above all, if art is a transfiguration, it has political consequences."[40] This sentiment could not be more relevant today, as we witness gruesome beheadings in videotaped spectacles that could be diagnosed as a refusal to examine the role of fantasy in constructions of reality, where the inability to represent sacrifice leads to real sacrifice, and where reality itself has become a commodity.

What is the difference between Caravaggio's painting of beheading in "David and Goliath" and recent videotapes of beheadings in Iraq? This question itself may be shocking because the primary difference couldn't be more obvious: one is art while the other makes a spectacle of gruesome murder. But, given psychoanalysis's insistence on the role of fantasy in perceptions of reality, can the difference be simply that of artifice versus reality? If artificial death abolishes the uncanny effect of real death, does this imply that the more realistic the representation the more uncanny it becomes? What about artists like August Raffet or Gericault, whom Kristeva discusses, and who used real severed heads and accident victims as their models?[41] And what of the artifice involved in the ritualistic staging and recording of the beheadings in Iraq? What of the staging involved in using green hoods and stacking prisoners in a pyramid for the camera at Abu Ghraib or standing a hooded prisoner on a box, arms outstretched attached to wires, reminiscent of crucifixion?

Where is the border between artifice and reality? Navigation of that border is precisely what is threatened by the contemporary fascination with reality television and live Internet Web cams. Freud is right when he states that the uncanny effect of the real is more powerful than artifice; but does the need for greater degrees of reality in violence and sexual victimization of others become perverse when representation becomes a form of acting out? Perhaps degrees of perversion can be measured only in terms of the suffering of its "objects."

Reality as Fetish

As evidenced by Christian and Islamic fundamentalists engaging in holy wars from Washington to Baghdad, from Gaza to Amsterdam, we are losing the ability to tell art from reality, the world of ideas from the real world. A filmmaker's or novelist's depiction of violence is taken as justification for literal violence; think of Dutch filmmaker Theo Van Gogh, who was brutally murdered for making movies critical of Islamic fundamentalism, or the death threats against Salman Rushdie after the publication of his novel, *Satanic Verses.*

We confuse images with reality and act on violent impulses rather than translating them into meaningful forms of representation and analyzing or elaborating on them. "Violence, addiction, criminality, or psychosomatic suffering," the "new maladies of the soul," as Julia Kristeva calls them, are sicknesses of the imagination.[42] As subjects of modern technological culture, we are losing the ability to imagine, and most importantly the ability to imagine the meaning of our own lives. Without the ability to articulate our violent fantasies, we end up acting on them—confusing fantasy with reality. This is to say that without the ability to imagine, interpret, and represent our desires and fears, our violent impulses can lead to either murder or suicide, abusing others or ourselves.

It may seem contradictory to claim that the society of the spectacle, which is based on images, works against imagination. After all, aren't television and film the products of imagination? While it is impossible to make categorical distinctions between forms of visual art in terms of checking or encouraging violence, it is possible to diagnose those images in terms of the unconscious fears and desires they represent. This analysis and diagnosis, like all interpretation, must be ongoing and provisional, readjusted for different contexts and historical periods.

Given the current popularity in the United States of reality television and action films high on violence and low on dialogue, it is important to draw a distinction between forms of media presentation that encourage interpretation and critical analysis and thereby compel the viewer to imagine alternatives, and those that don't. Instead of questioning stereotypes and challenging the viewer to rethink his/her position, media presentations that don't encourage critical self-reflection offer themselves up as reality in ways that reassure viewers of national and individual identity. I suggest that they do so by reifying reality through the presentation of a perpetual present rather than opening up the time for critical interpretation, a time that requires a historical context, along with a past and a future, a time of alternative realities and possible futures.

The popularity of reality television programs that show people engaging in extreme sadomasochistic acts or sexual encounters with strangers, along with true-confession talk shows in which guests reveal their most intimate and outrageous sexual lives, suggests that reality has become an obsession in the United States. Political theorist Susan Buck-Morss argues that spectacles anaesthetize us and thereby undermine the ability to act politically—and I would argue the ability to imagine otherwise that is a prerequisite for acting politically. Buck-Morss says that with the economy of the spectacle "a narcotic was made of reality itself."[43] And the more violent it is, the more real it is.[44] Cultural critic Slavoj Žižek maintains that "this violent effort to distill the pure Real from the elusive reality necessarily ends up in its opposite, in the obsession with pure appearance ... The key to this reversal resides in the ultimate impossibility to draw a clear distinction between deceptive reality and some firm positive kernel of the Real: every positive bit of reality is a priori suspicious... The pursuit of the Real thus equals total annihilation, a (self) destructive fury within which the only way to trace the distinction between semblance and the Real, is precisely to STAGE it in a fake spectacle."[45] This diagnosis of the Real aptly describes reality television, which is staged reality, reality become spectacle.

In the case of reality TV, viewers know that what they see is not real but just the same they "believe" that it is—they treat it as reality. The same disavowal seems to operate in relation to news of war—viewers believe that what they see is real but they also do not believe that it is real. Reality is produced and marketed to the point that the border between reality and fantasy has been blurred. It is not just that our perceptions of reality are always colored by our fantasies, but also that reality has become a version of fantasy. Reality has become a commodity that sells. The paradoxical logic of simultaneously knowing but not knowing that something is real is what psychoanalytic theory would identify as the logic of fetishism, complete with the disavowal of loss or separation. Reality has become a fetish.

The logic of the fetish is a logic of disavowal: the fetishist knows that it is not real, but just the same he believes that it is. He knows that his substitute object is not the be-all-and-end-all of his satisfaction and yet he believes that it is. Ultimately, the fetish is a substitute for the fantasy of wholeness and plenitude.[46] The media has fueled the fetishism that confuses reality and fantasy and disavows loss and separation, including the separation or distance necessary to sublimate loss into meaningful forms of signification; that is to say, rather than merely act on them, forms of signification can give meanings to our fears, desires, and suffering, When visual media presents itself as reality immediately accessible and in need of no interpretation, it encourages spectators to fetishize aggressive, violent, and sexual impulses rather than interpret them. And by turning reality into a fetish object we thereby disavow loss and separation. Indeed, Freud suggests that a fetish operates as a projection against loss and the psychical threat that it brings. The fetish protects the fantasy of wholeness.

To make this discussion more concrete, we might think of the debates over whether the news media should be allowed to show coffins of dead soldiers. The government withheld visual images of air-cargo holds full of coffins, and of their unloading. In the name of national security, they withheld the bulk of the photographs from Abu Ghraib. By not showing Americans dying and dead, or American engaging in abuse, they perpetuate the fantasy of wholeness and innocence that denies the real casualties of war. Both visual and print media rarely represent the death of either American military personnel or Iraqi civilians. The "security" at stake here is the illusion that Americans are not vulnerable or culpable. The flip side of this security, as we will see, is the discourse of emergency and crisis that justifies the use of extreme force in the name of security. The government projects American superiority in terms of both military might and moral right, while at the same time fomenting the sense of danger and threat that justifies extreme action in a state of emergency, in a nation at war.

Paranoid Patriotism

Since the attacks of September 11, 2001, the border between fantasy and reality has taken a paranoid form that points up the role of time in the confusion between the two. 9/11 has become a monument outside of time, as evidenced by the fact that popular media doesn't have to use the year, 2001, as its dating marker in referring to the event. Within the cultural imaginary of the United States, 9/11 acts as the moment of vulnerability when Americans lost our sense of security. 9/11 evokes nostalgia for safety that operates in the realm of fantasy as an invincibility that could not be lost because in fact we never had it. The loss of our sense of security has led not only to fantasies of invincibility and the notion that 9/11 took it away from Americans, but also to paranoid counterinvestments in nationalism and patriotism alongside paranoid fears of persecution and even paranoid delusions of grandeur.

Australian anthropologist Ghassan Hage describes a similar phenomenon in Israel, where the discourse of security dominates the social landscape. He says that Israel's search for "zero vulnerability" actually produces its opposite; rather than succeeding in eliminating any threat to security, the quest for this ultimately impossible goal leads to paranoia: "This search for zero vulnerability produces a gaze that sees threats everywhere and ends up reproducing the very vulnerability it is supposedly trying to overcome."[47] As Hage points out, this is exactly the aim of terrorism, to produce a sense of vulnerability and fear. But, ironically, what maintains and reproduces that fear is government and media warnings of possible threats; warnings of vulnerability make us feel vulnerable. This insecurity leads to what Hage calls "anthrax culture," where we are afraid of others menacing our borders, which in turn leads to a "warring and siege mentally" that demands the elimination of any potential threat—and threats are seen everywhere. Hage claims that "in this phobic culture where everything is viewed as either threatening and in need of extermination or threatened and in need of protection, there is an invasion of the order of the border."[48] Even the water we drink and the air we breath becomes suspicious, which is why Hage calls this phenomenon anthrax culture.

Within psychoanalytic theories of paranoia, fear of persecution is the flip side of delusions of grandeur. President Bush's 2005 inaugural address includes the rhetoric of grandeur that plays off of persecution and victimization: he says that he wants to conquer the *entire world* in order to bring freedom to all: "America, in this young century, proclaims liberty throughout all the world and to all the inhabitants thereof." Why? To protect America from hatred, resentment, and violence, and to secure us against a vulnerability that has its source in "whole regions of the world" that "simmer in resentment and tyranny" (Jan. 20, 2005). This paranoid patriotism is fed by a feeling of a lack of security that has as its unconscious partner the fantasy of invincibility.

Ultimately, however, the Bush administration defines security in terms of ownership. In his 2005 inaugural speech, Bush explicitly links homeland security and social security and goes on to say that economic security will be achieved through "an ownership society": "We will widen the ownership of homes and businesses, retirement savings and health insurance—preparing our people for the challenges of life in a free society." Within this rhetoric "to own" or "to possess" is "to secure." This notion of security as possession or ownership is part and parcel of a imperialist mentality; we can justify our imperialist ventures in the name of securing ourselves—through ownership. Securing ourselves by bringing freedom to the globe means owning it; and freedom becomes a euphemism for capitalist ventures that expand U.S. ownership. In this regard, it is telling that the word "secure" can also mean without care, even careless, and overconfident.

In the rhetoric of the Bush administration, America is secure, its wealth is secured, if its youngest citizens sacrifice themselves for ideals of freedom. In his inaugural address, President Bush also links self-sacrifice and self-governance to the greater wealth and character of the country: "In America's ideal of freedom, the public interest depends on private character.... Self-government relies, in the end, on the governing of the self." Much of this talk of ideals is in the context of praising the military and urging "our youngest citizens to believe the evidence of your eyes" that "evil is real and courage triumphs" so that they will "make the choice to serve in a cause larger than [their] own wants," to add "not just to the wealth of the country but to its character," which is obviously a recruitment pitch to join in the idealistic—or should we say "idolistic"—fight of Good versus Evil in order to add to the character and wealth of the country. Again the emphasis is on security and ownership, now as self-sacrifice and self-governance for the sake of the wealth of the country (or at least the privileged class, whose sons and daughters are not required to make this sacrifice).

In answer to questions about the Bush administration's rhetoric, Angela Davis maintains that we need to reconceptualize security in ways that resist the connection between security and ownership; capitalism produces not security but its opposite. Davis asks, "How can we help to make the world secure from the ravages of global capitalism?" She suggests that "this broader sense of security might involve debt relief for Africa; it would mean an end to the juggernaut of privatization that threatens the new society people in South Africa have been trying to build. It would also involve the shifting of priorities from the prison-industrial-complex to education, housing, health care."[49] In sum, security would come not from the ownership and increased privatization proposed by the Bush administration, but from the opposite. And rather than see security in terms of the wealth of the nation, we would have to see it in terms of the wealth and well-being of the world.

Within the Bush administration rhetoric, freedom means ownership and ownership means security. Homeland security replaces social security, which was originally envisioned as a remedy to the economic injustices of capitalism—now the United States has patriotism and an ownership society that use the rhetoric of freedom to advance the injustices of capitalism. Yet freedoms are simultaneously taken away in the name of Freedom-with-a-capital-F, through the Patriot Act; and the ownership society allows us to disown the violence necessary to secure that ownership, especially in Iraq and other parts of the world. With the Patriot Act here, and U.S.-inflicted violence and imprisonments elsewhere, the rhetoric or fantasy of Freedom replaces real freedoms. Now the foundation of civil society as Freud described it has been reversed: rather than substituting rituals and symbols for real murders, we substitute real murders for rituals and symbols; and in the end we cannot tell the difference.[50]

Spectacles of violence viewed within the United States displace the real violence inflicted by the United States elsewhere in the world. While they may horrify us even as they are presented on television as entertainment, these spectacles also allow us to disavow real violence elsewhere. Images of war—so many videotapes of beheadings and of prisoner abuses, and computer-generated images of high-tech warfare—turn war into a form of reality TV. In fact, ABC was considering airing a reality series that followed soldiers in Afghanistan but decided against it because "there would be enough mayhem covered by its news divisions"; and NBC aired a pilot for *War Stories*, a drama set in Iraq, but it was dropped because it might "undermine" their news operation.[51] While network television doesn't want shows to compete for viewers with their news programs, in an article entitled " 'Friends' and Enemies: The War as Situation Comedy," the *New York Times* reports that cable plans to air two new shows about war in Iraq, one drama, *Over There*, and one comedy, *Spirit of America*.[52] Viewers can now watch news programs (e.g., the nightly news), re-created simulations (e.g., made for TV *Saving Jessica Lynch*), and embedded journalist's reports (e.g., CNN special reports) alongside comedies and dramas about the war as entertainment.

The time period between presentation as news and representation as television shows is both collapsed and accelerated. In this way, violence and war are normalized as part of everyday life and entertainment. Every evening on the television news reports with live footage from war zones are presented along with simulations of war and violence and sitcoms, talk shows, etc. The flatness of the screen, so to speak, levels the differences between these forms and makes it difficult to distinguish between reality and fiction. Even the "reality" that is presented has been packaged and framed in ways that further undermine our ability to take a critical position on what we see (and don't see).

Perpetual Present

Both television and the Internet level differences; time and space become indeterminate. Like the landscape of American strip-malls, as we navigate the landscape of television we could be anywhere—every place looks alike. The leveling effect of television and the Internet further undermine our ability to take a critical position that allows us to see the frame around the images. Television news combines live satellite feed, recorded footage, commentary, news bars scrolling across the screen, and commercial breaks, all condensed into a present whose marketability depends upon its up-to-the-minute breaking news reporting. The Internet presents a slideshow of photo-stills and videos of war images along with celebrity fashions, and video footage of natural disasters along with the funniest moments captured on home video, all together with pop-up advertisements and the glut of images available through any Internet search.

Several media theorists have analyzed the time and space compression brought about by the speed and proximity of these images.[53] Arguably the most influential media theorist, Marshall McLuhan claims that "ours is a brand new world of allatonceness"; he warns that time has ceased and space has vanished.[54] Television collapses all time into the present such that it becomes difficult to interpret events in the context of the past or future. And the globalization of the media homogenizes all places and spaces into one type of package. A metaphor for the way in which global media packages emotions and desires in order to sell them around the world, a particular Federal Express television ad shows packages being delivered all over the world to all different locals and to different people speaking different languages. In spite of all of these differences, what the ad intends to show is that the packages are met with the same pleased reaction; geographical, linguistic, and cultural differences are irrelevant when it comes to receiving a package: thanks to global capitalism, we all get the same thing (because we are all waiting for the same thing).

Television telescopes the past and the future into an eternal present that reduces time and space into one common moment of instant gratification. A recent technique on news programs, especially CNN, employing simultaneous presentations compounds the effects of that condensation. Media scholar Andrew Hoskins argues that television news effectively "collapses memory, through a continual and pervasive visualizing of the world in the present":

> Like human memory [TV] tracks, selectively recalls, and alters the past as it re-represents it in real time. It collapses times and forges a "simultaneity of the non-simultaneous" (Brose 2002) through its real-time (television is always "live") presentation of the recent and/or distant past (recorded footage and the "news bar" scrolling along the bottom of the screen) with the present (the instantaneous "now" of news talk unfolding in the real-time of speaker and audience) and the extended present (the future tense and temporal references in news language constructing an eternal promise of what-is-yet-to-come). And it is these very complexities that serve to collapse memory into an overloaded shifting present.[55]

Analyzing news coverage of 9/11, and the outdoor news broadcasts prominent in that coverage, Hoskins says that on that day the New York "skyline reflected its 'extended present' and the determined though indeterminate response in the declared 'war against terrorism,' that is to say, a war without end."[56] The lack of interpretative commentary to contextualize and historicize the time and space of events creates the sense of an indeterminate time/space somehow outside of normal linear time. The understandable emotional reaction of reporters combined with the marketability of disaster put journalists in the position of witnesses to terror rather than news reporters.

The real tragedy was compounded by later media hysteria, including the infamous CNN advisory for New Yorkers to use plastic and duct-tape to seal themselves inside their apartments to prevent the effects of chemical weapons. In addition to the real horror of the attacks of September 11 was the imagined horror of media speculations on what could happen if terrorists attacked nuclear power plants, or released bio-pathogens into drinking water, or detonated chemical weapons in subways. Along with the government's various red, orange, and yellow alerts, the fantasies of disaster were almost as terrifying as the real thing.

Even now, years after the attack, the media and government keep reminding us of the danger, the threat, the urgency. Years later the state of emergency continues. The rhetoric of emergency, crisis, exceptional circumstances is used to justified military action and making exceptions to national and international law. In this indeterminate time/space created by the perpetual present of emergency, prisoners are detained indefinitely. Our national identity becomes linked to the time of emergency such that we are "a nation at war"; and it is this state of emergency that gives us a sense of nationalism and patriotism. Historian Victoria Hesford argues that the emphasis on the present comes at the expense of "a historicizing, futurial consciousness"; and this "tyranny of the present" "not only structured the Bush administration's response to the September 11th attacks, but also the re-workings of nationness complicit in that response," which is to say, the U.S. national identity as a "nation at war."[57] The nation at war operates within the time of crisis or emergency that extracts the present moment from its historical context, from any relation to past or future, and suspends its relation to narratives about that history. By declaring a state of emergency, we become justified in suspending law, particularly international law, in the name of national crisis. The time of emergency makes the present moment exceptional and therefore not bound to law. As Judith Butler observes, this state of emergency is indefinite and thereby justifies indefinite detention of prisoners (now called "detainees") and "war without end."[58]

The news market's obsession with real-time live reports and the latest breaking news, along with its telescoping of all time into the present, creates a perpetual present that is now used to justify perpetual war. The real-time live effect of images of war, combined with news programs' sketches, archival footage, and recreations of both real and possible terrorist attacks, fuels insecurity and fears that play into the paranoid patriotism that desires war as revenge. Insofar as they are produced and nourished by the perpetual present of television and Internet images, these fears and desires thinly veil an anxiety about absence and death. Paradoxically, the urgency of real-time live programming violently rips images out of context and fixes them in an eternal moment, the perpetual present, that collapses past, present, and future into one media moment. The urgency of "the now" and "the real" play into the sense of crisis that legitimates war. The emergency that was the exceptional situation becomes the rule; and colonial violence becomes the norm rather than an anomaly.[59]

It is telling that the one thing television avoids at all costs "dead air," or a blank screen. Television's (our) obsession with the real and the live stops life (and history) in its tracks; it fixes events and takes them out of context so that they become souvenirs or relics, dead things to be displayed in the spectacle of violence as entertainment. Not only does this spectacle displace the reality of death and violence, but also more importantly it effaces any responsibility for that violence. At once, the deaths of others are presented as less important than our deaths, and our responsibility for those deaths is minimized, not only in the dominant narratives used to justify war, but within the visual economy that effectively presents all violence, fictional or real, as part of the same flat but perpetual present.[60] At the same time that we commodify the real (and its violence), we disavow it. We see but at the same time we do not see.

Eternal Correctness

It is not just the structure of visual media or the marketability of immediate, real live broadcasts that levels history and undermines contextual or historical interpretations of events. The rhetoric of eternity and righteousness used by the Bush administration also collapses history into an eternal moment that can be used to place "our way of life" above all others.

In his famous prison speech of October 15, 1953, Fidel Castro claims that history will absolve him for the deaths resulting from his attack against Batista's regime: "La historia me absolverá." Ironically, George W. Bush (following Tony Blair) echoes Castro when he claims, "History will prove me right" for attacking Iraq. It becomes apparent in his 2005 inaugural address, however, that Bush does not mean human history but history from a "God's eye" view, from the point of view of eternity. Bush assimilates the rhetoric of history and historical materialism into the rhetoric of an eternal mission from God that is outside of both the linear history of the realm of meaning and the cyclical repetitive time of the unconscious, which is to say completely outside of human temporality. Although his inaugural speech is full of invocations of history—"the history we have seen together," freedom as "a force of history," and "this time in history"—ultimately the perspective of both judgment and justification is outside of history; it is eternal and therefore cannot be questioned.

It is the righteousness of absolute infinite Good that justifies any finite means for eradicating and punishing what Bush names "Evil" (he continues to use the rhetoric of Good and Evil; for example, in his September 11, 2006, speech he said that "on 9/11, our nation saw the face of evil"). In his speech, Bush invokes "the image of the maker of heaven and Earth," the "eternally right," and the "viewpoint of centuries" versus "the perspective of a single day"; his conclusion makes the juxtaposition between history and eternity clear: "History has an ebb and flow of justice, but history also has a visible direction set by liberty and the author of liberty," who is explicitly named several times as "God" or "a just God" (Bush continues to link freedom to God: in his speech of September 11, 2006, he concludes that we can be confident in our purpose "and faith in a loving God who made us free"). His attempts to stand outside of time disavow history. Moreover, he separates justice, which is associated with history, from liberty or freedom, which is associated with God as the author of liberty; and thereby justifies the perpetual war waged by a nation at war in the godly crusade to bring freedom or liberty to the entire globe. Within this rhetoric, human justice or the justice of history is subservient to God-given liberty, which can justify anything in the name of the "eternally right."

Bush is notorious for using religious rhetoric and invocations of God and righteousness, language that appeals to the eternal against the linear time of history and thereby confuses or conflates the ideal and the real. With the rhetoric of the "Axis of Evil" versus the "good of the American heart," the current administration idolizes Good and Evil and moves politics from the realm of history into the realm of the eternal and the moral or religious (and thereby out of the realm of the ethical and the political). The rhetoric of Good and Evil and "godly crusades" turns politics into religious fundamentalism.

Politics as religious fundamentalism—Christian or Muslim—becomes dogmatic because it refuses all questions. And dogmatism becomes deadly by closing off analysis of our own desires and fears. When questioning of our violent impulses is foreclosed, then acting on them becomes a dangerous reality. Instead of engaging in imaginary or symbolic rites of sacrifice, fundamentalists act out their violent fantasies in the real world, which leads the members of one religion to sacrifice the members of another. We see this today: Theo Van Gogh was killed for questioning Islam while

George W. Bush was re-elected with support from Christian fundamentalists to continue to wage what he calls his godly "crusade" against terror in
Iraq and around the world.[61] Religious extremists share the unquestioned
belief in Good versus Evil and that God or Allah is on their side. Such extremists see themselves on the side of purity and goodness fighting against
impurity and corruption, the holy against the infidels or heathens. They
employ rhetoric of unquestioned and unforgiving righteousness and dam-
nation.[62] The displacement of human history and temporality into "Eternal
Godly Truths" proves fatal when it enters the realm of politics. The Good
justifies killing in the name of universal principles of justice, democracy,
and freedom. The supposed eternal nature of the Good makes it immune
to questioning and pits it against history, particularly history conceived as
fluid and dynamic in relation to social contexts as they are governed by
sociopolitical circumstances.

In conclusion, paranoid patriotism operates by disavowing or effacing
both history and time by freezing the fluidity of time into eternal ideals of
Good and Evil on the one hand and the perpetual present of spectacle on
the other. Eternity and the perpetual present seemingly operate outside of
time and therefore outside of history. They not only exclude the historical
context within which they exist, but also do so in a way that effaces history
altogether insofar as they construct either a timeless eternal or a perpetual
present/presence. They also deny the very context that makes these notions
of eternity and presence possible. To attend to the history of the concepts
themselves would be to expose the power differentials that allow some people to dominate others. Analysis of the history of the use of these concepts,
particularly those of Good and Evil, and of Real, would eventually lead us
back to the history of imperialism and attempts to justify colonization, occupation, and subjugation.

Moreover, both the rhetoric of eternity and the rhetoric of the perpetual
present disavow the historical processes that are essential to human temporality and shape not only our values and ideals (of Good and Evil), but
also our desires (for security) and fears (of death and loss). By denying historical context in the full sense of social contexts and power differentials,
and by denying unconscious desires and fears, both the rhetoric of eternity
and the rhetoric of perpetual present mystify history and truth. Insofar as
this rhetoric effaces history it leaves us with "empty empathy" rather than
witnessing, in the full and double sense of witnessing to the social contexts that shape individuals and their choices and to the dynamic conscious

and unconscious processes that motivate us. Unlike empty empathy, this form of witnessing is a process of perpetual questioning and interpretation rather than a dogmatic closure. Interpretation and analysis can perform the function of time-shifting, but not like the VCR that makes life more convenient and simpler. On the contrary, interpretation as temporal go-between makes life less ready-to-hand and more complex. It dislodges the past and present in relation to an indeterminate future. It "disembeds" the past, present, and future in order to analyze their relations both to social contexts and to unconscious desires and fears.

Full Witnessing

In *Witnessing*, I elaborate a notion of witnessing in its double sense: as being eyewitness to historical facts, and as bearing witness to what cannot be seen. Of these two poles, that of eye-witnessing is associated with history and the social context of the agents involved in specific events, what we might call subject-position. Attention to social context addresses the ways in which an individual is constituted by and within his or her circumstances (for example, most young people who join the military do so because they are poor and have few career choices). Paradoxically, even while news reports focus on individuals, attention to the ways in which individuals and the choices they make are shaped by their sociohistorical context is usually lacking. Rather than focus on the sociohistorical context or conditions that shape the individual, these reports assume that these individuals have absolute freedom to choose the lives that they lead. By not focusing on social context, news reports construct individuals outside of history.

Even when news reports do attend to issues like race, gender, or class, they rarely analyze the ways in which they are constituted within sociohistorical contexts, and the media is rarely self-reflective in considering its own role in constructing identities through its rhetoric. As feminist historian Joan Scott argues, "Making visible the experience of a different group exposes the existence of repressive mechanisms, but not their inner workings or logics; we know that difference exists, but we don't understand it as constituted relationally. For that we need to attend to the historical processes that, through discourse, position individuals and produce their experiences."[63] News that focuses on individuals out of context disavows the history of those involved. These fragmented images of individuals provide neither a historical context nor a sense of the social contexts through which individual identity and choices are shaped.

Ignoring social contexts in relation to history is part and parcel of the logic of colonialism that makes it easy to blame victims for their victimization. Chandra Talpade Mohanty suggests that traditional notions of history as linear and teleological, moving from origin to end, cannot account for the dynamics that give rise to this history. She argues that the notion of history as linear and evolutionary, moving from more primitive to more civilized, has a colonial history that is effaced in its propagation.[64] Mohanty argues that as a result of the evolutionary notion of progress and of history, "other civilizations or tribal cultures are seen as 'contemporary ancestors,' the past the West has already lived out."[65] The use of the rhetoric of "bringing democracy" to "whole regions of the world" that "simmer in resentment and tyranny" and freedom to "women of cover" continues this colonial legacy that treats other civilizations as past versions of ourselves who need to be modernized by Western technologies and ideologies—thereby justifying occupation and warfare.[66] This is the same colonial attitude that leads prison guards to treat Iraqi prisoners like objects, animals, and sex toys; and moreover to take pictures as souvenirs, as birthday gifts, and as pornography for use in their own sexual activities. Recall that Charles Grainer, the "ring leader" of the Abu Ghraib abuses, claims to have given his then-girlfriend Lynndie England, also involved in the abuses, photographs of Iraqi prisoners forced to simulate masturbation as a "birthday gift."[67]

Colonial or imperialistic rhetoric and attitudes not only efface the social contexts of history by assuming an evolutionary notion of time as progress, but also efface time by assuming a transparent subject and reality easily viewed through the lens of a camera. Colonial logic not only reduces the eyewitness to a vulgar actor engaged in the pornography of looking at what he dominates but also reduces bearing witness to war to an endless flow of digital images that appear in the perpetual present of television and the Internet. This endless flow of images collapses the time and space necessary for critical reflection, interpretation, elaboration, or what psychoanalysts call "working-through." The perpetual present/presence of the spectacle of violence compromises the witness in both senses, as eyewitness and as bearing witness to something that cannot be seen.

That "something that cannot be seen" is multidimensional and associated with the unconscious, which operates according to the cyclical time of repetition and working-through. It is what is outside of the frame of the photographs; it is the agency of colonial subjects debased and objectified through abuse and recordings of it. It is the invisible ideologies at work in producing and legitimating imperialism and war. It is the fears and phobias exacerbated by media hysteria and by government paranoia that our enemies are around every corner. At bottom, that something that cannot be seen is our unconscious desires and fears, which manifest themselves in various ways in what we can see and what we do. Working through these desires and fears is crucial to understanding our own investment in violence and war. At its most transformative, working-through is enabled by various forms of interpretation or analysis. Working-through is not "through" in the sense of being done with, but in the sense of a passage, a going, a movement. This is why working-through relies on interpretation, which comes from the Latin *inter*, or "between," and *per*, or "go." Interpretation is the go-between, the negotiator. And negotiating between bodies and words, pleasures and meaning, between what can and cannot be seen, is the infinite task of human beings. Humanity exists in between being and meaning, between the real and the ideal; and the psyche occupies this precarious in-between space.

This form of interpretation as witnessing requires witnessing to the process of witnessing itself, witnessing as an opening rather than a closure, witnessing as perpetual questioning. This perpetual questioning and openness to alternative interpretations must be first and foremost directed toward our own actions, attitudes, and beliefs. Only by interrogating our own unconscious motivations can we ever be vigilant enough in our quest for justice; and this interrogation must necessarily be never-ending. Only by finding ways to both articulate and elaborate on our unconscious aggressive impulses is there is hope of breaking the cycle of simple repetition of violence.

Witnessing as opening onto both subjectivity and subject positions can counterbalance "empty empathy" that plays on emotions but short-circuits understanding and acting. Recall Ann Kaplan's diagnosis of focusing on individual feelings apart from their social and political contexts; this type of eyewitness account produces "empty empathy" that pulls at our emotions but does not give us any way to interpret the trauma that we see. In this regard, the eyewitness position of the embedded reporter or the human interest story shows us heartbreak and misery but does not give us the critical and interpretive tools with which to make sense of it. Kaplan opposes "empty empathy" to witnessing: " 'Witnessing' happens when an essay or film not only aims to move the viewer emotionally but also without sensationalizing or overwhelming her with feeling that enables rather than undermines understanding and interpretation. 'Witnessing' involves not just empathy and motivation to help, but understanding the structure of injustice—that an injustice has taken place—rather than focusing on a specific case."[68] Witnessing in the double sense of eyewitnessing and bearing witness not only to what is not seen but also what cannot be seen opens up possibilities of interpretation closed off by embedded reporting.

Witnessing in this sense is an ongoing process of critical analysis and perpetual questioning that contextualizes and recontextualizes what and how we see. It requires vigilant attention to what we see and the meaning of what we see. We cannot simply take what we see at face value; rather we must move beyond what we recognize in visual images to what is beyond recognition: the subjectivity and agency, along with the social and political context or subject positions, of the "objects" of our gaze, and our own desires and fears, both conscious and unconscious, that motive our actions in relation to others. We must witness to the subjectivity and subject positions of ourselves and others, which necessarily takes us beyond mere eyewitness testimony or images.

The notion of witnessing in its full and double sense is instructive in analyzing the tensions that arise when reporters are eyewitnesses as well as the double violence of the visual image. As we have seen, when reporters act as eyewitnesses to war and trauma, their immediate emotional reactions preside over critical commentary that might situate the events in which they now participate. As a result, investigative journalism becomes an emotional appeal without adequate engagement with both the subject positions of the reporters or the other people involved. In addition, images or narrative that challenge our stereotypes, preconceptions, or expectations are nonexistent or crippled. Such challenges are essential to witnessing beyond recognition, witnessing beyond preconceived expectations ... what we might call thinking outside of the box—the television or computer screen.

As I argue elsewhere, ethics—or making politics ethical—requires accounting for the unconscious, which is why psychoanalytic concepts are useful for social analysis.[69] If we are not transparent to ourselves, our bodies and behaviors demand incessant interpretation. If a part of ourselves always remains inaccessible and to a greater or lesser extent resists any *one* interpretation, then we will be compelled to continually call into question our own motives and desires. And only when we engage in this continual self-interrogation is there hope that we can become an ethical society, only then is there hope for anything approximating justice.

Ultimately, witnessing to the unconscious as what cannot be seen in our experience is witnessing to the impossibility of ever completely recognizing or understanding ourselves; it is witnessing to the otherness within, witnessing to something beyond recognition. This form of witnessing requires witnessing to the process of witnessing itself, to witnessing as an opening rather than a closure, to witnessing as perpetual questioning. This perpetual questioning and openness to alternative interpretations must be first and foremost directed toward our own actions, attitudes, and beliefs. Our interpretations and elaborations of history, then, require attention not only to the historicity of subject-positions but also to the temporality of subjectivity, a temporality associated with the unconscious and its cyclical repetitive rhythms.

Historian Dominick LaCapra calls the time of the unconscious "repetitive temporality," which necessitates an open future and open debates over the status of the past. He suggests that "a psychoanalytical informed notion such as repetitive temporality (or history as displacement) ... counteracts historicist teleology and redemptive or messianic narratives, and it has a hypothetical, revisionary status that is always in need of further specification and open to debate."[70] This is not to say that we need to simply repeat the same unconscious patterns without interrogating, interpreting, analyzing, and elaborating them. On the contrary, only by finding ways to both sublimate our unconscious aggressive impulses along with elaborating them is there is hope of breaking the cycle of simple repetition.[71] It is crucial to this endeavor to acknowledge the repetitive temporality of the unconscious that operates behind the scenes of the linear and evolutionary time of history as it is traditionally conceived. If witnessing in the sense of eyewitness, complete with sociohistorical subject-position, transforms our notion of static history into dynamic historicity, witnessing in the sense of bearing witness to the unconscious, complete with repressed fears and desires, transforms our notion of Eternal truth into interminable analysis.

The hope—and we must maintain hope—is that perpetual questioning can stop perpetual war.

Innocence, Vulnerability, and Violence

If the teenagers from rural United States involved in prisoner abuse at Abu Ghraib are just average kids in an extreme situation "having fun," then we need to consider how mainstream American culture produces these fun-loving individuals who can abuse others while maintaining their innocence. If we can explain, even excuse, violence in the name of fun—just joking, just having fun—then perhaps we need to investigate our notion of fun and the ways in which it exonerates us from responsibility for violence.

The Nike slogan "Just do it" seems more appropriate to a fun-loving culture than "Don't just do it—think about it first." The emphasis on *fun* in American culture, which blossomed with the media age and television advertising, works against questioning and interpretation. In the media and at the movies, fun is usually associated with action and/or bodily sensations that give immediate gratification. In general, as a culture, we want more fun and we want it now ... the sooner, the better ... we don't want to wait ... we hate to wait. Reflecting on the meaning of fun and what we deem "fun," however, takes time; it is not immediate and perhaps not always fun.

In thinking about fun, and what it means to "just have fun," it is telling that all of the various definitions of *fun*, both as a noun and as a verb, in the *Oxford English Dictionary* involve either making fun at someone's expense, fooling another, or boisterousness, which is defined as roughness or violence. The first definitions of *fun* as both noun and verb are cheat (or to cheat), trick (or to trick), and hoax (or to hoax). Does this etymological discovery indicate an essential connection between fun and violence toward others? It seems as if many of our sporting events and much of our media entertainment include violence, even if it is the well-regulated violence of football and boxing or the well-choreographed violence of the movies.

In this chapter I take up such questions as: What is the relationship between our notion of fun and our notion of innocence? How can there be a difference between moral innocence and legal innocence? What is our ideal of innocence and how does it function in contemporary discussions of war, terror, and torture? I argue that the contemporary notion of law is being reduced to regulations and disciplinary codes that do not and cannot give robust meaning to our emotional lives and moral sensibilities. As a result our society is creating increasing numbers of what I call "abysmal individuals," who suffer from a split between law—broadly conceived as that which gives form and structure to social life—and personal embodied sensations of pain and pleasure. Using Freud's theory of childhood sadism combined with a Foucaultian focus on material and institutional power relations that produce law as a mere disciplinary technique, I diagnose an imagined regression to a childlike state of innocence before guilt or responsibility in order to help explain how young soldiers at Abu Ghraib can engage in abuse seemingly as innocent fun. My attempt to understand the place of Abu Ghraib within American culture leads to an analysis of our valorization of innocence and ignorance. Such notions of innocence and ignorance not only become the grounds on which we morally (if not legally) excuse abusive behavior as "fun," but also become part of the justification for condoning some forms of violence while condemning others within the rhetoric of war.

The distinction between legitimate and illegitimate violence trades on underlying assumptions about the relationship between culture and nature, and technology and bodies, wherein bodies are imagined as natural and innocent. This is one reason why suicide bombers armed only with box-cutters who brought down the Twin Towers, hit the Pentagon, and downed an airplane in Pennsylvania, along with the "body bombers" who continue to kill innocent civilians, not only make us all feel vulnerable but also seem mind-boggling to us.[1] But, as we have seen, this sense of vulnerability quickly gives way to the demand for revenge and violent war. In this chapter, then, I explore the connection between innocence, vulnerability, and war. In the end, I again focus on women suicide bombers in order to make the case that in addition to the political and economic stakes of violent aggression and violent resistance are the ethical stakes of creating a meaningful life.

Law Become Management

If there is a crisis of Western culture, it is a crisis of meaning. Our affective and emotional lives have become detached from the cultural institutions—schools, churches, governments—that should give them meaning. This disconnect between emotions and possible venues for the articulation or sublimation of emotions can result in violence toward oneself (from cutting or hanging games to anorexia) or violence toward others (from shootings at schools to sexual abuse at Abu Ghraib).

The civil laws that should help us live meaningful lives together as societies, nations, and citizens of the earth are becoming mere regulations that can be bought and sold like anything else. Laws—whether they are principles of ethics, religious commandments or rituals, civil codes, codes of honor, school rules, or even the Geneva Convention—are becoming nothing more than hoops to jump through on our way to pursuing as much wealth as quickly as possible, to the point of death. Laws, generally conceived to include customs and traditions that could give form to pleasure and pain, that could give meaning to our bodily sensations as we live together, instead become regulations to be manipulated, when they aren't penal codes used to segregate and discipline so-called undesirable elements. Law becomes a way of managing bodies, especially those that we deem violent.[2]

Although our nation was once conceived of as a welfare state that could provide for all of its citizens, we are now living in a penal state that provides for some at the expense of others.[3] The American dream of living a good life is available to fewer, while the prison industry has become a multi-billon dollar venture purportedly designed to protect the lifestyles of those few. As Angela Davis demonstrates, the prison industry has also become a major export of the United States.[4] The fact that some people have considerably more wealth than others makes them more eager to protect it by locking up those who might threaten it. In the words of social scientist Ghassan Hage,

"The latest cycle of capitalist accumulation, the modalities of class exploitation it has made necessary, and the resulting change in the quality of work
and precariousness of people's hold on their employment have all led to a
general climate of insecurity in the face of the future. Increasingly, there is
a sense of society's shrinking capacity to provide a good life to everyone. As
a result, a defensive attitude of guarding whatever good life is left supplants
the enjoyment of that good life."[5] The "haves" see the "have-nots" as threats
to their lifestyle and their primary concern becomes guarding their goods
against those who don't have them. But, as Hage suggests, this not only
leads to increasing incarceration and exploitation of poor people, but also
diminishes the meaning of life for middle class and rich people who spend
all of their time worrying about their goods ... getting them and protecting
them. Material goods easily become part of ideological notions of Good
that are used to justify lifestyles that depend upon wide economic dispari-
ties. The easy movement from goods to Good allows us to justify "guarding
our stuff" in the name of justice. This sense of "barbarians at the gate" is
fed by the growing divide between Earth's rich and poor. And law becomes
another means of controlling those "barbarians."

It is not just that "laws are made to be broken," but that our conception
of law itself is broken. Finding legal loopholes has become an industry unto
itself. It is telling that the word "loophole" originally referred to a small slit
or hole in a fortified wall for firing guns: the law has become a fortified wall
into which we drill holes, loopholes, for honing and aiming our legalisms
against others while protecting ourselves and our wealth. Interpreting law
is being reduced to finding loopholes, which is to say finding omissions
in the law that allow otherwise unlawful acts to be carried out within the
terms of the law. The activity of interpretation crucial to having a meaningful life is being reduced to the sophist's pleasure in finding loopholes;
interpretation has become a mere instrument used to justify surveillance,
confinement, violence, and torture. As evidence of the level of manipula-
tion of law-become-regulation, one can point to the enormous amount of
time and energy the Bush administration has spent finding loopholes in
the Geneva Convention in order to justify torture, as well as in legal wran-
gling to redefine torture itself. Through such machinations law itself is
made devoid of meaning, becoming nothing more than a strategy to win
or at least avoid losing the battle over the right to control both material and
ideological goods. The letter of the law has become disconnected from its
spirit. This disconnect between letter and spirit in the law is a symptom

of a more general disconnect between sensation and meaning in a culture that just wants to have fun.

This hurry to have fun operates as the counterpoint to American Puritanism, which turns on the harsh repression of bodily pleasure. This repressive tendency is manifest in both policing technologies and professional hyper-productivity. For example, surveillance technologies have advanced to the point where we can target a single person for assassination using global positioning satellites and moving violations can be issued automatically to drivers captured on video cameras running stoplights even when no one else is around. At the same time, Americans work long hours trying to get ahead in an economy that values efficiency and profits over meaning.

On the other side of law-become-the-science-of-management are ever more violent forms of entertainment: spectacles, scandals, and sexcapades. We alternate between regulations and scandals. It is this reduction of law to regulation and management that leads to the disassociation between bodily sensations—pain and pleasure—and law. The cleavage between law and desire, or meaning and bodily sensation, can produce teenage torturers who abuse prisoners seemingly in all innocence, as they claim at their trials, "just for fun."

Law and order no longer give structure to life so that we can live together in meaningful ways. Rather, law and order are being reduced to regulatory agencies that multiply rules and the bureaucracy of order for its own sake—or, more accurately, to ensure orderly consumption in a society for whom the meaning of life is produced by commercial television or the Internet. In *Hate and Forgiveness*, Julia Kristeva suggests that what she calls "the drama of Abu Ghraib tragically reveals that our civilization not only fails to produce [an] integration of the symbolic Law in the deep strata of [the psyche] that governs sexual pleasure, but that maybe, it [also] aggravates the disintegration of Law and desire."[6] She says that it is not the army or such and such administration that has failed, but rather it is the integration of the symbolic Law in the psychic apparatus that has failed. In her account, symbolic law can be thought of as social structures generally, including civil laws, language, and cultural traditions; basically, any kind of structure that allows people to communicate with each other or share a social space. The order provided by these social structures, language in particular, makes our experiences meaningful for ourselves and for others.

Although my own thinking about the relationship between law and sensation is influenced and informed by Kristeva's diagnosis of the split between law and desire, I disagree that the problem is one of integration. When diagnosing the disintegration of the law in relation to emotional life, Kristeva suggests that it is a matter of integration. But, doesn't integration imply once again freedom as calculus, a culture or globe made whole through the integration of its parts? Perhaps we should conceive of the relationship between different elements as interaction instead of integration. Kristeva suggests as much in her discussion of rights for the disabled when she says, "I distrust the term 'integration' of the handicapped: it feels like charity towards those who don't have the same rights of others. I prefer 'interaction' which expresses politics becoming ethics, by extending the political pact up to the frontiers of life."[7]

In this regard, we should be mindful of at least two senses of "integration": the mathematical process of finding the solution for a differential equation; and producing behavior compatible with one's environment, on the one hand, or opening society or culture to all without erasing their differences, on the other. We should be wary of the rhetoric of integration that proposes formal equality without giving meaning to the freedoms opened up by that equality. This notion of integration risks turning individuals into simple variables within an equation rather than acknowledging that it is their singularity that gives life meaning. The problem is not that we do not integrate law conceived of as regulation, prohibition, or penal code into our emotional lives. Rather, it our conception of law itself. How can a regulation or penal code designed to manage and discipline bodies give any enabling form to our emotional lives? Rather than trying to stage an integration or assimilation of these regulations or punishing codes into our psychic lives, we need alternative forms of law that work to support the articulation of bodily sensations that might allow us to communicate and to live together. We need to critically examine our very conception of law and its function in our lives.

The failure of law to give structure to desire, or to give meaning to bodily sensation, is not the result of a lapse in law or the weakening of prohibitions. On the contrary: It is not that we don't have enough laws or enough regulations prohibiting desires or pleasures.[8] Rather, it is that the very notion of law as regulation or penal code does not give form to bodily experiences of desire and sensation, either in the lives of individuals or as we live together. The pervasiveness of surveillance and punitive technologies in all aspects of life undermines rather than strengthens the power of law to provide meaning. I want to reiterate that "Law" here means something much broader than what we usually think of when we say the word. Everything that gives shape to social life is part of symbolic law. When symbolic law becomes nothing more than regulations, penal codes, and management techniques, then it ceases to give form to experience.

Without the structure or organization provided by symbolic law—especially language—we cannot articulate our experiences in order to make them meaningful in the context of our lives, both as individuals and as a society. As a result, we are left with raw sensations of pain and pleasure whose meaning alludes us. Symbolic law is being reduced to regulation and management techniques that police without giving form to desire or sensation; and without form, our affects and sensations remain trapped at the level of the body imagined as cut off from representation and from culture or politics. Through medicine and herbal remedies, behavior modification therapies, and new forms of diet and exercise, we attempt to manage our anxiety or stress without interpreting the meaning of these phenomena. But in order to bring robust meaning to our feelings and sensations, we need to articulate them, to interpret them, to question them. We need to understand even our most basic bodily sensations as part of the world of human meaning.

Contemporary culture with its regulations and media spectacles does not give meaning to our lives and leaves us feeling alienated. As we have seen in the previous chapter, as visual media replace narrative media, we lose the ability to translate bodily experience into meaningful forms; this is in part a result of the decontextualization of images and in part because we lack visual literacy. The call for interpretation through which bodily sensations become meaningful returns us to the question of innocence. For within assumptions about the body cut off from culture or politics is the association of the body with nature: natural innocence and natural violence, which is to say, an innocent sort of violence.

Childlike Innocence: "Dumb and Dumber"

We usually associate both fun and innocence with children. American culture seems to idealize the innocent and fun-loving nature of kids.[9] Part of their innocence comes from the fact that children believe anything—they are gullible; and another part is that children will do anything—they are shameless. This combination of gullibility and shamelessness not only makes for fun, but also for funny scenes as entertainment at home and on television and in films. We laugh at children doing things that we would find offensive in adults. Sometimes it is funny to see a little body and a little voice saying and doing nasty, even violent, things.

Innocence associated with childhood is not only valorized within American culture but seemingly definitive of it. We pride ourselves on our innocence. And we continue to feel menaced by events that threaten our innocence: Vietnam, 9/11, Abu Ghraib, Guantánamo. We talk about the loss of American innocence in relation to these events, even while we continue to insist on it. Childlike innocence works as an inoculant against responsibility and guilt. If we are innocent and ignorant, then we cannot be held responsible and cannot be found guilty. The defendants at Abu Ghraib claimed that they were just having fun. They also claimed that they didn't know that forcing prisoners to eat pork or stripping them violated Muslim religious beliefs. This defense should not surprise us in a culture that takes pride in its ignorance, which is part and parcel of its imagined innocence. Think of the box office hit movie *Forrest Gump*, in which Tom Hanks plays the lead character, a lovable but clueless innocent who accidentally does all kinds of good things. His ignorance and innocence, his mistakes even, bring good things to all. He is not responsible for his actions insofar as he does not intend them, yet his innocence is the agency of benevolence. The film seems to say that innocence and ignorance are good qualities—if only we could all be more like Forrest Gump, the world would be a better place. We idealize innocence to the point of stupidity. Think of the film *Dumb and Dumber*, where the comedy stems from stupid behaviors that often involve forms of physical violence. Think too of shelf after shelf of books and manuals entitled "Idiot's Guide to X" or "X for Dummies." We demand that the complexities of life be described in the simplest possible terms. We revel in our image of ourselves as idiots and dummies. We are ignorant and proud of it!

Our ignorance is telling. What we want to know and what we don't care to find out should tell us something about our values and priorities. Innocence-as-ignorance protects us against culpability. Following 9/11, paradoxically, the media reported on our innocence and vulnerability along with our loss of innocence. Within the logic of this fantasy of innocence, to be innocent is to be invulnerable and without guilt; while to be vulnerable, to be the victim of an attack, takes away our innocence. In fact, the threat from attack is not just a threat to our lives but also to our innocence. Can we *understand* something like the 9/11 attack and maintain our innocence/ ignorance? Doesn't interpreting what happened to us require some reflection on the U.S. role in global politics? And doesn't such reflection challenge our notion of ourselves as innocents? Even now we don't have to spend much time reflecting on the current political situation to realize that behind the rhetoric of American benevolence delivering democracy to the globe there are rich corporations waiting in the wings to reconstruct the infrastructures of the recipients of our generosity.

Innocence and Violence

Ironically perhaps, in addition to the association between children and innocence is an association between children and instinctual or natural violence. In Freud's theories of children's relation to sex, childhood innocence mingles with sexuality. In *Three Essays on the Theory of Sexuality*, Freud argues that small children are without "shame, disgust, and morality" and therefore do not restrain their "instincts of scopophilia [voyeurism], exhibitionism, and cruelty," which manifest themselves as "satisfaction in exposing their bodies," "curiosity to see other people's genitals," and "cruelty towards animals and playmates," and make children "eager spectators of the processes of micturition and defecation."[10] As children grow up, they learn to control their impulses rather than act on them. They find alternate ways to express their anger and aggression, more socially acceptable ways. They learn to act according to social laws and codes of behavior. When children, or adults, do not sublimate aggressive impulses into socially acceptable behavior (sports, art, work, etc.) they may act on them, even relish scopophilia, exhibitionism, and cruelty.

If proper or socially acceptable pleasures are the result of ordering violent impulses, then regression to an infantile state prior to that constraint circumvents the gap between what Freud calls the reality principle—what society requires we do to live together—and what he calls the pleasure principles—what our bodies want. The regressed or infantile individual does not have to wait to satisfy his or her pleasure within a socially proscribed code of behavior. Rather, the regressed individual reverts to unrestrained pleasure within his or her emotional life even while acknowledging a harsh

disciplinary structure in other aspects of life. In this way, reality and pleasure are segregated and compartmentalized. Individuals and culture can
foster conservative mores, sexual promiscuity, and sadomasochistic violence at the same time.

We can thus engage in the rhetoric of tolerance and global freedom
while our military uses sex, loud music, and dogs as torture strategies in
part of what is openly called the "occupation of Iraq." And our politicians
can turn outrage at the abuse of prisoners into outrage at "humanitarian
do-gooders right now crawling all over these prisons looking for human
rights violations," in the words of one senator. This senator echoed the sentiments of many Americans when he suggested that the end justifies the
means, even if that means is explicitly opposed to the fundamental values
of democracy and freedom; he said, "We have a war to win, and we need to
keep our talents concentrated on winning the war as opposed to prisoner
treatment."[11] In this way of thinking, any form of abuse or punishment is
justified by the intensity of the threat, which is imagined as nothing short
of evil; in the struggle between good and evil, the "humanitarian do-gooders" get in the way of some greater good, namely winning a war. Criminal
guilt or innocence (in respect to both the prisoners and the abusive guards)
is deemed irrelevant in relation to our moral virtue. National, military, and
international laws are seen as impediments to our quest for righteous revenge. Legal innocence or guilt is superceded by moral innocence or guilt.
Our innocence as those wounded and wronged by the attacks of 9/11 seemingly renders legal innocence irrelevant.

If their innocent smiles weren't enough, their testimony at trial suggests that the women involved in the Abu Ghraib abuse truly believed they
were "just having fun" and that they were therefore somehow (morally)
innocent even if they were legally guilty. Pfc. Lynndie England reportedly
said that reservists took the photographs while "they were joking around,
having fun" and at her trail she said that they piled up detainees and took
pictures of naked prisoners for the "amusement" of her then-boyfriend Pvt.
Charles Graner (one newspaper headline reads "We did it for fun: Female
guard explains Iraq abuse"); after taking photographs of England holding
the now infamous leash around a prisoners neck, Graner e-mailed the picture home, writing "look what I made Lynndie do."[12]

The military judge, Col. James Pohl, declared a mistrial in England's
court-martial on the grounds that she "can't have it both ways," saying,
"You can only plead guilty if you believe you are guilty. If you plead guilty,

you can't put on evidence that you're not guilty."[13] It is noteworthy that the military judge heard England and Graner testifying that she was both guilty and innocent at the same time. Even before Graner testified that England was just following orders and that the force they used was legitimate—testimony that resulted in the mistrial—the judge had expressed misgivings about England's guilty plea after she testified that she thought the leash picture was okay because Graner said it was.[14] England testified that she thought that what she did was "having fun," "joking around," "OK"; but as part of her guilty plea she also testified that she knew what she did was wrong: she said "You don't wrap a leash around somebody's neck and tell them to crawl; I mean, that's wrong."[15]

England's own ambiguity over her innocence or guilt, and her lawyer's disappointment when she was forced to plead innocent, suggests a deeper ambivalence over the notion of innocence. It makes manifest a split between legal guilt or innocence and moral guilt or innocence that helps explain the discrepancies in the testimony. England and her lawyers decided that she would plead guilty in order to plea-bargain her sentence, which she could not do if she pleaded innocent. In a sense, her guilt in front of the law was merely a strategy to get leniency; on the practical level it means that she spends less time in jail while on the ideological level it demonstrates that she feels guilty and repentant. She admits legal guilt while still harboring a sense of moral innocence—it was just a joke, she was just following orders. Furthermore, this ambivalence over her innocence suggests that having fun and joking around, at least in this case, can be linked with abuse and wrongdoing.

This breach between law and virtue, between legal and moral innocence, is symptomatic of a disconnect between our conception of law and our experience. Law ceases to give structure and organization to social and civil life, or to enable peaceful coexistence among different people. Rather, law is becoming mere regulation that prohibits but does not provide robust meaning for our experiences as a society. Nietzsche, Freud, and others have argued that civil codes and laws restrict our natural instincts. Existentialist philosophers like Dostoevsky and Sartre suggested that the individual is essentially opposed to the social and that therefore on a fundamental level all social institutions and laws curtail individual freedom. Taking this extreme position, however, not only overlooks the fact that human beings are from birth social beings and therefore social structures and institutions are necessary to human life, but also that these structures make life meaningful.

Language, for example, is a social institution or practice that is governed by rules and laws that make us intelligible to one another. If we conceive of law in the broadest sense, then language and all forms of signification fall under the rubric of Law. Law can and should support the articulation of experience into meaningful forms that can be shared with others; and it is that sharing, that social aspect of law as support, that enables articulation of experience. In psychoanalytic terms, this articulation or translation of bodily experience into forms of signification like language—or sports, art, or dance, etc.—is called sublimation. We could say, then, that our contemporary conception of law no longer includes its crucial sublimatory function.

Abysmal Individuals

Echoing Susan Sontag's phrase "The photographs are us," Julia Kristeva claims that the so-called black sheep of Abu Ghraib, the few bad apples, are not exceptional but "average inhabitants of the globalized planet of humanoids trained" by reality shows and the Internet.[16] These abysmal individuals, as we might call them, are not exceptions but rather the product of a culture in which innocence and even ignorance are valorized.

It is as if these so-called black sheep, these regressed or abysmal individuals, occupy an abyss between law and desire, taking refuge from harsh regulations through regression to an infantile state of innocence. These individuals cordon off regulations and keep them separate from their sexual and emotional lives, where they retreat into what Freud calls "polymorphous perversion," or immediate bodily pleasure without guilt. To be more precise, they retreat into a realm of bodily sensations cut off from law—law that would give form or meaning to those very sensations. Moreover, this retreat is in part triggered by increasing regulations and more severe management of bodies (e.g., in the military, in the strict codes of fundamentalist religions). It is not that they/we have not integrated symbolic law into psychic or emotional life, but that symbolic law itself has ceased to provide meaning or order for psychic, emotional, or sensory experiences. They/ we retreat to a presubjective and preobjective psychic dynamic, a childlike state of innocence where there is no "I" (subject) who is responsible for his or her actions toward others (the objects of their actions). In this childlike state there is no responsibility and therefore no guilt. The body has aggressive impulses and we act on them ... without waiting, without thinking, without considering what they mean or where they come from.

When symbolic law or social institutions, including and most especial-ly language, give form to bodily experiences and thereby also give them meaning for our lives, then we have access to symbolic substitutes for vio-lent or aggressive impulses: we exercise, participate in sports, paint pic-tures, dance, write poetry, talk to friends, etc. But when the body is associ-ated with natural instincts that are imagined as opposed to society, laws, and ethics or politics, then the body is seen as beyond our control. Going back to Abu Ghraib, recall that some commentators said that this sort of sexual violence and what they called "whore house behavior" was *natural* when you put young women and men together; they suggested that natural sexual instincts cannot be controlled and that Abu Ghraib was the result of bodies doing what they do naturally.

This conception of bodies is extremely problematic because it extracts bodies from the realm of meaning and relegates them to a sphere that lies outside human civilization. On this view, we have bodies but we are not responsible for them. Paradoxically, we both separate ourselves from our bodies—we cannot control them because they are ruled by animal instincts—and reduce all experience to bodily sensation without mean-ing—we measure fun in terms of intense bodily experiences. What these two extremes share is the evacuation of meaning from the body. This split between sensation and meaning leads to feelings of emptiness and mean-inglessness that drive so many of us to therapy and pharmaceuticals ... or, at the extreme, to violence as a form of entertainment, toward the self and toward others.

This disconnect of symbolic Law from emotional life results in "inno-cent" parties who, on the psychic level, escape guilt by regressing to a time before guilt, a time before proper subjects who take proper objects, which is to say a time before responsibility. These "innocent" subjects dwell, even wallow, in wretched acts with guiltless glee. They become cheerleaders of abjection for whom sadomasochistic violence toward themselves and others becomes the prerequisite for a good party.[17] It is not exactly that these "innocent" individuals don't "know the difference between right and wrong," but that by erotizing the abject, the taboo, the improper, they pu-rify it and thereby purify themselves. This is to say, they purify it of both law and guilt by relegating it to the realm of the body imagined as outside the realm of ethics or politics, where there is supposedly no right or wrong because there is no meaning.[18] (Think of the phrase "I didn't mean any-thing by it"—these acts appear as meaningless fun; and meaningless acts or bodily sensations appear to be the definition of fun imagined as the nat-ural domain of bodies, especially young bodies). The desire for the abject, the unseemly, even disgusting, becomes a defense against contamination by it. Their sexualization of torture and eroticization of prisoners turns ev-erything into sex; and sex is fun. They are not torturing or committing war crimes, they are just having fun. In an odd way, their/our sexualization of everything, their/our "polymorphous perversity" through which everything becomes sex, their/our promiscuity protect them/us from facing their/our own culpability. The sensational spectacle of scandal turns their torture into a perverse form of entertainment that incites outrage and shocks even as it titillates. Instead of turning our outrage into political protest or ac-tion, we turn the abuse at Abu Ghraib into a spectacular sex scandal, kids "just having fun" or fraternity "pranks" (themselves remarkable in their violence, which is tolerated, even endorsed by our culture).[19]

Sex is "Natural"

Sex operates as an excuse when it is seen as a "natural instinct" beyond our control. Sex is seen as an aspect of our bodies that is associated with animality and therefore with nature rather than with culture. Although the techniques and practices of sex may vary from culture to culture, we still conceive of sex as merely instinct. This element of our bodily being is relegated to the natural sphere imagined as distinct from, even at odds with, the social or cultural sphere. Paradoxically perhaps, we associate shamelessness about sex with both children and with perverts, the for-mer because they are supposedly just acting on their normal or natural instincts and the latter because they are supposedly abnormal and mon-strosities of nature. The connection between sex and war, between eroti-cization and objectification, again makes uncanny this hard and fast dis-tinction between nature and culture, between bodies and technology. We witness the use of sex as a technique of war used along with some of the most advanced technologies known to man. The ambiguous place of sex, between nature and culture, reminds us again of the doubleness of our being that makes the return of the repressed sexual body so uncanny and therefore so threatening.

It seems that we idealize bodily instincts as they are expressed without shame in children; and childlike behavior or attitudes can exonerate or excuse childlike adults or teenagers from culpability. Furthermore, it is assumed that there are bodily impulses with which we are born that ultimately cannot be even in part controlled by social forces; even if they can be redirected or constrained they are always present and threaten to reappear in their original violent forms. As we have seen, this seems to be the rhetoric of some who attributed abuses at Abu Ghraib to "natural" sexual instincts that result from a co-ed military where male and female soldiers live and work together. This very conception of a natural body supports our ideas of childhood innocence and of childhood violence.

Our concept of nature itself connotes innocence—nature is what it is and cannot be otherwise, and therefore it does not make sense to blame nature. We might ask, can we blame (in a moral sense) the tornado or the forest fire for their destruction? But what does it mean when we attribute *naturalness* to people? Even Freud links instincts (or what he calls drives) to culture and society. Human beings are born into social situations; no baby can live without other people who take care of it. So the baby's body is already part of a social system that governs if not determines its bodily desires and "instincts." Right away it gets used to certain smells, sounds, sights, tastes of its culture that become the background for its most basic experiences.

French philosopher Michel Foucault challenged what he took to be the Victorian notion that desires, especially sexual desires, are natural and only secondarily repressed by culture. He argued that desires are not so much retrained by cultural prohibitions and taboos as produced by them. For example, our articulation of what practices (especially sexual practices) are forbidden (by the church, the school, the government, the law, etc.) reiterate those practices, sometimes in graphic detail. These descriptions of what is prohibited, fueled by and fueling the imagination, conjure the very acts that they supposedly seek to abolish. Foucault also argues that advances in technology and scientific discourse, whether in biology or the science of management and engineering, produce desires and fears. For example, various technologies that allow us to "see" the microscopic world modulate the realm of the visible that changes as technologies change; what we once thought of as real and evident becomes fantasy and illusion as technologies change; scientific worldviews change with transformations in technology (for example, more advanced telescopes have lead scientists to conclude that Pluto is not a planet after all). So too, technological transformations affect our desires. For example, the possibility of recording moving visual images is relatively new. The government, law enforcement agencies, and the military have developed recording technologies to enhance surveillance techniques. But the same technologies that allow law enforcement to watch and/ or record from a remote location produce new forms of the desire to watch and to be seen, what Freud calls voyeurism/scopophilia and exhibitionism. The low-tech "flasher" of the 1970s becomes today's high-tech live Web-cam exhibitionist. Technology also has changed the ways that we make war; from high-tech weaponry used in surgical strikes to communication and information technologies upon which terrorists rely to spread terror, technology is not only used to inflict violence but also shapes our relationship to violence.

The implication of both a Freudian and a Foucaultian analysis of desire for our discussion of Abu Ghraib, and violence more generally, is that the desire for violence and the forms that this desire takes are intimately connected to the milieu of our culture, in particular its technologies and the institutions through which they are deployed: there is a reciprocal relationship between desires or affects associated with the body, and laws, words, or other symbolic forms associated with society. The upshot is not only that nature and culture are reciprocally constitutive forces, but also that the very terms "nature" and "culture" are contested terms whose definitions have political ramifications. Moreover, as we have seen, many of the strange and unsettling images from Abu Ghraib and women's violence put into crisis any neat distinction between nature and culture by making manifest the ambiguity between these two categories within which we live. In terms of Freudian psychoanalytic theory, we could say that the opposition between these terms is a symptom of the repression of this ambiguity; while in terms of Foucaultian discourse analysis we might say the fixity of the two is the effect of biopower. At stake in both repression and biopower is the regulation of bodies and pleasures.

While trying to articulate and negotiate the tensions between psychoanalytic theory and discourse analysis is productive in itself, my aim here is to think through the meaning of Abu Ghraib, both in terms of the psychic economy of our culture and in terms of the technologies that produce and reproduce that economy. What is at stake in our notions of innocence and violence? And how does that lead to debates over legitimate and illegitimate violence? Legitimate and illegitimate force? What does it mean to be legitimate, to be sanctioned by law, especially when law has been reduced to regulation, the science of management, and penal codes?

Even if we find violence "in nature," the situation is complicated by what we identify as *nature* and how, and what we identify as *violence* and how ... and why. We can investigate our relation to violence in terms of the psychic economy of violence as it is inherently connected to the cultures within which it is produced, reproduced, and distributed. Furthermore, the American idealization of innocence as it relates to violence can and should be examined in order to begin to understand some of the ways in which, implicitly if not explicitly, we justify and excuse our own violence as legitimate even while we condemn the violence of others as illegitimate.

Legitimate and Illegitimate Violence?

One issue in the current "war against terror" is who is allowed to possess high-tech weaponry and who is not, who is allowed to possess weapons of mass destructions and who is not. The war in Iraq ostensibly began because U.S. intelligence (mistakenly) reported that Saddam Hussein possessed weapons of mass destruction. Never mind that the United States and most other technologically developed countries have weapons of mass destruction. Never mind that the United States is the only country to have used nuclear weapons in war, which affected the Japanese people in horrific and deadly ways. Increasingly the rhetoric surrounding U.S. warfare and imperialist ventures centers on preventing "rogue" nations from developing nuclear weapons.[20] On the fifth anniversary of the terrorist attacks on the World Trade Center in Manhattan, President Bush said that the war on terror is the "calling of our generation" and nothing less than "a struggle for civilization" against "radical dictators armed with nuclear weapons."[21] And in a speech before the United Nations criticizing Iran, Bush linked liberty to not pursuing nuclear weapons and terrorism to pursuing them, suggesting that only countries that fall in line behind the United States' nuclear weapons can be free. Bush said, "The greatest obstacle to this future is that your rulers have chosen to deny you liberty and to use your nation's resources to fund terrorism, and fuel extremism, and pursuer nuclear weapons."[22] The easy slippage between liberty, terrorism, and nuclear weapons is telling in a speech delivered by the "leader of the free world" and the only superpower to have used nuclear weapons in war.

Complete with mushroom cloud–like explosions shown over and over again on television, the terror attacks of September 11, 2001, conjured the fear of nuclear weapons.[23] Reviewing the media coverage of the attacks on the Twin Towers, journalist Tom Engelhardt remarks on the numerous comparisons between 9/11 and the threat of nuclear weapons. The attacks themselves were compared to Pearl Harbor, the strike that brought the United States into the war with Japan during World War II, which in turn saw the world's first use of nuclear weapons, to destroy the Japanese cites of Hiroshima and Nagasaki; that is to say, the attacks of 9/11 were compared with attacks that were seen as acts of war that could justify the use of nuclear weapons in response. The aftermath of the attacks on the Twin Towers was also compared to a nuclear event: Tom Brokaw of NBC said that it looked "like a nuclear winter in lower Manhattan," a sentiment echoed in print media; and on September 12 many newspapers used the headline "The Day After," the title of a 1983 movie about nuclear Armageddon. As Engelhardt and others have argued, Hollywood movies have been full of apocalyptic visions that conjure fears of nuclear holocaust ever since we dropped the atomic bomb. We are haunted by the fear that the awesome killing power we created will be used against us. As President Bush's memorial speech five years after 9/11 suggests, we are afraid of imaginary dictators armed with nuclear weapons pointing right at the United States.

In order to prevent what is typically called "the spread of nuclear weapons," we are willing to wage war to prevent other countries, especially developing countries, from joining the ranks of those who have them. The rhetoric of "spreading" suggests that nuclear weapons are like diseases or noxious weeds rather than weapons of mass destruction, whose creation and deployment catapulted the United States to the status of superpower. The circular reasoning goes something like this: we are on the side of right and goodness, so should have nuclear weapons; "they" are on the side of wrong and evil, so should not have nuclear weapons. Of course, since we do have nuclear weapons, we are in a position to define right and wrong, good and evil in self-serving terms that legitimate our own use of violence while condemning violence used by others.

The possession of nuclear weapons, then, is seen as legitimate for some countries but not for others, while the possession of nuclear weapons is never legitimate for individuals, only for nation-states. In an important sense, the United States is going to war over the development and distribution of high-tech weaponry. Among others, one significant fact that distinguishes what we call "terrorism" from what we call "war" or "legitimate force" is the use of advanced technologies of war. As Cavarero argues, "The political lexicon of the West, by distinguishing between war and terrorism, assumes that only the violent (high-tech) performances of the Western Empire deserve the name of war. You can have a war on terrorism, as we are told, but not a war of terrorists."[24] War is seen as legitimate violence, while terrorism is illegitimate; one reason is that we idealize violence in relation to our advanced technologies that make it possible to kill without being killed—the so-called surgical airstrike for example that connotes the precision of a surgeon removing a cancerous tumor. Cavarero points out that bodies are no longer the protagonists of war properly fought.

> Television broadcasting, by authorizing only certain types of images, allows us to think that the modern war is clean and aseptic because of its technological precision, electronic surgery, and other means of politeness. As a matter of fact, as television watchers, we see devastation and desperation, but we see very seldom disfigured corpses and, amazingly enough, we are also kept from seeing the coffins of our dead warriors. People still die, but human bodies, replaced by technology, are no longer the protagonists of war, or at least, of the specific modality of violence and destruction that, according to the current vocabulary of the Western emprise, is the only one to lawfully deserve the old and glorious name of war.[25]

In modern warfare high-tech weaponry displaces bodies in combat. We imagine war as a video game where our troops handle remote controls that "take-out" the enemy, seemingly without the blood and guts of older forms of war. Of course, this is an illusion created by technologies of war that "remote-kill" and by a visual culture in which fantasies of war in the movies are as close to bloody bodies as most of us (in post-industrial developed countries) ever get. The media coverage of the first Gulf War, fed to the television networks by the military, seemed to substantiate our sense of virtual bloodless, disembodied warfare.

War with real bodies fighting and killing each other seems like a thing of the past; it seems like a barbaric way to wage war. Deadly force is imagined as high-tech precision violence that can be commanded with the push of a button. Deadly force that results from bodies rather than technology is not only illegitimate but also horrifying—we ask, "What kind of psychopath would use their own body to blow up other people?" We are especially appalled by suicide bombers who seem to value killing over their own lives. Even while we honor our own dead as heroes sacrificed for the sake of higher values, we cannot imagine those other killers as sacrificing themselves for higher values; their bodies don't count as bodies that can be sacrificed.[26] Rather, their bodies are seen as weapons, treacherous, illegitimate, cruel weapons that fall outside of the political sphere and into the realm of the monstrous and unnatural.

How can a few guys with box-cutters cause so much destruction? If box-cutters can be weapons of mass destruction, what about nail clippers, tennis shoes, Gatorade bottles, or baby formula … or maybe even the babies themselves? If the body can be a weapon, then we are surrounded by weapons; we cannot tell the difference between weapons and the things or people in our midst every day. Suddenly everything and everyone becomes threatening. The idea that the body can be a weapon or that something as low-tech as a box-cutter can take down an airplane not only boggles the mind but also seems wrong—the use of everyday objects in this way is just plain evil … too sinister for words. This attitude suggests that *good* people use high-tech bombs to blow up people, preferably other soldiers who are manning military targets. It also suggests that we feel somehow threatened by bodies themselves; that bodies used as weapons are especially uncanny because they conjure a deeper ambivalence we feel about our own bodies as well as the bodies of others. Insofar as bodies are mortal and all bodies die, they are all in a sense ticking time-bombs waiting to kill us. Within the history of Western thought bodies are figured as finite, inconsistent, even irrational, and so they have been conceived of as opposed to civilization and culture. Part of the subtext of the exclusion of the body from politics is its unpredictability, that it could "go off" at any minute. This is one reason suicide bombers, or "body-bombers" as Cavarero calls them, are particularly uncanny. With body-bombers, the body literally explodes back into the realm of politics.

In recent rhetoric, more than identifying a particular form of political violence, the label "terrorist" connotes a psychopath who commits horrific violence beyond the pale of human society and politics.[27] Terrorists are figured as monsters without any human compassion or ethical values. To call an act a terrorist act, to call a person a terrorist, to call an organization a terrorist group expels them from the realm of the political into the realm of the pathological. There is "normal," "civilized" violence and then there is "abnormal," "sick," and "barbaric" violence. But, as Ghassan Hage emphasizes, "we need to question that way we are invited to uncritically think of a particular form of violence as 'the worst possible kind of violence' merely by classifying it as 'terrorist.'" The ways that the classification "terrorist" is used normalize some forms of violence and pathologize others. It thus becomes an inflammatory term that not only describes a particular form of violence but also legitimates another form of violence, namely the high-tech warfare of Western militaries. Hage maintains that "the struggle between states and opposing groups [is]: first, over the distribution of means of violence and second, and more importantly, over the classification of the forms of violence in the world, particularly over what constitutes legitimate violence."[28] The fight operates on the material level of the distribution of wealth, in particular high-tech weaponry, and on the symbolic level in terms of who has the authority to define *legitimate* force. "Legitimate" means legal; recently we have seen how the most powerful can redefine what constitutes legitimate force by redefining torture and international law. If it is simply a matter of the more powerful defining the terms of engagement, then it is merely a case of "might makes right," and our virtuous stand is nothing more than posturing on the part of the powerful.

Hage points out that what we call terrorist groups never call themselves terrorists; rather they call themselves revolutionaries, rebels, martyrs, nationalists, or freedom fighters. He claims that terrorism is a "violence of last resort" that in many cases results from the will to resist colonial domination or foreign occupation in spite of a lack of resources or high-tech weaponry. He quotes a Palestinian Australian saying, "Let the Americans give us the monopoly over nuclear power in the region and the strongest army there is, and we are happy to do 'incursions' and hunt down wanted Israeli terrorists by demolishing their houses and 'accidentally' killing civilians. Who would want to be a suicide bomber if such a luxurious mode of fighting is available to us?"[29] Part of the struggle, then, is precisely over who will have and who won't have access to "luxurious" high-tech weaponry. Those that do have access, the wealthy nations, have not only the military might to physically force their case but also the symbolic capital to define the terms of the struggle on an ideological level. They are in the position of power in terms of both the weapons of war and the rhetoric of war. With high-tech weapons they can dominate the material landscape, but with the power of rhetoric they can also dominate the symbolic landscape. They control and distribute both the armaments of war and the ideology of war using high-tech weaponry and high-tech media. This is to say, they have the power not only to execute deadly force but also to justify it with the rhetoric of saving civilization from barbarians, good versus evil, humane versus monstrous, and legitimate versus illegitimate violence.

Technology both produces and reproduces the material and intellectual terrain of the contemporary landscape. On the one hand, technology provides the instruments or vehicles through which we experience our world—almost all facets of our everyday lives are mediated by technology, from electric toothbrushes, breast-milk pumps, and hair clubs for men, to televisions, airplanes, and computers. On the other hand, the technological form of mediation gives rise to a way of looking at the world, a worldview, that philosophers like Martin Heidegger and Hannah Arendt among others have associated with instrumental reason—everything in our world, including our own bodies, other people, and other living beings become nothing more than the raw material with which to make high-tech instruments. They are no longer seen as ends in themselves, as having their own value, but rather as having value only insofar as they serve to advance our technologies. Technology becomes a value in itself.

Applying this line of thinking to contemporary warfare, Cavarero argues that "technology aims at replacing, covering, and neutralizing the traditional role of the fighting bodies.... The contemporary scenario of violence and devastation presents us with a spreading and intermittent battlefield in which both high-level technology and bare bodies play the role of destructive weapons. However, according to the Western political canon corroborated by the engineering skills of late modernity, only technology is allowed to claim the correct and legitimate status of weapon. Although dreadful, because of its power of producing a higher amount of death and destruction, technological weapons, unlike body-bombers, are easily inscribed in the Western symbolical order that connects politics to war and provides a theoretical and narrative support for legitimating this connection."[30] Bare bodies, as Cavarero calls them, are excluded from the realm of the properly political and therefore from the realm of legitimate war, which is seen as an outgrowth of the political. Or, to put it simply, bodies are imagined as part of nature and therefore never completely assimilated into culture, while politics is imagined as the most organized form of culture, which removes us from the realm of nature altogether.

Yet what is most remarkable about these bare bodies is that they are *not* bare; they are *not* natural; they are *not* innocent. Rather, they are armed and dangerous. They are, as Cavarero suggests, young mothers who become killers. In this regard, they are *more than* the return of the repressed natural body within Western politics. What is more dangerous than a natural body is a body that won't stay put, a body that moves between nature and culture, a body become a political statement. Indeed, what these women suicide bombers make manifest that unsettles Western politics is the way in which the body is always political; there is no bare body, no natural body. The greatest threat, then, is the *ambiguity of the body* as existing between nature and culture, between the physical and the technological.

As we have seen, in her analysis of the role of the body in metaphors of politics—e.g., the "body politic"—Cavarero shows how real flesh and blood bodies have been associated with women and excluded from the realm of the properly political while properly political bodies are seen as male bodies abstracted from everyday existence. Western politics' valuation of abstract or virtual bodies over the messiness of real ones is part and parcel of our investment in advanced technologies. Our psychic and material financial investment in technology, in this case high-tech weapons with which to defend our body politic, both produces and reproduces the exclusion of real bodies from the realm of politics. This is one reason the body appears as a threat to politics. Cavarero says, "Bodies embedded, as instruments of low-tech level, in the system of high-technology weaponry ... the body as such, the mere body transformed into a moral weapon appears instead as totally irregular and, so to speak, disloyal, illegitimate, treacherous. This doesn't depend—as we often are told—on the scandal of human beings who seem to neglect the value of their individual life—in Italian history [and the history of the West in general], for example, there are many cases of patriotic heroes, martyrs of the nation, who immolate their life for the sake of the community. It rather depends on the scandal of lethal weapons that consist of bare and non-technological bodies."[31] What is disloyal and treacherous about these bodies become weapons, however, is not merely the fact that they are bare and nontechnological—the exploding belt may be low-tech, but it is still technology. Rather, alongside the threat of physical violence comes the threat of the explosion of ambiguity onto the scene of meaning.

The centrality of visual media to both the culture and the effectiveness of suicide bombers indicates that these violent acts are intended for mass distribution via communication and information technologies. The video recordings that suicide bombers make beforehand are circulated both to honor the "martyr" and to recruit more "martyrs." And the terror of these attacks, which actually do not kill as many people as high-tech weaponry, is spread through media reports, especially television and the

Internet. Al Qaeda is notorious for delivering video recordings of its leaders condemning the United States and calling for Jihad. And Jihadists are increasingly using the Internet to recruit; they turn American technology against itself.[32] So while these "body-bombers" menace high-tech Western culture with the return of the repressed body to the realm of politics, they also rely on Western technology to deliver their message. Their homicidal acts become terrorism in part because they aim them at the realm of information exchange—the symbolic realm—as well as at material bodies. The body returns as political; and it is the ambiguous status between nature and culture, between life-giving mother and death-dealing bomber, between being and meaning, that makes these acts not just violent but also abject and horrifying.

Kristeva's description of the abject is apt here. She maintains that the abject is not just what is disgusting or dirty but rather what calls into question the boundaries of the clean and proper. The abject is in-between, the double, which cannot be neatly contained.[33] Kristeva says that the abject is "a terror that dissembles, a hatred that smiles, a passion that uses the body for barter instead of inflaming it, a debtor who sells you up, a friend who stabs you."[34] Certainly this description fits the perky girls engaged in abuse at Abu Ghraib and the pony-tailed girls blowing up themselves and others; their smiles dissemble; they are not what they seem.

While Cavarero identifies the idealization of a virtual technological (male) body over and against a real natural (female) body, she does not discuss the role of technology in creating this prejudice. The issue of the relation between technology and bodies is complex. Technology is often seen as one means to control and even discipline unruly or diseased bodies; for example, we develop ultra high-tech modes of surgery to treat diseases and illness. As we have seen, the technologies with which we cure bodies are condensed with those that destroy bodies, as in the use of the metaphors of surgery for military strikes. Technology is also used to monitor and manage criminals and even terrorists. The use of surveillance technology is widespread, from the cash machine on the corner, to the prison, to satellite surveillance of our enemies. As our world becomes more technological, we become more dependent on, and invested, in technology. Not only is our material world affected, but our mental landscape changes as well. And it is this change in our ideas that is more difficult to diagnose. As we have seen, we come to prefer technological or virtual bodies to real ones to the point that we feel betrayed or threatened by flesh and blood. At the same time we feel alienated from our bodies in this technologically mediated world, and we then crave more intense bodily sensations, which can lead some people to commit sadomasochistic violence toward themselves or others. We become more limited in the ways that we imagine ourselves as human beings living together. We adopt a technological approach to life that is imagined at odds with what we still maintain as natural bodies excluded from the realm of politics. In this way bodies and politics are seen as opposed to one another. The consequences of this idea—or perhaps we should call it an assumption—are grave in terms of actual life-and-death struggles. And we feel threatened when the ambiguity of the relationship between bodies and politics is made manifest.

We claim to value life itself, when actually we value some lives over others. Moreover, our conception of life is reduced to what Italian philosopher Giorgio Agamben calls "bare life" rather than quality of life. Life in and of itself is seen as a value that exists outside of the realm of politics. Life is imagined as "bare" or without qualities or cultural significance. Supposedly, it is what it is by nature. This way of thinking leads us to make political decisions in the name of "life"—decisions about abortion, euthanasia, and war—that value life in itself over the quality of life, mere survival over meaningful life. The very split between survival and quality of life has to be rethought once we acknowledge the ambiguities of life.

Our assumption about the value of bare life or mere survival, and our quest to protect life at all costs (well, some lives anyway), is part of what makes suicide bombers or "body-bombers" so horrifying within the Western imaginary. Suicide bombers make explicit the connection between the body and politics that has been denied within Western politics. They insist that the body is political and reinsert it into the realm of politics in a brutally violent way. They obviously value something other than mere survival or bare life because they are willing to kill themselves for their cause. (In his study of suicide bombers Christoph Reuter discovers that they are not crazed fanatics but well-educated young adults seeking to exact revenge on a more powerful enemy by using their lives as weapons.)[35] But this violent return of bodies to politics is all the more shocking because of Western assumptions about the opposition between natural bodies and cultural politics. These actions bring the ambiguity of bodies back into politics.

Agamben makes a persuasive case that Western politics excludes what he calls "bare life" or what we might think of as natural or biological bodies.[36] The natural or bare body is imagined as being outside of the realm of politics—how can culture or politics change the fundamental physicality of life?, we ask. In this way we continue to separate nature from politics. We deny the ways in which our very *notion of nature*—what is natural and what is not—is political. Agamben argues that the exclusion of bare life from politics (or the inclusion of bare life or the body within politics *as excluded*) leads to what he calls a logic of exception, which makes some lives valuable and other lives worthless. The logic runs something like this: if life exists prior to society and prior to the law, if it is outside of politics, then those in power can simply decide who lives and who dies using the rhetoric of exception. In other words, if law cannot govern life and death, then the decision of who will live and who will die, who will be killed and who will be saved, is a discretionary decision that disguises itself as a preordained or god-given decision in the name of a truth or justice that exists outside of the law. (We have analyzed President Bush's abstract appeals to eternity and a view outside of human history ordained by God.) The point is that the assumption that life or bodies are not political is used to justify so-called exceptions to the law that allow for killing and torture of those bodies deemed treacherous or evil.

The logic of exception seems to be the fundamental logic of the war against terror. For example, the abuse at Abu Ghraib or at Guantánamo Bay was said to be the result of *exceptional* individuals, the few bad apples. The prisoners held in Iraq and Cuba are not even called prisoners; rather they are called "detainees" because, as we are told, these are *exceptional* times that require *exceptional* measures for these *exceptionally* bad, even monstrous, individuals. President Bush and Vice President Cheney have argued that "the terrorism threat requires that the president have wide power to decide who could be held and how they should be treated"; and Defense Secretary Rumsfeld had his aides shred documents from officials who "called for a return to the minimum standards of treatment in the Geneva Conventions and for eventually closing the detention center at Guantánamo Bay, Cuba."[37] They insist that the president must have discretionary powers to make decisions about terrorists outside of national or international law. Terrorism is described as outside of the realm of politics, as evil; and therefore our normal ("good") means of war making don't apply because terrorism is an exception. This is why the administration maintained that the Geneva Convention was outdated and didn't apply to terrorism (Attorney General Alberto Gonzales called the Geneva Convention "quaint"); in other words, they argued that terrorism is an exception to international laws. The very space of the military base in Cuba is exceptional: the U.S. military runs a prison on the shores of one of its supposed enemies.[38] And we use these exceptional spaces to hold exceptionally evil enemies (we don't even call them criminals since that would imply that they are within the law) so that we can exercise exceptional methods of interrogation and torture because we live in an exceptional time. The urgency of exception, of emergency, is used to justify breaking the law.

The issue of bare life exempted from the realm of politics brings us back to the discussion of innocence. We imagine that bodily pleasures and pains are innocent in the sense that they are not part of the moral or political world. It is the assumption of the separation of the body from politics that conjures its innocence. It is imagined as innocent because it is not political. The paradox of imagining bodies as innocently outside of politics becomes manifest in discussions of killing of innocent civilians in war. First, it becomes obvious that although we claim to value all life, we maintain a hierarchy of lives that are worth saving. Our own lives are worth more than the lives of others. The lives of innocent civilians are worth more than the lives of combatants. The lives of American civilians are worth more than the lives of enemy civilians; for example we continue to hear about the 3,000 people killed on 9/11, but we do not hear about the as many as 100,000 Iraqis who died as a result of the first Gulf War or the 70,000–600,000 Iraqi civilians who have been killed so far in the current war.[39] The lives of enemy combatants are not even worth tallying up on the score card of warfare (for example, we don't want to know how many Iraqi soldiers we killed). And the lives of terrorists who aren't even considered combatants or soldiers are worthless. Judith Butler argues that we see some lives as worth grieving and others as not worth grieving.[40] Certainly, we don't grieve for our enemies. And for all of the rhetorical concern about not killing innocent civilians in Iraqi, if we are unwilling to even ponder how many civilians have been killed, do we really grieve those deaths either?

One of the aspects of terrorist violence considered most outrageous is that it is directed toward *innocent civilians*.[41] Perhaps here we should examine the notion of "innocence," especially as it relates to the different roles of the military and of civilians: military personnel protect and secure the comfortable lives of civilians, who benefit from military operations and occupations elsewhere—especially in the case of military superpowers that exercise force throughout the world in order to maintain their economic superiority and "way of life." In a thought-provoking statement, Ghassan

Hage challenges the distinction between soldiers and innocent civilians as it functions in violence between Israel and Palestine: "The PSBs (Palestinian Suicide Bombers) disrupt the ability of the colonizers to consolidate a 'normal peaceful life' inside the colonial settler state of Israel. As such they do not respect the Israeli colonizer's division of labor between the military who engage in protecting and facilitating the process of colonization and the civilian population who can peacefully enjoy the fruits of this process."[42] On the other hand, if guilt is the opposite of innocence, then why would we think that it is worse when our enemies harm innocent civilians than when they harm our soldiers? What does it suggest about our ideas of soldiers (or combatants, as they are now called)? Presumably, their lives are sacrificed so that the rest of us can maintain our style of life, the fruits of their labor. If civilians are innocent, what are soldiers, particularly our own soldiers? What makes civilians more "innocent" than the soldiers who fight for them?

Innocence and Vulnerability

The innocence of civilians is associated with their vulnerability. Children are especially innocent and vulnerable, and it is heart-wrenching when children are the innocent victims of war or terrorism. Immediately after the terrorist attacks on the World Trade Center, many news reports kept returning to the fact that children died in a daycare center in the towers. Even if children are or will be the beneficiaries of imperialist violence and exploitation, they, more than others, have not (yet) chosen this way of life.

But children's innocence, it seems, is associated with their vulnerability even more than with their lack of choice. They are dependent upon others for their care and well-being, and they are also vulnerable to others. In *Precarious Life*, Judith Butler argues that we have a primary vulnerability that comes with being human; more specifically, it comes with being born as a human infant completely beholden to others for survival. She claims that this primary vulnerability, associated with infants, is constitutive of humanity.[43] Although infancy lasts longer in humans than in other animals, however, the vulnerability of newborns is not unique to humans. The fact that we can be wounded by, or wound, others is also not unique to humans. We share this vulnerability with all living creatures. If, as Butler suggests, recognizing that our vulnerability is something we share with others can make us less violent toward them, then perhaps recognizing that vulnerability is something we share with all living beings can make us less violent toward nonhumans as well, animals and other inhabitants of the earth. While it may be that recognizing our shared vulnerability will make us more accepting of each other, it is important to critically analyze the rhetoric of vulnerability immediately following the terrorist attacks of September 11, 2001. Moreover, philosophically it is crucial to question the notion that vulnerability is constitutive of humanity, not just because we share vulnerability with all creatures but more particularly because it is not our vulnerability per se that distinguishes humans from other creatures; and most especially because in its history the very notion of vulnerability is inherently linked to violence.

The word "vulnerable" comes from the Latin word *vulnerabilis*, which means "wounding, injurious." The older, archaic, definition of *vulnerable* in the Oxford English Dictionary is "Having power to wound; wounding"; the current definition is "That may be wounded; susceptible of receiving wounds or physical injury." *Vulnerable* can thus mean both the power to wound or *wounding* and the capacity to receive wounds or *wounded*. It is apt, then, that the most frequent word to appear immediately following the attacks of September 11 was "vulnerable": America was wounded and wanting to wound those responsible for the attacks. Journalist Tom Engelhardt researched the newspaper coverage immediately following the attacks on the Twin Towers, starting with September 12, 2001. He concludes that "one of the most common words over those days in the [New York] *Times* and elsewhere was 'vulnerable'"; and the word that surfaced fastest on its heels was "war."[44] The lightening move from vulnerability to war suggests that feelings of vulnerability can trigger fear, hatred, and violence. Psychologically, it is true that violence toward others is often a defense against one's own sense of insecurity. More than this, however, the very concept of vulnerability contains within it violence toward others associated with war—wounding and wounded. It is this violence at the heart of the concept of vulnerability that should make us question a philosophy that sees vulnerability as constitutive of humanity. Although it is undeniable that human beings are capable of violence, even "unthinkable" violence, is it that which makes us human? Or, on the contrary, is it the ability to forgive and to move beyond violence that makes us human? Is violence or forgiveness more uniquely human? Elsewhere, I argue that it is forgiveness that is constitutive of humanity.[45]

Certainly, denying vulnerability and holding on to the illusion of invincibility and absolute security can lead to violent acts of war. We have seen how this happens when strength in the face of crisis is reduced to estimation of military might. Hatred and the urge for revenge can be seen as a manifestation of fear, fear of our own vulnerability. Victimization of others literally puts our own vulnerability onto others. We become the bully instead of the playground idiot. It is not surprising, then, that privates in the military, themselves subjected to hazing and humiliation as part of basic training, would act out these same rituals of humiliation and subordination on others in order to establish their own authority. *But just because we can or do wound others when we are wounded, does not mean that we have to do so.* While the denial of vulnerability may help explain human violence, that does not mean that being wounded or wounding is constitutive of humanity or definitive of being human. Indeed, in order to move beyond war and violence, it is necessary to imagine humanity defined not in terms of its power to wound but in terms of its power to heal.

Julia Kristeva also invokes vulnerability in her latest work, *Hate and Forgiveness*. There she associates the uncanny effect of others with vulnerability. She raises the question of "how to inscribe in the conception of the human itself—and, consequently in philosophy and political practice—the constitutive part played by destructivity, vulnerability, disequilibrium which are integral to the identity of the human species and the singularity of the speaking subject?"[46] She claims that along with liberty, equality, and fraternity, vulnerability is a fourth term that we inherit from Enlightenment humanism.[47] Speaking of the disabled, and extending her analysis to racism, classism, and religious persecution, she suggests a narcissistic wound that constitutes humanity as a scar at the suture of being and meaning. It is our ambiguous position in between nature and culture, animal and human, being and meaning, that makes us vulnerable, and also free. Precisely that which makes us human and opens up a world of meaning also makes us vulnerable.

As Kristeva describes it, however, this vulnerability is not primarily the result of being infants whose bodies can be wounded by others, or having bodies that can be wounded (à la Butler), but rather exists because we occupy a place between being and meaning, between bodies and words. In Kristeva's account, the gap between bodies and words, the ways in which words are never quite adequate to capture bodily experience, is figured as a wound. And it is this wound that is the seat of our vulnerability. We are wounding and wounded because we occupy the ambiguous space between bodies and meanings. She suggests that the uncanny encounter with another puts us face to face with our own vulnerability "with and for others." And it is the fear and denial of our own vulnerability that causes us to hate and exploit the vulnerability of others. She asks, then, how can we acknowledge that to be human is to be vulnerable? In other words, how can we accept our own vulnerability without violently projecting it onto others whom we oppress and torture or alternatively "civilize" and "protect"?

Asking about the role of vulnerability in human experience, about the role of the capacity to wound and to be wounded, is crucial to thinking through not only our capacity for, but also our pleasure in, violence. Unless we can answer that question by imagining humanity otherwise than wounded and wounding, we will not move away from violence. As I argue elsewhere, *what makes us human is not the split between being and meaning that alienates us from ourselves and others, or leaves us wounded and wounding, but rather the forgiveness that makes it possible to transcend alienation and violence,* if always only temporarily, through creative sublimation in language or signification. Moving away from Kristeva's metaphor of the wound or scar, we must be able to imagine occupying the ambiguous place between being and meaning, between nature and culture, between body and technology, as precisely what allows us to live beyond violence and vulnerability, beyond wounding and being wounded. We translate our own particularity/singularity, our finitude and limitation, our "wounded" bodies with our own unconscious desires and fears, into words and thereby unite bodily being and articulations of the meaning of that being; we become beings who mean. Forgiveness, then, is the acknowledgment that, for humans, being is meaning, and rich and full meaning becomes the power to heal.[48]

We connect our own violent impulses to our emotional lives in productive ways by interpreting them rather than merely acting on them. By interpreting our hatred and loathing as a response to our own vulnerability—our wounding and wounds—we gain the critical distance necessary to prevent ourselves from acting on them. We turn our fear and loathing into words so that we can live with them and with the others who inspire them. Rather than act on instinct or aggressive urges—whether sexual or violent—we stop to question our own emotions and actions. Rather than wallow in sadomasochistic pleasure in violence toward ourselves and others, we transform bodily pleasures into joy through interpretation. By giving meaning to our pleasures they become joy. By giving meaning to our sorrows they become tolerable; they can even become beautiful works of art. After all, satisfying bodily impulses does not in itself produce a satisfying life. Meaning and purpose in life come through the continual translation of pleasure and pain into social structures of meaning that allow us not only to live together and to communicate but also to love each other. As Kristeva says, psychic life is an "infinite quest for meaning, a *bios* transversal of *zoë*, a biography with and for others."[49] Curiosity and interpretation can be the source of joy that takes us beyond the realm of finite sensuous pleasures or pains and puts us in touch with the realm of infinite meaning. This joy in playing with words gives meaning to our violent impulses, now expressed in words rather than in actions. The articulation of our violent emotions transforms hate into forgiveness and allows us to live with our own vulnerability and tendencies toward violence without killing ourselves or others.

Meaning Against Death

When continued questioning and interpretation are the heart of representation, it is a form of translation through which meaning is given to "bare life" as the gift that bestows humanity. But this translation requires time and energy, scarce commodities in today's global economy, where questioning is considered inefficient, a poor use of time, and interpretation is a waste of resources unless it results in profits recognized by the value hierarchies of global capitalism. Ultimately, what must be called into question and constantly reassessed is the meaning of our actions, particularly our pleasure in violence. Through representation accompanied by critical interpretation, we can give a meaning to our violent impulses that may help us avoid acting on them.

Our obsession with speed and faster and faster technologies, inducing more and more stress, sacrifices curiosity to efficiency. Because it takes time and energy, and its profits are not immediately grasped, curiosity is not marketable in the new world order. Within this order, meaning becomes a commodity like any other that is valuable only if it can be marketed, distributed, and sold at a profit. The fungibility of meaning, however, places it within an economy of exchange that devalues its benefit to life, which cannot be calculated. The gift of meaning is in excess of the economy of exchange. For within the economy of exchange the dynamic and poetic operations of metaphorical substitution or sublimation are reduced to products or things. Consumer culture proliferates the empty desire for products that create their own needs and only ever lead to partial, incomplete, and therefore short-lived satisfactions. The rich are idolized for their wealth and property—they are individuals with things. Individuals themselves become fungible, as their organs or babies are sold to the highest bidder, illegally or legally sanctioned through brokers and insurance companies. Monetary value stands in for ethical values.

But these objects that we crave can't touch the more profound longing for meaningful lives that comes not through a hunger for consumer goods but rather through a passion for life. Unlike hunger, passion cannot be temporarily satisfied. Unlike the thirst for wealth and things, passion has no object; it is not defined in terms of possession and calculations. Passion gives more energy than it takes, in excess of calculations and exchange value. Passion for life is what we risk losing when we reduce freedom to the free market and peace to a leveling universalism that subjects the planet to regulatory norms. Within freedom defined in terms of the free market, anything goes: both strict prohibitions (like those touted by the Christian Right or Muslim fundamentalists) and wild promiscuity (like we see in confessional memoirs and Internet porn) are marketable. Within this economy, violent sadomasochistic abuses are performed and photographed in all innocence as "just having fun" at the expense of others.

The world of representation has become disconnected from our affective or psychic lives; the result is an inability to represent (and thereby live) our emotional lives outside of the economy of spectacle. Expressions of affect and emotion take the form of violent images or outrageous confessions of sexual exploits. Our psychic lives are overrun with images of sex and violence on television, at the movies, or on the Internet, while the idealized romance and everyday lives of movie stars become our prosthetic fantasies. Imagination, creativity, and sublimation are at stake in the colonization of our fantasy lives by media images. Indeed, the possibility of creativity, imagination, and representation are impeded by the standardized expressions of mass media. Media images become substitute selves, substitute affects, that impede rather than facilitate the transfer of bodily sensations and affects into signification.[50] Images, seemingly transparent, substitute for questioning and interpreting the meaning of the body and therefore of life. The psyche or soul itself hangs in the balance.[51]

What is lacking or threatened by modern forms of regression is not just the integration of law into emotional life but any interaction between pleasure and joy. Bodily pleasures at the level of our physical existence are cut off from the joy enabled by the realm of meaning. Joy is reduced to pleasures unto death because pleasure is cut adrift from meaning. We shop until we drop ... or we engage in dangerous practices of cutting, hanging, suffocation, etc., in order to feel something in our bodies ... or we abuse, torture, or kill others to ward off our own feelings of bodily vulnerability. Rather than circumscribing our bodies with meaning, contemporary versions of law have become techniques designed to manage, regulate, and spy in order to more efficiently contain. Within this military-industrial consumer culture, we mess around in the abject space between images and reality to the point of a perverse regression to infantile pleasures in sadomasochistic violence toward ourselves and others. Within this culture of spectacle and death, the only way to imagine sexual fulfillment and satisfaction with life is through possession and violence. When, like Mr. and Mrs. Smith, we can only imagine pleasure as brutalized, bruised, and bleeding bodies, perverse pleasure replaces passion for life.

"Amorous Disasters"?

How does passion for life turn into passion for death? Perhaps the most fascinating manifestations of passion for death are women suicide bombers, called *shahidas*, the Arabic word for feminine martyr. Historically, women within patriarchal cultures have been denied access to education and positions of power. They have been relegated to the realm of procreation, to a natural role as the bearers of life; women are associated with giving birth and nurturing children. So how then do they become the bearers of death?

In her book *Army of Roses*, Barbara Victor chronicles the lives of some women suicide bombers and discovers that most of them have been shunned by their families because they do not fulfill their designated functions as wives and mothers.[52] Some of them are barren and cannot have children or choose not to, others have been shamed by rape or sexual assault, and others are divorced or without husbands. Many of them have been given the seemingly "poisonous" gift of Western education, which leaves them caught in a no-man's land between opposing values of two cultures. They are in the impossible situation of trying to navigate one set of prohibitions and another, to the extent that for some it seems that martyrdom becomes not only the way to reach paradise but also the way to gain recognition from their society.

Reuter's history of suicide bombers, which focuses primarily on male suicide bombers, indicates that these well-educated young people see themselves in a hopeless situation, fighting against a much stronger enemy, and resort to suicide bombing as a way to make their lives matter, to make a difference. Rather than looking for virgins in paradise, as the Western media characterizes them, according to Reuter these passionate young people sacrifice their lives to be remembered as heroic figures. In his analysis of Palestinian suicide bombers, Ghassan Hage too maintains that suicide bombing is a last resort in a fight against colonization; but, he argues, it becomes part of a culture of martyrdom because both material and symbolic resources are so limited by the colonial situation. In other words, martyrdom becomes a way of gaining symbolic cultural capital when one's culture is perceived as being under siege. In a situation where both material and symbolic resources are controlled by dominant forces, resistance becomes valued, even heroic. It becomes ritualized to the point that suicide bombers make videotapes before their killings to be circulated afterward, along with posters and pictures of these "martyrs for justice" in the face of seemingly invincible Western arsenals.

In the case of women suicide bombers, Victor's account suggests that for the most part these are excellent students who want more from their lives than simply being the good woman as defined by tradition. But everything in their surrounding environment, especially their families, is hostile to this aspect of their personalities. In a sense they redeem themselves in the eyes of their traditions by sacrificing themselves for their society. Rather than sacrifice their personal freedoms to fit into the restrictions placed on them by patriarchal culture (like so many women do in the "East" and the "West"), they sacrifice themselves for that culture in another, more absolute way. Julia Kristeva argues that these women (and women in general) have been relegated to the realm of procreation or physical being (*zoë*) and denied access to representation (*bios*). She concludes that as a result these women occupy the two incompatible universes of family and school, a dilemma that creates in them "double personalities" or "psychic cleavage" that renders them politically vulnerable to the rhetoric of extremists.[53]

Yet insofar as they are, in Kristeva's words, "sent off to sacrifice and martyrdom in imitation of the warlike man and possessor of power," they are killing in the name of principles that have excluded them; the representatives of life are sent to kill. This is to say that the very culture that reduces them to the bearers of life now makes them the bearers of death.[54] In her speech before UNESCO in December 2002, Kristeva comments on *shahidas*: "Some currents of classic Islam do not hesitate to pander to this alleged 'equality' between the sexes, without ever envisaging the sexual and subjective difference of the woman, revelator of new life values and creativity!"[55] She provocatively suggests that the *shahidas* represent the triumph of a culture of death that values women's biology over biography, reproductive life over meaningful life. Even when through education and technology women are freed from compulsory reproduction, they are still not necessarily free for biography or representing their lives beyond reproduction.

Traditionally in both Islamic and Christian cultures, women have been associated with biological life and denied access to the biographical or political, that is to say the realm of meaning; they have been associated with procreation as the survival of the species and not as the creation of new values and new meaning for life. In different ways, fundamentalisms in both traditions continue to victimize or ostracize women who do not serve the procreative function as circumscribed by patriarchal religious law. Based on Victor's *Army of Roses*, Kristeva speculates that "these are amorous disasters—pregnancy outside of marriage, sterility, desire for phallic equality with the man (like the woman-nihilists who committed suicide in the cause of the Russian Revolution)—which influence the vocation of shahidas."[56]

While the enlisted women whose photographs have been associated with war in Iraq may not be amorous disasters, they are poor women who typically joined the military to avoid the poverty that can lead to various sorts of "amorous disasters." Think of Lynndie England, pregnant by Abu Ghraib "ring-leader" Charles Graner (who later married another soldier indicted for abuse, Megan Ambuhl) at the time she was charged with the abuses at Abu Ghraib. England's story could be one of amorous disaster. With her baby son in her arms at her trial, she was bitter about Graner's marriage to Ambuhl. And it was Graner's testimony that undermined her defense and lead to the retrial in which she was convicted. In an article entitled "Behind Failed Abu Ghraib Plea, A Tangle of Bonds and Betrayals," journalist Kate Zernike described the soap opera–like scene: "In a military courtroom in Texas last week was a spectacle worthy of 'As the World Turns': Pfc. Lynndie R. England, the defendant, holding her 7-month-old baby; the imprisoned father, Pvt. Charles A. Graner Jr., giving testimony that ruined what lawyers said was her best shot at leniency; and waiting outside, another defendant from the notorious abuses at Abu Ghraib prison in Iraq, Megan M. Ambuhl, who had recently wed Private Graner—a marriage Private England learned about only days before."[57]

As Victor and Reuter note in their research on suicide bombers, many of them are from middle-class families. Victor suggests, and Kristeva argues that it is their middle-class access to Western education that puts them in the no-man's land between two cultures, which leads them to desperate acts of suicide and murder. The situation of poor women in the United States military is radically different in some ways in that they join up in order to gain access to middle-class education, which will give them opportunities to escape poverty and the rural lives back home. What these women share, however, is the necessity to continue to navigate patriarchal conventions and institutions—in the case of these American young women, the military. As different as the traditions of these cultures may be, in both women's roles are defined in relation to their bodies, which may be expectations of marriage followed by pregnancy and child-rearing, or as we have seen in American popular culture, associations between women and sex.

While Victor's and Kristeva's analyses go some distance in giving us a perspective on these women that acknowledges the significance of their sociohistorical contexts, or subject positions, we must also keep in mind that these women are participating in the traditionally masculine activities of war. While it is crucial to analyze the ways in which their acts are governed, even overdetermined, by their circumstances as women in patriarchal cultures, it is also important not to displace their public persona back into the domestic sphere. They may be "amorous disasters," as Kristeva says, but theirs are not just private or domestic disasters but also public disasters that trade on war and hate and not just love, or failed love. The very question of the meanings of love and hate, particularly as they come to bear on women's public and private lives, is at stake.

What we need is not just the rhetoric of equality—equal opportunity killers—which has been used to justify violence, but rather a new discourse of the meaning and joy of life, not life as mere biology but also as biography, not merely *zoë* (biological life) but also *bios* (recounted life, or biography). Fundamentalisms may use the rhetoric of women's equality to valorize women's suicidal violence, but they do not give women freedom to re-create what it means to be a woman. If women have been freed from age-old restrictions on their freedom, restrictions that justified their lives only in terms of the biology of procreation, then we need discourses that provide new justifications for women's lives that move beyond procreation. Otherwise, at the extreme, women are free only to kill themselves.

In one sense the *shahida* can be seen as a symptom of patriarchal restrictions within which the only meaningful place left to women who do not conform to the ideals of motherhood and femininity is martyrdom. She represents the return of the repressed uncanniness of human procreation, of human life and death, which, straddling nature and technology, on the frontier between biology and biography, cannot be assimilated into, or circumscribed by, patriarchal social codes. This uncanny aspect of our existence has been relegated to women, maternity, and female sexuality. And as women begin to occupy the position that we have built for them discursively, that is to say the position of deadly weapon, it should be no surprise that the return of the repressed explodes in our face.

Do They Jump, or Are They Pushed?

This account of the situation of these women is reminiscent of Gayatri Spivak's discussion of the paradoxical position of subaltern women, caught between a modern world in terms of which their traditions seemingly render them passive objects and traditions that seemingly make them agents, but only of their own suicide.[58] Discussing the traditional Indian ritual of *sati*, in which widows throw themselves on the burning funeral pyres of their husbands, Spivak shows how, within the rhetoric of the traditionalists, these women are free agents who chose to burn themselves; but within the rhetoric of Western feminists, these women are the victims of repressive and deadly patriarchal customs of a "backward" culture. The double-bind in this situation is that while we don't want to perpetuate the stereotype that women are merely passive helpless victims who don't possess any agency of their own, we also don't want to embrace a practice that not only serves patriarchal inheritance laws but moreover kills women. So, which is it? Do these women jump onto the burning pyres of their own free will, or does their culture push them, so to speak? On Spivak's analysis, it is precisely our stereotypes of women, and subaltern women in particular, that constructs this dilemma in which women do have agency, but only the agency to kill themselves.

In the case of women suicide bombers, we see a similar phenomenon. On the one hand, feminists want to insist that these women have agency, in this case powerful political agency with which to resist colonization. On the other hand, feminists want to insist that these women are compelled to martyr themselves by social circumstances that leave them only this extreme option to redeem themselves in the eyes of their traditions. On this view, undesirable women are sacrificed to traditional law as their last attempt at redemption. Their difference can be forgiven only through their sacrifice as a form of purification ritual. But this notion of forgiveness is merely the flip side of vengeance—it is a perversion that idolizes sacrifice and killing. We could say that forgiveness is precisely what these women lack and that lack of forgiveness leads to depression and suicide.[59] A more life-affirming type of forgiveness comes through an interpretation that gives enabling and robust meaning to life. This alternative notion of forgiveness operates outside the economy of vengeance or judgment to offer meaning to life without the necessity of sacrifice. Forgiveness offers a renegotiation with laws and traditions such that meaning supports the singularity of each individual rather than prohibiting it.

The enlisted women now associated with war in Iraq—Lynndie England, Megan Ambuhl, Jessica Lynch—in their own way may be "amorous disasters" insofar as they joined the military to escape poverty, to leave rural American, to see the world, and to have a better life. The army provided an alternative to staying in their small towns, getting married, and having children right after high school like many of their school mates. And recall the soap opera stories of the women involved in the criminal activities at Abu Ghraib, where their military careers ended in the midst of "amorous disasters" of pregnancy, betrayal, and separation by prison. Once again we could ask, what is the meaning of consent, of freedom, in a situation that leaves so few options? Once again we could ask, did they jump, or were they pushed?

But this either/or proposition reduces women's agency merely to the freedom to kill themselves and others. There must be an alternative way to conceive of freedom, so that our only opportunity is not reduced to equal access to violence. It is too simple to think that these women, or any individuals, exist in isolation from their society and the norms and values around them, or that individuals are completely determined by their culture like programmed robots. This dichotomous way of thinking is connected to the split between being and meaning, bodies and politics, discussed earlier. We imagine determinism as something like laws of nature that turn us into machines; at the same time we imagine human culture or the political sphere as completely free, to the point that life and death matters are decided at the discretion of those in power. Within this oppositional way of thinking, determinism, passivity, bodies, being are on one side of the equation while freedom, agency, minds, meaning are on the other: one pole is defined against the other, such that ultimately to be free is to be free from the body. Think for example of the women's movement, which continues to struggle with the biological fact that women get pregnant and give birth to children; the meaning of that "fact" is precisely what is at stake in debates over women's roles in society, government, politics, and the military. Our experience, however, is not so black-and-white. We are neither merely natural bodies nor political stooges. Rather, we are human beings whose lives are meaningful precisely because of the ambiguities of existence.

It might be helpful to note that Kristeva's discussion of "amorous disasters" is embedded in her discussion of freedom. Recall from chapter three that Kristeva delineates two senses of freedom that we inherit from the Enlightenment: freedom imagined as the result of the autonomous individual's agency, which operates according to a logic of cause and effect that she associates with instrumental reasoning; and freedom to create meaning by virtue of our existence embedded in relationships with others and otherness, including our own unconscious fears and desires. This second version of freedom cannot be thought of in terms of any traditional logic of cause and effect, the very logic that operates in the law become science of management. As we have seen, when law is reduced to regulation or management technique it cannot provide full and robust meaning for our lives and instead is reduced to disciplinary practices in so many penal codes. These codes may be researched and designed in accordance with the latest technology for the most effective management of bodies, in particular those deemed "undesirable," but they do not take into consideration the role of either societal or unconscious forces (which may amount to the same thing). To avoid the unhappy choice between "jumping and being pushed," we need to conceive of freedom beyond the free market in which individuals supposedly sink or swim based solely on their own free will, translated now into exchange value on the market. On the market, every thing, including human life, is fungible and can be translated into calculable risks and profit margins. This version of freedom, as we have seen, is at odds with any consideration of the singularity of individuals that makes each unique and different from all others; it is also at odds with the fact that their well-being depends on support from others and from society.

In Kristeva's discussion of the so-called amorous disasters of women suicide bombers and two versions of freedom, she returns again to the Enlightenment philosopher Immanuel Kant, specifically to the two pillars of peace from his essay on "Perpetual Peace." Like she did with the two notions of freedom, Kristeva describes what she takes to be Kant's two pillars of peace: "first, that of universality—*all men are equal* and all must be saved. Second is the principle of *protection of human life*, sustained by the love of the life of each."[60] She insists that although we are far from achieving economic justice for all, it is the second pillar and not the first that is in the most danger today: "Yet whatever the weaknesses, the efforts for realizing social, economic, and political justice have never in the history of humanity been as considerable and widespread. But it is the second pillar of the imaginary of peace that seems to me today to suffer most gravely: The love of life eludes us; there is no longer a discourse for it."[61] It is not just economic, racial, and religious inequalities that prevent peace—although these are immense—but also the lack of a discourse of the love of life. The culture of death fosters war over peace because we are losing the ability to imagine the meaning of life beyond mere survival or profit-margins and; therefore we can no longer imagine ways to embrace life.

Economic justice and the distribution of wealth, however, cannot be separated from questions of meaning. Increasingly the resources and wealth of the earth are owned by fewer individuals while most of the world's population lives in poverty. While the majority of the citizens of the planet struggle to survive, privileged middle-class and rich individuals increasingly feel their lifestyles threatened by poor people. They guard their possessions with gated communities, security systems, and high-tech prisons. At the same time they complain of feeling depressed and exhausted from spending all of their time accumulating wealth, which ultimately leaves them with feelings of meaninglessness. They/we have sacrificed the quality of life—the good life—for goods and services. The distribution of resources is thus related to questions of meaning in complex ways that affect the "haves" differently from the "have-nots." As we have seen, within patriarchal cultures and institutions both the distribution of resources and the distribution of meaning affect women differently than men.

As Kristeva describes it, life as "amorous disaster" is a result of women liberated from traditional roles that reduced the meaning of their lives to procreation, but who are not able to create new justifications for life. Even as women and others gain the negative freedom from prohibitions, how do they gain the positive freedom to create the meaning of their lives anew? What does their unique biological difference mean outside of a discourse that reduces them to procreation? How can their uniqueness be articulated in creative forms of representation that give meaning to their singularity beyond an economy of abjection, in which women's bodies are either shunned or eroticized? If women are freed from the restrictions of patriarchal cultures, we might ask "free for what"? If they are no longer "pushed," are they now only free to "jump"? Or can we imagine beginning to re-create what it means to be a woman, a man, an American, a citizen of the world? Yes, but only if we begin to think the "unthinkable"—9/11, Abu Ghraib, women suicide bombers—and bring these "undesirable" bodies and events back into the realm of meaning. Only then can we hope to imagine otherwise ... to imagine a world at peace rather than a world at war.

Conclusion

Witnessing Ethics Again

In the context of criticizing the Bush administration's foreign policies, retired Army colonel Lawrence Wilkerson said that he could understand the "bestiality that comes over men when they're asked to use force for the state."[1] Did he really mean "bestiality"? While one meaning of the word "bestiality" is "humans behaving like animals," more commonly it means humans having sex with animals. Did Wilkerson mean to suggest that during war soldiers turn their enemies and prisoners of war into animals by sexualizing them—think of Abu Ghraib. Or did he mean that soldiers themselves behave like animals? Or both?

In the media surrounding the "scandal" at Abu Ghraib, both the soldiers and the prisoners were variously referred to as "animals" and "beasts." The abusive guards were called "beasts" for their inhumane treatment of prisoners. And those same guards reportedly claimed that "left on their own," the prisoners behaved like "animals." One of the most infamous photographs from Abu Ghraib shows Pfc. Lynndie England holding the end of a leash tied around a prisoner's neck. The image suggests that she is treating the prisoner like a dog; in testimony, several prison guards reportedly said that they were ordered to treat the prisoners like "dogs," instructions that they interpreted to include making them bark like dogs. The photographs of abuse also show guards using dogs to threaten naked prisoners, which even Saddam Hussein made a point of claiming did not happen when he was responsible for Abu Ghraib. Mississippi senator Trent Lott justified the use of dogs, saying, "Hey, nothing wrong with holding a dog up there.... This is not Sunday school; this is interrogation ... you don't get information that will save American lives by withholding pancakes."[2] These scenes of war are filled with real and metaphorical dogs ... not to mention Sunday school and pancakes.

The Dogs of War; or, Let Them Eat Pancakes!

The dogs in this story are not the ones that we imagine as man's best friend; rather they are imagined as ferocious attack dogs or pathetic stray dogs left to die in the street: dogs as victimizers and as victims. These dogs do not even evince the pathos of the poor dogs chained to roofs and abandoned to Hurricane Katrina. These are the dogs of war.

It is in this context of war that Col. Wilkerson can imagine humans behaving like beasts. The rhetoric of war is full of beasts in order to justify the "naturalness" of war; images of dogs doing what they supposedly do by nature, when "left on their own," become perverse reassurance that we are behaving naturally too, that it is only natural that we would have enemies and kill and torture them. The power of the metaphor, however, is that through comparison it also underlines the difference: we *are not* dogs; we can behave *like* dogs only because ultimately we are unlike them. Metaphors of beasts and animals are not new to war. Think of descriptions of Nazis who behaved like "beasts" (were they also the "black sheep" of the German people, just following orders?) rounding up Jews who went to slaughter like "sheep" or "cattle," who were also treated like "dogs," even worse than dogs. As we have seen, the so-called beasts at Abu Ghraib who did shocking things to prisoners are also called the "black sheep" of the army, the few "bad apples." The dog metaphors—along with sheep and apples—falsely reassure us that the photographs from Abu Ghraib are *not* us![3]

We are not the beasts, the sheep, the dogs. Yet those photographs continue to haunt us precisely because we recognize both the abusers and the abused not as beasts or dogs, but as human, all too human. It is the humanness of this violence that makes it so uncanny. We are animals, to be sure. We are creatures, beings in the world, among other living beings.

But we are also animals or beings who mean. To be human is to inhabit a world of meaning and a meaningful world. Perhaps more than denying the entrance of the body into politics, we deny the entrance of meaning into politics, or more precisely, we deny the ambiguity between body and meaning as it affects politics. Paradoxically, the realm of politics has been reduced to actions and policies that are seemingly self-evident, even natural, and don't require interpretation: good versus evil. Contemporary media with their real-time reporting, embedded journalism, and fictional simulations of events contribute to the lack of interpretation that results in a crisis of meaning. We don't question what we see because seeing is believing. Yet, as Mark Danner concludes in *Torture and Truth*, "the scandal is not about uncovering what is hidden, it is about seeing what is already there—and acting on it. It is not about information; it is about politics."[4]

The Scandal of What We See

The impression that we cannot see what is right in front of our eyes echoes throughout contemporary discussions of the meaning and power of violence. We have access to photographs, military orders, so-called torture memos, even insider exposés because contemporary technology and media make exposure of terror and torture widespread. But, as we have seen throughout this book, rather than inspiring action or changing attitudes, these images lead instead to empty empathy and apathy or, worse, to the perpetuation of violence. Journalist Mark Danner concludes that "this makes Abu Ghraib a peculiarly contemporary kind of scandal: like other scandals that have erupted during the Iraq war and the war on terror, it is not about revelation or disclosure but about the failure, once wrongdoing is disclosed, of politicians, officials, the press, and, ultimately, citizens to act."[5]

This failure, however, as we have seen, is not just a failure of action but also a failure of meaning. In a culture that values action over meaning, it is, ironically, the lack of meaning that results in a lack of action. If we do not act because we will not allow ourselves to see what we see, as Danner suggests, it is because we witness trauma and extreme violence as a spectacle without interpreting meaning, not only for the lives of others but also for our own lives. We see violence on television and at the movies, but we do not investigate our own investment in violence, both real and imagined. The "scandal," as Danner calls it, is precisely that we turn violence into scandal, into media spectacle—and thereby shield ourselves from the implications and meaning of violence for our everyday lives. Politics itself has become the spectacle of one scandal after another, reported in the media alongside other scandals of violence, infidelity, and sexual promiscuity among the rich and famous. In this way, as we have seen, violence is not only normalized as a natural and therefore unquestioned part of our everyday experience, but also turned into entertainment. Even horrifying images like the destruction of the Twin Towers are rebroadcast over and over again, while news media work to get the scoop and present it in a format that sells, a format that competes well against other entertainment offered at the same time.

Not seeing, then, is not just about information (which, as we have seen, is always presented from a particular perspective and too often ripped out of context), and it is also not just about politics (which has become scandalous spectacle that reduces meaning to clichés and sound-bites)—it is also about technologies for reporting information and packaging politics. Reporting techniques like embedded reporting and real-time live news reports that do not contextualize the trauma they present create a sense of "empty empathy" that produces an emotional response without the critical distance necessary to interpret either the images or one's reaction to them. Even while political discourse is full of inflated rhetoric of good and evil and moral values, it closes off any discussion of ethics.[6] As we have seen, the rhetoric of good versus evil, of "us versus them," leaves us with a violent struggle to the death in which politics has been evacuated of meaning and morality is reduced to cheerleading for one side or the other.

Stereotypes and myths are essential to the effectiveness of this rhetoric. Politicians and the media play on age-old myths and traditional stereotypes in order to fuel hatred and the desire for death and killing. As we have seen, the focus on women's involvement in violence plays on uncanny stereotypes that for centuries have linked women, particularly their sexuality, with danger. The use of problematic stereotypical images of women as virgins or whores, or as damsels in distress or man-hating lesbians, dampens our reactions to torture, abuse, and killing. Images of women as they are used by the media to create a spectacle of sex and violence—a spectacle familiar to us from Hollywood fantasies and Internet pornography—displace violence from the realm of war and terror to the realm of sex and sexuality. The characterization of women as naturally dangerous and naturally sexual takes deadly violence out of the context of war and puts it into the context of bodies, female bodies, linked with nature. This combination of sex and violence is popular on television and at the box office, where much of the content continues to revolve around women's bodies. While we are glued to the media spectacle of sex and violence, also we feel disgust at the violence, but on some level we can learn to live with it ... we are used to living with it ... it doesn't touch us ... in fact perhaps we even crave it ... we become addicted to it.

As we have seen, however, these images of women at war continue to haunt us; they are uncanny manifestations of the ambiguous role of bodies, particularly women's bodies, between nature and culture, as bare reproductive bodies or technological bodies, imagined as both the bearers of life and the bearers of death. These images, as the media surrounding them indicate, make manifest the various levels of ambiguity with which we live, ambiguities that we would rather deny so that we can continue to justify our own violence, either as exceptional (those black sheep and bad apples again), or as necessary and legitimate force to stop terrorism (extreme measures for an exceptional situation). What do we see in these visual and narrative images and why? How do we respond to what we see?

Judith Butler concludes her reflections on violence in *Precarious Life* by insisting that "the task at hand is to establish modes of public seeing and hearing that might well respond to the cry of the human within the sphere of appearance, a sphere in which the trace of the cry has become hyperbolically inflated to rationalize a gluttonous nationalism, or fully obliterated, where both alternatives turn out to be the same."[7] Butler suggests that while we may see and hear "the cry of the human," at the same time we do *not* see and hear it because, as she maintains, we do not *recognize* it as human. Ghassan Hage also asks, "What kind of social conditions must avail and what kind of history must a people have internalized to make them lose this capacity of seeing the other in his or her humanness?"[8] Hage too suggests that we do not see, because we do not *recognize*, the humanity of the other.

What would it mean to see or hear the humanity or humanness in the images presented to us in the media? In the case of the photographs from Abu Ghraib or the testimony of Army insiders from Guantánamo, is it that we do not see or hear the victims—and the perpetrators—as human? Is it, as both Butler and Hage argue, that we do not *recognize* their humanity?

Or is there rather something more at stake than recognition in explaining and overcoming violence? Is there something in these images, in these events, in our response to them—our responsibility for them—that takes us beyond recognition? We might formulate the question this way: what is the relationship between recognition of another's humanity and response to it? Are these one and the same? Or, on the contrary, is it rather that we do indeed recognize the other's humanity and that is precisely why we engage in insistent disavowals of our own violence as well as hyperbolic justifications for it?

Beyond Recognition

Both Butler and Hage, along with many other contemporary theorists, explain violence in terms of a struggle for recognition, a struggle to be recognized as part of humanity. More than this, they both suggest that reciprocal or mutual recognition is a necessary ideal for overcoming violence. Butler articulates this struggle in terms of the constitutive power of norms and describes recognition itself as a performance that enacts and confers (in this case) humanity.[9] Hage discusses the distribution of recognition in terms of the meaningfulness of life. He maintains that "society is characterized by a deep inequality in the distribution of meaningfulness," which he associates with "the losers in the symbolic struggle for recognition," to humanity.[10]

In spite of their gloomy portrayals of the dreadful consequences of losing the struggle for recognition, however, both Butler and Hage continue to embrace the Hegelian ideal of reciprocal or mutual recognition. In spite of the fact that they catalogue in gory detail many of the casualties in this struggle, they continue to have faith in the ideal. Elsewhere I have argued that by so doing, they continue to promote an ideal that is not only unattainable but also and moreover politically suspect, because the struggle or need for recognition is a by-product of colonial violence in the first place.[11] Why do we continue to hold on to the ideal of mutual recognition, even while we reject so many other nineteenth-century ideals because they were part of the colonial enterprise? More to the point here: why do we continue to imagine humanity as a struggle, a fight, a war? How can we get beyond violence if the best hope we have for overcoming it is violence itself, the so-called struggle for recognition?

When we look at the photographs from Abu Ghraib and hear about the abuses at Guantánamo we may have different reactions: we may work to justify them, explain them away, or redefine torture; we may see them as "just having fun" or necessary or "legitimate force." In all of these cases we may recognize our own culpability but simultaneously disavow that recognition; we know it is wrong but continue to insist on our innocence. Like Lynndie England at her trail, we maintain both our guilt and our innocence, both that we know and that we didn't know. It is this ambiguity between knowledge and ignorance, guilt and innocence, between violence and fun, between bodily impulses and law, that foils the enterprise of recognition. In other words, unconscious desires and fears are the spoilers in recognizing "the cry of the human."

At bottom, it is *not* a lack of the recognition of the other's humanity or humanness that leads to violence, torture, and killing. The military guards who tortured prisoners at Abu Ghraib or Guantánamo Bay recognized their victims as human; they also recognized them as enemy combatants or terrorists; and they dehumanized them with their rhetoric and actions. Still, their rhetoric and actions, complete with elaborate metaphors, rationalizations, and teams of lawyers redefining torture, all suggest that the *problem* is precisely that they/we *do recognize* the humanity of their/ our victims, which is why they/we then have to invest so much time and energy in justifying the torturing and killing of these people. We have to create a rhetoric and a fantasy with which we can deny what we know and justify what we do in spite of that knowledge—that we are torturing and killing other human beings. If we truly believed that they were dogs, then we wouldn't need to justify, rationalize, or explain our treatment of them (except to the world of dog-lovers!); and we wouldn't have to order the military interrogators to treat them *like* dogs. Certainly Lynndie England did not really think that the man on the leash was a dog and not a person. Rather, it is precisely because she recognized his humanity, that treating him *like* a dog was so humiliating for him (and therefore so much *fun*, because, as we have seen, in this case our notion of fun is inherently linked to humiliating others).

The question, then, is not one of recognition—that if we recognized (in either the epistemological sense of Hage or the political sense of Butler) these other people as humans, we would treat them differently.[12] We can epistemologically and politically recognize them as humans and still torture them and kill them. The question is how and why we deny what we recognize in order to justify torture and killing. This is the question that I addressed in the first part of this book, wherein I examined the ways in which traditional stereotypes of women not only serve to "soften the blow" of images of torture, but also to explain the torture as either the work of a few perverted individuals or the natural consequence of the presence of women in the military. Either way, it is explained away as sexual rather than violent or criminal. In the case of women suicide bombers, as we have seen, their violence is also linked with the supposed natural violence and deceptiveness of women, associated with what they wear and the imagined fluidity of female bodies. In the case of women involved in war, stereotypes both increase the fear and danger associated with women and displace violence onto sex, turning war crimes into "amorous disasters" or love-triangles. Moreover, the connection between sex and violence can make these horrible acts seem like "just having fun." The question, then, becomes not just how and why we justify violence, but how and why we seem to enjoy it! This question of the meaning of violence in our cultural imaginary demands that we pay attention to unconscious desires and fears, as I discussed in the last part of this book.

Given the violence of humans against humans, it is not enough to recognize humanity if what that means is to "fight the good fight" or keep up the struggle for recognition. If winning the war over recognition is the only way to end violence, then violence becomes the only means to peace. We are all too familiar with the deadly logic of "peace-keeping forces" waging war. With recognition, the best we can hope for is that we recognize that there is something in our relationships with others that is always beyond the struggle, violence and war, which requires recognizing the limits of recognition itself. Constantly reassessing the limits of our own recognition compels us to continue to examine and question our own desires and fears in relation to others. It is precisely when we think that we understand others that we have stopped having a relationship with them and have started having a relationship only with our fantasies of them. This is true for relations not only with so-called enemies, but also with friends and loved ones.

The question, then, is not how to win the struggle for recognition or how to recognize the humanity of others. Rather, the question is, What does it mean that we imagine human relations as a struggle in the first place? What are the implications for ethics and politics of seeing and describing human relations as fundamentally and inherently violent? This is the more general question at stake in the specific questions raised in this book: What does it mean that we figure women as weapons of war? What does that tell us about how we conceive of female sexuality as dangerous? What does it mean that we conceive of freedom as sexual freedom defined in terms of the free market? How do we interpret the effects of embedded reporting or reality television on our sense of ourselves and others? These are questions of meaning and interpretation that take us beyond recognition. Our analysis of these questions and the rhetoric surrounding war and violence suggests that in the end we cannot answer these questions with reciprocal recognition. While the struggle for recognition might help to explain war and violence, when it is taken as the norm for human relationships, then it also normalizes war and violence.

War and violence exist and human beings are capable of inflicting and suffering astounding violence, but this violence is not definitive of humanity. Rather, it is the ability to move beyond violence that makes us human. We can commit violent acts, but we can also analyze and interpret our violent impulses to prevent ourselves from acting on them, to prevent the repetition of the cycle of violence. Our first reaction when wounded might be to seek revenge. But the time of critical reflection and interpretation of our own stake in violence can be just enough time to stop that deadly reflex.

Free for What?

As we have seen, we are not merely *zoë*, biological life, but also *bios*, recounted life. The meaning of our lives, of our bodies, of our *zoë* is created through interpretation, through *bios*. This interpretation is ongoing, and only perpetual analysis nourishes the meaning through which we live, the meaning of life.

When individuals are cut off from the possibility of making meaning for their lives, however, their freedom is curtailed in ways that go beyond rights and civil laws and touch their/our very souls. As we have seen, freedom has become a cliché. Global freedom has been defined in terms of opening up free trade and free markets—that is, as the freedom to shop. But as Western material goods and ideals of the Good become increasingly available and impossible to avoid around the world, we have to wonder what kind of freedom we are offering and, in turn, what kind of freedom we have at home. For example, the definition of women's liberation elsewhere not only is reduced to the freedom to shop but also displaces women's oppression here. Are we free to create and re-create the very stereotypes of women and traditions that continue to dominate diverse patriarchal landscapes?

The freedom to create and re-create the meaning of one's own life, most especially one's own body, is essential to living a meaningful life. Freedom from constraints or freedom of movement is a necessary but not sufficient condition for creating meaning and articulating the singularity of each individual life as part of a community. More than the freedom from constraint, we also need the positive freedom to create value and meaning for our lives. Women need the freedom to revalue the connection between biology and biography in their lives both as individuals and within their cultures. As we have seen, women may now be freed from traditional roles as mothers and housewives, but the meaning of their bodies as women is still restrained by age-old stereotypes of virgin, whore, weapon, danger, and duplicity. And the body that has traditionally defined women—the maternal or pregnant body—continues to be in some ways the most suspicious. So while it is true that women have gained more material freedom and civil rights, still they must have the freedom to create the meaning of their lives and of their bodies. In addition to material freedom and civil rights, they need the freedom to become the producers of cultural meaning; they need what legal theorist Drucilla Cornell calls freedom in the *imaginary domain*.[13]

As I have argued elsewhere, creating meaning is not jumping outside of one's cultural confines altogether but rather finding support for the singularity of each individual's experiences and embodiment, complete with sociohistorical context, within culture, language, and various meaning-making enterprises.[14] We might call this form of meaning-making "witnessing to one's life." As we have seen, "witnessing" has both the juridical connotations of seeing with one's own eyes and the political connotations of testifying to that which cannot be seen, or "bearing witness." It is this double meaning that makes witnessing such a powerful notion for bringing together the ethical and political dimensions of life. The double meaning of witnessing—*eyewitness* testimony based on first-hand knowledge, on the one hand, and *bearing witness* to something beyond recognition that can't be seen, on the other—opens up the possibility of a new conception of ethics that is supported by the very tension between history and the unconscious.

Even as we continually evaluate and reinterpret what we see (the finite embodied lives of individuals in particular sociohistorical contexts), we also continually evaluate and interpret what we cannot see (the unconscious dynamics that remain hidden). The hope is that by interpreting our desire for violence we can prevent acting on it. This form of incessant interpretation necessitates accounting for unconscious as well as conscious desires and fears. Behind the visible world that we recognize is the invisible world of unconscious motivations, which is why our quest to understand violence takes us beyond what we see and toward what we can only witness.

The tension between eyewitness testimony and bearing witness, between history and the unconscious, is the dynamic operator that moves us beyond the melancholic choice between either empty empathy or traumatic repetition of violence.[15] Both senses of witnessing—the juridical sense of witnessing what you can see and the political sense of bearing witness to what cannot be seen—come together in the ethical-political sense of witnessing: witnessing to the horrors of the war, torture, abuse, and oppression. This sense of witnessing not only involves testifying to the events observed, the historical facts—what Danner calls the information— but also to the meaning of those events, which goes beyond what the eyes can see.

Images offer us a perspective on reality, but unless we make an effort to interpret the meaning of these images, this perspective remains invisible. Thanks to recording and imaging technologies, we can see pictures or footage of Abu Ghraib or beheadings or the results of suicide bombings; but these images reveal neither sociohistorical context—the conscious motivations for violence—nor the unconscious motivations for such violence. These images may shock and appall, but they also challenge us to interpret our own investments in violence, to give meaning to this violence in the hopes of preventing it. Rather than leaving us with a purely emotional response that resists interpretation—trauma as spectacle—or inciting the unthinking repetition of violence—as revenge—the doublet of sociohistorical and unconscious meaning can help short-circuit the economy of violence, particularly as it has become part and parcel of the economy of the spectacle.

In addition, witnessing to sociopolitical and unconscious investments in violence is necessary for rethinking our conception of law as punishment or regulation, in what is increasingly becoming a penal society. The exploration of conscious and unconscious motivations for violence requires that we ask who profits from violence and how; who profits from law as punishment and regulation or the incarceration of increasing numbers of black men? Analyzing both the material and psychological profits from violence can help us identify what is at stake in continued abuse, torture, and killing. It is the first step in owning-up to our own investments in violence in order to develop political policies and ethical attitudes that circumvent violence and exploitation. Obviously this would entail a radical change in the distribution of both wealth and meaning. It would mean imaging a law against profiting from the suffering of others, a law that enables community rather than managing it or reducing it to a group of isolated individuals contractually bound only by rules of market exchange.

Exploring the unconscious dimension of our experiences and actions can work to forestall merely acting on violent desires and fears. Rather than "just do it," we think about it first. The time and space required by this process of questioning and interpretation not only slow down our violent reactions but also allow us to see what is not visible in media images: which is to say, both our political/economic and our unconscious and disavowed investments in those images. We need to assess and reassess our own investments in images of sex and violence and they ways in which those investments signal unthought fears and desires. We need to avow the ways in which we profit both materially and psychologically from violence toward others. By contemplating our pleasures and fears, and moreover by articulating them, we can begin to short-circuit some of the effects of the economy of the spectacle and law become mere regulation. We must become visually literate. Moreover, through the process of meaning-making, we will begin to articulate bodily sensations of pleasure and pain in ways that help us understand the connection between these sensations and the cultural institutions and values that produce and reproduce them. In other words, we will reconnect *zoë* and *bios* in ways that give meaning to bodily sensations within the realm of politics, now become ethical. This type of meaning-making is the freedom to explore and give form to the singularity of each individual that resides in the ambiguous space and time in-between body and technology, *zoë* and *bios*, nature and culture: namely, the psyche.

The freedom that comes from creating and recreating the meaning of one's life rests on *response-ability* to oneself and others. Our ability to respond to ourselves and others in ways that open up rather than close off the possibility of response requires articulating bodily sensations of pleasure and pain and unconscious desires and fears. Certainly torture, killing, and war close down response in extreme ways. Witnessing sociohistorical, political, and economic contexts as well as unconscious desires and fears complicates simple notions of responsibility. Responsibility becomes the ability to respond and the obligation to open up the possibility of response from oneself and others. One of the most radical aspects of witnessing ethics is that we are responsible for forces beyond our control; but ethics is not about control. In a sense, witnessing ethics is owning-up rather than owning.

At this point we might ask how we can imagine making politics ethical. Instead of expressing moral outrage or righteous indignation, what if our politicians, and their domestic and foreign policies, were ethically responsible? Instead of aiming at securing financial interests that privilege the few over the many, what if our politicians created public policies that demonstrated ethical responsibility? If ethics entails interacting with others and the environment in ways that open up the possibility of response, which is to say meaningful life, then an ethical politics would necessarily transform the dynamics, goals, and techniques of political interactions both domestically and abroad.

Witnessing ethics become politics would change the way that we think about freedom and security. Rather than link security to ownership and wealth, to the protection of property, as President Bush did in his State of the Union address, we would imagine security in terms of the freedom for all inhabitants of the planet to have resources with which to live. This would mean not only the material resources necessary to ensure survival but also access to various social and cultural institutions that foster and enable the psychic resources necessary to imagine and create a meaningful life. Not just our own security would be at stake, but the security of all inhabitants of the planet—which would also have implications for thinking about animals, the environment, and isolationist foreign policies. If we think of ethical responsibility in terms of responding to others and the environment—by virtue of whom/which we survive and even thrive—then we have to rethink the many ways in which maintaining our "way of life," our ethos, currently exploits others and the environment.

Witnessing ethics implies a politics of response. And this politics of response in turn entails attending to both the physical realm of material resources and the psychic realm of spiritual resources. Since witnessing ethics is the result of a productive tension between how we are governed by historical situations and how our ability to act transcends any one of those particular events, it is already political. In other words, witnessing is concerned with the political situations of individuals, with the social and historical events that shape their lives and make them who they are. In this regard, witnessing ethics challenges any sharp separation between ethics and politics insofar as ethical response must consider subject positions, which is to say political circumstances. Attention to subject positions requires contextualizing our own and other's beliefs, desires, and actions before responding to them. Attention to the meaning of those beliefs, desires, and actions, however, takes us beyond the material and historical situations that govern our lives to the meaning of those lives. Because individuals do not exist outside of social and political contexts, every relation between individuals is not only a matter of ethics but also of politics. Even the face-to-face relation between two individuals, or the intimate love relation of a couple, takes place within and is possible only by virtue of a social-political setting. Insofar as relations and obligations between individuals are engendered by their social-political context, any ethics implies a politics; and in turn, political justice requires that politics becomes ethical.

Within the framework of witnessing, a politics of security become ethical would require considering both the material and the psychic factors that threaten not only our own security but also the security of others and of the earth. Recall the words of Angela Davis: "One of our main challenges is to reconceptualize the notion of 'security.' How can we help to make the world secure from the ravages of global capitalism? This broader sense of security might involve debt relief for Africa... . It would also involve the shifting of priorities from the prison-industrial-complex to education, housing, health-care."[16] We would have to imagine our security as being inherently linked not to our own wealth, but to the welfare of all people. We would have to imagine our own freedom linked to the freedom of others. As Simone de Beauvoir suggests in her *Ethics of Ambiguity*, none of us are free until all of us are free—because how can we say that to be human is to be free when some people are imprisoned, physically or psychically.[17]

Ethics requires owning up to residing in the ambiguous space between good and evil. It requires taking responsibility for our own ambivalence toward violence. Moreover, it requires owning up to the ways in which we profit both materially and psychologically from the suffering of others. We need an ethical politics, which is to say a politics beyond recognition. We need a way of imagining governments and nations that open up rather than close down response-ability, the ability of ourselves and others to respond in nonviolent, even generous ways. We need a politics that witnesses to the ways in which politics becomes a disavowal of ethics; the hope is that by acknowledging our disavowed investments, we can change not only our actions but also our ideas and even our fantasies. This also implies that we take responsibility not only for our actions, but also for our ideas and for our fantasies. Imagining politics otherwise will require perpetual analysis of the role of violence not only in our foreign and domestic policies but also in our cultural imaginary.

To rethink politics as beyond recognition, we must consider the psychic forces that operate behind the scene—or perhaps we should say behind the screen (computer screen, television screen)—of what we witness with our eyes. It is not just that these images flatten the space and time of the psyche by presenting events in two dimensions. After all, we can imagine two-dimensional images inspiring reflection on history and society or conjuring the psychic dimension of life. But, as we have seen, the pornographic way of seeing everything as scandal or spectacle—as sex—renders the sociohistorical and psychic dimensions of violence invisible. Furthermore, pornographic ways of looking easily become trophy-viewing, wherein images are taken and distributed as trophies or souvenirs of war.

As Ghassan Hage argues, with the move from a welfare state to a penal state, we no longer value social explanations—and I would add psychological explanations—for understanding violence.[18] For if we did insist on seeing the frame, the context, the social, political, economic, and psychological stakes, then we could no longer easily justify detaining people indefinitely, or punishing, torturing, or killing them. It is much easier to figure them as evil and dispose of them than to analyze our own political and psychological investment in their disappearance, exploitation, or suffering. Reacting or acting out without considering these complexities may seem easier, but in this case our obsession with speed and efficiency leads to death.

Rather than trying to deny the complexities of life by seeing everything in black and white, in terms of good and evil, us and them, we must explore not only the ways in which our lives depend on those ambiguities but also the ways in which without those ambiguities, life made is empty and ultimately meaningless. When we do not examine our own ambivalence toward violence, we allow freedom, justice, and democracy to become nothing but clichés, or worse, the justification for torture, killing, and war. Without the ability to step back and interpret the relation between the "few bad apples" or "black sheep" and the culture that breeds them, we risk sending our hopes for peace "to the dogs."[19]

Notes

Introduction

1. Alvarez 2006.
2. See Alvarez 2006.
3. In *Witnessing: Beyond Recognition* (2001), I define pornographic looking as follows: "Pornographic seeing is voyeuristic looking that treats the seen or looked at as an object for one's own pleasure or entertainment. The seer considers only his own interests and maintains a willful ignorance about the subject-positions of those he watches. The seer also maintains a willful ignorance about the interconnection or interrelationship between himself and what he sees. His gaze is one-way since he discounts the other's ability to see. For him, the other is to be seen and not subject enough to look. Except insofar as it relates to his own pleasure, the voyeur is not concerned with the effect of his watching on *his object*. This type of seeing or vision divides the world into seers and seen, subjects and objects. The seer remains in control of the scene of sight, while the seen is there for him.... The myth that the relationship to the seen is as an object of sight, even a spectacle there for one's own enjoyment, denies the interconnection between the seer and the world seen and ignores the responsibility of seeing. Seeing is an activity, which like any other brings with it responsibilities.

When it involves other human beings, then it brings with it ethical, social, and political responsibilities. Pornographic seeing denies the seer's responsibility for seeing and what is seen by denying the seer's connection to what he sees. Pornographic seeing treats others as objects for the subject, as the subject's rightful property. The subject is entitled to treat other as spectacle; his freedom and rights guarantee that he can take others as objects."

4. Apparently the Republicans can imagine victory in the war, or at least a homecoming celebration—which might not amount to the same thing. They have put aside $20 million dollars for a celebration to "commemorate success in Iraq." Reported in the *New York Times*; see Shanker 2006.

5. See Mazzetti 2006.

1. Women—The Secret Weapon of Modern Warfare?

1. See Stefan Heymann, *Sidelights on the Koch Affair*.
2. See Brittain 2006.
3. See Johnson 2003, p. 75.
4. In his work on torture, criminologist Ronald Crelinsten concludes, "I am unaware of any research on women as torturers. I have come across occasional references to regimes that do use women torturers, such as the Islamic Republic of Iran, but to my knowledge there has not been any systematic study of whether or how women are recruited or trained as torturers. This gap in the literature suggests a host of interesting research questions and agendas related to gender and gross human rights violations" (Crelinsten 2003, p. 316).
5. See Freud 1919, p. 245.
6. Freud 1900, p. 238.
7. Freud 1913a, p. 522.
8. Parker 2004, p. D2.
9. Ray Blumhorst, quoted in Parker 2004, p. D2.
10. George Neumeyr, quoted in Marshall 2004, p. 10.
11. See Warner 2004, p. 75.
12. Black 2004, p. B4. See also Ehrenreich 2004.
13. Warner 2004, p. 75.
14. Thomas 2004, p. 10. See also Scripps 2004; Cuniberti 2004; D'Amico 2004.
15. Thomas 2004, p. 10; my emphasis.

16. Sontag 2004, p. 27.

17. Ollove 2004, p. A18.

18. See Joan Dayan 2004, which documents the changing definition of torture.

19. Dowd 2005, p. A17.

20. Saar 2005, pp. 222–228.

21. Ibid., p. 228.

22. Novak 2005, p. 33.

23. See Kristeva 2002, "Powers of Horror."

24. Davis 2005, p. 58.

25. Saar 2005, pp. 229–230.

26. Steward 2005.

27. Dodds 2005a, p. 11.

28. Ibid.

29. Ibid.

30. See Dodds 2005b, p. 15; *News Journal* 2005, p. 04A; Novak 2005, p. 33; Jacoby 2005, p. 11.

31. Novak 2005, p. 33.

32. See Freud 1919, pp. 244–245.

33. Sontag 2004, p. 29.

34. Cloud 2004, p. 306 n. 85.

35. Carby 2004, p. 4.

36. Jaber 2003, p. 1.

37. Ibid.

38. See Black 2004, p. 4, and Cocco 2004, p. A51.

39. Victor 2003, p. 3.

40. Daraghmeh 2003, p. A22.

41. Sheik Yusef al-Qaradawi, quoted in Bennet 2003, p. 1.

42. Victor 2003, p. 19.

43. See for example Lloyd 1984 and Cavarero 2002.

44. Cavarero 2006.

45. Cavarero 2006.

46. Hage 2003, pp. 70, 76; Hage is specifically discussing Palestinian suicide bombers.

47. Reuter 2004, pp. 160–161 (my emphasis). Eelam is the name the Tamils use to refer to the independent homeland on the island of Sri Lanka for which they fight.

48. Fanon 1967. See also my analysis of Fanon's essay on the veil in *The Colonization of Psychic Space* (Oliver 2004).

49. See Cavarero 2002; see also Lloyd 1984.
50. Daraghmeh 2003, p. A22.
51. See Spivak 1988; cf. Cooke 2002, Cloud 2003, Abu-Lughod 2002.
52. See Abu-Lughod 2002, p. 784; cf. Viner 2002, Ahmed 1992.
53. See Abu-Lughod 2002, p. 784; cf. Larzeg 1994.
54. See Abu-Lughod 2002, p. 783.
55. See also my discussion of Malek Alloula's *The Colonial Harem* in ch. 4 below. For now, however, consider how conservative politicians employ, and thereby trouble, feminist rhetoric even as they cut programs that help women, including welfare, planned parenthood, and affirmative action. As journalist Katherine Viner points out, "On his very first day in the Oval office, [Bush] cut off funding to any international family-planning organizations which offer abortion services or counseling (likely to cost the lives of thousands of women and children); this year he renamed January 22—the anniversary of Roe vs. Wade which permitted abortion on demand—as National Sanctity of Human Life Day and compared abortion to terrorism: 'On September 11, we saw clearly that evil exists in this world, and that it does not value life.... Now we are engaged in a fight against evil and tyranny to preserve and protect life" (Viner 2002).
56. Quoted in Abu-Lughod 2002, p. 748.
57. Quoted in Cloud 2003.
58. Ryan 2002, p. D3.
59. See Parker 2003, p. 21.
60. Quoted in Eig 2003, p. A1.
61. See Bragg 2003, p. 122.
62. Rich 2003, p. 2.1.
63. McAlister 2003.
64. Ibid.
65. Bragg 2003, p. 103.
66. Ibid., p. 119.
67. Kristof 2003, p. A31.
68. Kristof 2003, p. A31.
69. See Bragg 2003, p. 154.
70. Chow 1989, p. 84.
71. Ibid.; my emphasis.
72. McAlister 2003.
73. Ibid.
74. Ibid.
75. Kristof 2003, p. A31.

2. Sexual Freedom as Global Freedom?

1. Cf. Saffire 2001, p. 22.
2. For a discussion of the increasing numbers of women and mothers diagnosed with and treated for depression in terms of women's oppression, see my *The Colonization of Psychic Space* (Oliver 2004).
3. See for example Enloe 1990; Abu-Lughod 2002; Brooten 2004.
4. "HPV is responsible for at least 70 percent of the cases of cervical cancer, which is diagnosed in 10,000 American women a year and kills 4,000"; see Pollitt 2005.
5. Pollitt 2005.
6. See Spivak 1988; cf. Cooke 2002, Cloud 2003, Abu-Lughod 2002, Franks 2003, Hawthorn and Bronwyn 2003, Viner 2002, Luthra 2007. See also Davis 2005, p. 68, and Butler 2004, p. 41.
7. See Chatterjee 1989 and 1993.
8. For example, see Abu-Lughod 1998, Ahmed 1992, Larzeg 1994, Haddad and Esposito 1998, and Yamani 1996, among others.
9. Ahmed 1992.
10. Quoted in Saffire 2001, p. 22. Judith Butler remarks that Bush's concern with feminism gauges the success of feminism as a colonial project—bringing feminism (along with democracy) to all parts of the globe (Butler 2004, p. 41).
11. *New York Times*, June 29, 2005, A19.
12. Dowd 2005b.
13. See Givhan 2005.
14. See Najmabadi 2000, p. 40.
15. See www.time.com/time/photoessays/afghanwomen/1.html; 11/24/2001; frame 1.
16. Cloud 2003, p. 295.
17. See Kolhatkar 2002, p. 34.
18. For example, see Kolhatkar 2002, Abu-Lughod 2002, Cloud 2003, Luthra 2007, Franks 2003.
19. Kolhatkar 2002, p. 34.
20. Abu-Lughod 2002.
21. Abu-Lughod 1998.
22. Ibid., p. 9.
23. Ibid., p. 13.
24. See Aziz 2004.

25. See Mohanty 1987, p. 30.
26. For example Abu-Lughod 1998, Ahmed 1992, Chatterjee 1989, Enloe 1990, Stoler 1995, McClintock 1995, Haddad 1998, Larzeg 1994, Spivak 1988, Yamani 1996.
27. Abu-Lughod 1998, p. 7.
28. See Mcveigh 2005, p. 20; these remarks were made by Reuel Gerecht of the American Enterprise Institute, a Washington think tank, in response to the report from Amnesty International given by Amnesty's secretary general, Irene Khan.
29. Reported in Richter 2005, p. A10.
30. Reported in Weisman 2005, p. A1.
31. Collier 1995, p. 162.
32. For an analysis of the Promise Keepers movement, see Oliver 1998.
33. Reported in Kilborn 2005.
34. Cited in Abu-Lughod 1998, p. 7.
35. For a discussion of medicine in relation to disciplining the maternal body, see Oliver 1997.
36. See Edwards and Field-Hendrey 1996. See also *Monthly Labor Review Online,* June 10, 2005, "Editor's Desk."
37. For a sustained discussion of the relation between oppression and depression in middle-class women, see Oliver 2004.
38. See Novak 2005, p. 33; cf. Dodds 2005a, Dowd 2005a.
39. See Ollove 2004; see also Steward 2005.
40. Dowd 2005a.
41. Victoria Hesford argues that contemporary feminism is "haunted" by the ghost of the "figure of the feminist-as-lesbian." She quotes Susan Douglas: "We know what feminists are. They are shrill, overly aggressive, man-hating, ball-busting, selfish, hairy extremists, deliberately unattractive women with absolutely no sense of humor who see sexism at every turn ... a band of wild lesbians" (Hesford 2005, pp. 227–228).
42. Herbert 1998, p. 55.
43. Hampf 2004, p. 16.
44. Ibid., p. 18.
45. Ibid., p. 16.
46. Bragg 2003, p. 28.
47. Ibid., p. 41.
48. Ibid., p. 42.
49. Cf. Rich 2003, p. 1.

50. Bragg 2003, p. 122.
51. Spivak 1988, p. 298.
52. Sontag 2004, p. 28.
53. Spivak 1988, p. 299.
54. Abu-Lughod 1998, p. 13.
55. Kristeva 2005a, p . 30.
56. Kristeva 2005a, p. 30.
57. Kristeva 2005a, p. 31.
58. Kristeva 1998, p. 152.

3. Perpetual War, Real Live Coverage!

1. See Chaudhary 2005, esp. pp. 70 and 75.
2. Sontag 2004, p. 27.
3. Carby 2004, p. 3.
4. Ibid., p. 3.
5. Ibid., p. 3.
6. Alloula 1986, p. 28.
7. See Alloula 1986, p. 5.
8. Alloula 1986, p. 122.
9. Sontag 2004, p. 28.
10. Chaudhary 2005, p. 70.
11. Ibid.
12. Ibid., p. 95.
13. For my description of pornographic looking, see Introduction, note 4 above.
14. Kant 1795, pp. 106–107.
15. Sontag 2004.
16. Kaplan 2005, p. 97.
17. Chaudhary 2005, p. 77.
18. Berger 1980, p. 39.
19. Ibid., p. 40.
20. Ibid.
21. Kaplan 2005, p. 94.
22. Ibid., p. 99.
23. Massing 2004, pp. 10–11.
24. Ibid., p. 10.
25. Ibid., p. 81.

26. Butler 2005, p. 822.

27. Massing 2004, p. 82.

28. Ibid., p. 84.

29. Sontag 2003, p. 26.

30. Butler 2005, p. 826.

31. Hoskins 2004, p. 114.

32. Kaplan 2005, p. 94.

33. Thanks to Cynthia Willett for pointing out this comparison to me.

34. See Whitlock 2006. Psychologist Janis Whitlock reports that self-injury is increasing dramatically among adolescents and young adults. She attributes some of this to Internet sites that create a community of cutters and other self-injurers. See also Whitlock 2006b.

35. The psychotherapist is Susan Baker of Gerystone Psychological Center in Lancaster, Penn.; reported in Espenshade 2004.

36. See Herman 2006.

37. Davis 2005, p. 51.

38. See Center for American Progress 2004.

39. Cf. Agamben 1998.

40. Kristeva 1998, p. 110; all translations of *Visions capitales* are my own in consultation with a translation by Sarah Hansen.

41. Kristeva 1998, passim.

42. Kristeva 2002, pp. 203–209.

43. Buck-Morss 1991, p. 22.

44. As Žižek says, "The real in its extreme violence is the price to be paid for peeling off the deceiving layers of reality," a reality that became suspect in the nineteenth century with the so-called masters of suspicion, Nietzsche, Marx, and Freud. See Žižek 2001.

45. Žižek 2001. Žižek's analysis of the spectacle is based on the writings of Alain Badiou.

46. For Freud, this fantasy comes from the infant's belief not only that the mother is all-powerful (the phallic mother) but also that she uses that power to meet the infant's needs. Once the infant realizes that the mother is not all powerful, that she does not exist merely to meet his or her needs— or to put it more generally that wholeness and plenitude are illusions— then the infant or adult might resort to a fetish substitute through which s/he disavows the loss of wholeness and a denial of separation (or in Freud's vocabulary, the denial of castration).

47. Hage 2003, p. 81.

48. Ibid., p. 86.

49. Davis 2005, p. 89. Davis argues that after 9/11, we sought solidarity through national rather than global identity.

50. In *Totem and Taboo* and other works, Freud argues that civil society began when humans sublimated their aggressive instincts and substituted their urge to kill into rituals and totems that reinforced taboos or laws to prevent such actions.

51. Reported in Waxman 2005, p. 23.

52. Ibid.

53. McLuhan and Fiore 1967, p. 63. For example, Harvey (1989) describes "time-space compression"; Giddens (1990) describes "time-space distantiation"; Virilio (1994) describes a "paradoxical presence"; Wark (1994) discusses "CNN news strategy of pure speed"; Huyssen (1995) identifies "emerging new structures of temporality"; and Hoskins (2004) diagnoses a "collapse of memory."

54. McLuhan and Fiore 1967.

55. Hoskins 2004, p. 110.

56. Ibid., p. 114.

57. Hesford 2007.

58. Butler 2004, pp. 64, 79. Butler works with Giorgio Agamben's notion of emergency and exception as the sources of contemporary sovereignty.

59. Italian philosopher Giorgio Agamben argues that contemporary state sovereignty is the result of this logic of the exception become the rule (see Agamben 1998). Derek Gregory extends Agamben's analysis to colonial sovereignty in relation to the war in Iraq and the Abu Ghraib prison abuses in particular (see Gregory 2006).

60. For discussions of how the deaths of Iraqis is not reported or downplayed in the media, see Tom Engelhardt's series on news coverage of Iraq, especially "What Do We Call the Enemy?" August 18, 2004.

61. See Suskind 2004, p. 47.

62. This righteous rhetoric, however, runs counter to the media and counter to the media culture of spectacle whose bread and butter is scandal, sex, and perversion, as well as lack of security and lack of self-governance, that is to say risky behaviors and the loss of self-control. Rigid ideals of Good and Evil are the flip side of the sadomasochistic enjoyment of violence that we analyzed in the last chapter. The more violent the punishment for lack of righteousness becomes, the more violent the resistance to it.

63. Scott 1992, p. 25.

64. Mohanty 1987, p. 30.
65. Ibid.
66. Chandra Mohanty uses the phrase "contemporary ancestors" (1987).
67. Reported in Zernike 2005, p. A14.
68. Kaplan 2005, p. 22. Kaplan uses the notion of witnessing that I develop in my book entitled *Witnessing*, along with the notion as it is developed in Dori Laub and Shoshana Felman's book *Testimony*.
69. Oliver 2004.
70. LaCapra 1994, p. 9.
71. See Oliver 2001 and 2004.

4. Innocence, Vulnerability, and Violence

1. Adriana Cavarero calls women suicide bombers "body-bombers"; see Cavarero 2006.
2. In *Discipline and Punish*, Michel Foucault argues that the definitions of "criminal" and "insane" have changed over time in conjunction with government and societal attempts to control certain populations. The recent incarceration of Arabs without due process could be seen as the latest example of population management ostensibly for the sake of national security, where, as we will see, this security is defined in terms of protecting our property and lifestyle even if it means supporting our economy through war. Angela Davis (2003) continues Foucault's analysis of prisons, applying it to prisons in the United States, which in most cases contain and manage black male bodies.
3. Ghassan Hage says that "the rise and dominance of neoliberal economic policy and its substitution of the welfare state by a penal state is a well-documented and researched phenomenon today, especially in the United States, where this penal state has become a particularly salient feature of the social structure" (Hage 2003, p. 85). See also Marc Mauer, *Race to Incarcerate* (New York: New Press, 1999).
4. See Davis 2003.
5. Hage 2003, p. 86.
6. Kristeva 2005a, p. 347.
7. Ibid., p. 102.
8. Kristeva diagnoses what she calls the new "malady of civilization" as a failure to integrate the symbolic Law into the psychic apparatus (2005a, p.

347). In *New Maladies of the Soul* she described these "maladies of the soul" as failures of representation caused by a split between word and affect (meaning and body) that is intensified by media culture with its saturation of images (2002, pp. 207, 443–444).

9. For a fascinating sociohistorical account of images of children as innocent in American culture, see Gary Cross's *The Cute and the Cool* (2004).

10. Freud 1919, pp. 268–269.

11. Reported in the *Washington Post*, May 12 and 28, 2004; see Babington 2004 and Dewar 2004a.

12. See *Herald Sun* 2005; Zernike 2005; Harris 2005.

13. Hart and Serrano 2005.

14. Fuoco 2005.

15. *Herald Sun* 2005.

16. Kristeva 2005a, p. 346.

17. In *Power of Horrors* Kristeva describes the uncanny effect of the other, who becomes the catalyst for the return of repressed otherness—the abject—in the self that provokes hatred and loathing, which in turn can lead either to acting out against others or to sublimating the experience of uncanny otherness through representation. Successfully negotiating and renegotiating abjection sets up the precarious border between self and other; but when the "subject" remains stuck at the level of abjection, confusion between self and other can be both threatening to the extreme of phobia and arousing to the extreme of perversion. It is the polymorphous perversion of this regressed state that can lead to sexual pleasure in violating others. Eroticizing the abject becomes a form of purification that protects the abysmal subject from "contamination" from its phobic object/other. See Kristeva 2002, pp. 225–263.

18. In *Homor Sacer* Italian philosopher Giorgio Agamben introduces the notion of "bare life." He argues that Western politics constitutes itself through the exclusion of "bare life," which sets up a structure of exception upon which sovereign power sustains itself. Bare life, or the biological body in itself, is imagined as being outside of politics and therefore excepted from law. This makes some lives (imagined as bare life) or bodies of supreme value and some completely worthless, as decided by the sovereign power. This is to say that if life or the body is imagined as lying in the realm of nature outside of culture or politics, then it can be either killed or revered without recourse to reason or law. Agamben defines bare life as that which can be killed without sacrifice or homicide, which is to say that which has no value whatsoever. His analysis of bare life could be related to the war in Iraq and the torture of

prisoners at Abu Ghraib and Guantánamo Bay, wherein the bodies of those prisoners are treated as worthless, while the U.S. soldiers who are killed in action are seen as making the ultimate sacrifice. See Agamben 1998.

19. See Sontag 2004, p. 28.

20. For a "deconstruction" of the notion of rogue states in relation to Western notions of sovereignty, see Derrida 2005.

21. President George W. Bush's speech on September 11, 2006, in Shanksville, Penn.; as reported by Terence Hunt of the Associated Press, "Bush Vows to Fight 'to the End': War on Terrorism Is Calling of Our Generation ...," in the *Tennessean*, Sept. 12, 2006, 1.

22. Reported in the *New York Times*, Wednesday, Sept. 20, 2006; Rutenberg and Cooper 2006, A1.

23. Tom Engelhardt makes this argument in an article entitled "9/11 in a Movie-Made World" (Engelhardt 2006). He reviews the press coverage immediately following the 9/11 terrorist attacks and remarks on the numerous comparisons between 9/11 and apocalyptic Hollywood films and between 9/11 and the threat of nuclear weapons.

24. Cavarero 2006.

25. Ibid.

26. Judith Butler makes this argument in much greater detail (2004).

27. For recent discussions of how to define terrorism, see the collection of essays in Coady and O'Keefe 2003.

28. Hage 2003, pp. 71–72.

29. Ibid., p. 73.

30. Cavarero 2006.

31. Ibid.

32. See Fattah 2006.

33. Kristeva describes that abject: "It is thus no lack of cleanliness or health that causes abjection but what disturbs identity, system, order. What does not respect borders, positions, rules. The in-between, the ambiguous, the composite" (2002, p. 232).

34. Kristeva 2002, p. 232.

35. See Reuter 2004.

36. See Agamben 1998.

37. See Golden 2006.

38. For an insightful application of Agamben's logic of exception to Abu Ghraib and Guantánamo Bay prisons, see Gregory 2006. Cf. Judith Butler's use of Agamben's theory of exception and bare life in *Precarious Life* (2004).

39. See post-gazette.com, *Pittsburgh Post-Gazette*, Sunday, Feb. 16, 2003, where Jack Kelly, Post-Gazette national security writer, reports the controversy around statistics on casualties in the Gulf War in "U.S. News: Estimates of Deaths in First War Still in Dispute"; therein, Beth Daponte, now considered the leading authority on Iraqi casualties in the Gulf War, puts the number who died as a result of the war at over 200,000, with more than half of those civilians. Dan Chapman reports in the Atlanta *Journal-Constitution*, March 22, 2003, "War in the Gulf," p. 11A, that the number of Iraqi soldiers killed in the Gulf War was 100,000 and 300,00 wounded and 35,000 civilians killed. See also Iraq Body Count (iraqbodycount.net), which at the time of writing put the Iraqi deaths in the current war at between 43,145 and 47,921. Robert Dreyfuss and Dave Gilson compiled the following statistics—through January 2007—for the death toll in Iraq for the April 2007 issue of *Mother Jones* magazine: U.S. soldiers 3,021; British soldiers 129; other coalition soldiers 123; Iraqi soldiers/police 5,965; Iraqi civilians 70,100–601,00 (est.); defense contractors 665; journalists 146. They also report that the war costs taxpayers $1.9 billion dollars per week, or $275 million dollars per day (Dreyfuss and Gilson 2007, pp. 59, 62). In his five-year anniversary speech on September 11, 2006, President Bush remembered not only the 3,000 U.S. citizens who died on 9/11 but also the 3,000 U.S. soldiers who had died so far in Iraq.

40. See Butler 2004 and 1993.

41. It is noteworthy that several discussions of "just war" theory that focus on the issue of killing innocent civilians during war do not question the use of the word "innocent" in this context; nor do they reflect on the relationship between soldiers and civilians as a division of labor. See, for example, Jeffrie Murphy, "The Killing of the Innocent" (1986) and Robert Holmes, *On War and Morality* (1989). For a historical account of changing conceptions of civilians in relation to war, see Richard Hartigan's *The Forgotten Victim* (1982).

42. Hage 2003, pp. 68–69.

43. See Butler 2004, esp. pp. xiv and 31.

44. Engelhardt 2006, p. 17.

45. In *The Colonization of Psychic Space*, I conclude, "Our exploration suggests that forgiveness and acceptance ... [are] definitive of the human condition and subjectivity" (Oliver 2004, p. 197).

46. Kristeva 2005a, p. 115. Kristeva has dealt with destructivity throughout her work, especially in *Powers of Horror*, where she describes the negotiation

with the abject as a stage in the process of becoming a subject by excluding that which threatens the borders of proper identity. Starting with her earliest work, she insists on the role of negativity in psychic life. In *Revolution in Poetic Language* she calls negativity the fourth term of the dialectic; negativity is the driving force of psychic life. In *Intimate Revolt* she maintains that it is questioning that transforms negativity into something other than merely negation or negation of negation; through endless questioning, negativity is transformed from a destructive or merely discriminatory force that separates self and other, inside and outside, and becomes the positive force of creativity and the nourishing of psychic space. The negativity of drive force becomes the positive force of signification through repetition and response from the other; it becomes the sublimation of drive force into language.

47. Kristeva 2005, p. 115.

48. See Oliver 2004.

49. Kristeva 2005, p. 115.

50. Kristeva predicts, "If drugs do not take over your life, your wounds are 'healed' with images, and before you can speak about your states of the soul, you drown them in the world of mass media. The image has an extraordinary power to harness your anxieties and desires, to take on their intensity and to suspend their meaning. It works by itself. As a result, the psychic life of modern individuals wavers between somatic symptoms (getting sick and going to the hospital) and the visual depiction of their desires (daydreaming in front of the TV). In such a situation, psychic life is blocked, inhibited, and destroyed" (2002, p. 207; see also pp. 443–444).

51. See Kristeva, *New Maladies of the Soul* (2002).

52. Victor 2003.

53. Kristeva 2005, pp. 89–90.

54. Ibid.

55. Kristeva 2007.

56. Ibid.

57. Zernike 2005.

58. Spivak 1988.

59. See Oliver 2004.

60. Kristeva 2007; 2005, p. 424.

61. Kristeva 2007; 2005, pp. 424–425.

Notes

Conclusion

1. Weisman 2005.
2. See Dewar and Hsu 2004 and Follman 2004a.
3. This is an allusion to Sontag 2004. I take up Sontag's analysis earlier in the book.
4. Danner 2004, p. xiv.
5. Ibid.
6. For a discussion of the tension between morality and ethics, see Oliver 2004, conclusion.
7. Butler 2004, p. 147. See also her conclusion in Butler 2005: "Perhaps our inability to see what we see is also of critical concern."
8. Hage 2003, p. 85.
9. Butler 2004, pp. 43–44.
10. Hage 2003, pp. 78–79. Hage makes use of the theories of French sociologist Pierre Bourdieu.
11. In *Witnessing* (2001) I argue that the recognition model of identity is part and parcel of colonialism. I challenge what has become a fundamental tenet of this trend in debates over multiculturalism, namely, that social struggles are struggles for recognition. Testimonies from the aftermath of the Holocaust and from slavery, and now from the military occupation of Iraq and indefinite detention at Guantánamo Bay, do not merely articulate a demand to be recognized or to be seen. Rather, they witness to pathos beyond recognition. The victims of violence and torture are not merely seeking visibility and recognition, but they are also seeking witnesses to horrors beyond recognition. If, as I suggest, those "othered" by dominant culture are seeking not only, or even primarily, recognition but also witnessing to something beyond recognition, then our notions of recognition must be reevaluated. Certainly notions of recognition that throw us back into a Hegelian master-slave relationship do not help us to overcome domination. If recognition is conceived of as being conferred on others by some dominant group, then it merely repeats the dynamic of hierarchies, privilege, and domination. Even if oppressed people are making demands for recognition, insofar as those who are dominant are empowered to confer it, we are thrown back into the hierarchy of domination. This is to say that if the operations of recognition require a recognizer and a recognizee, then we have done no more than replicate the master-slave, subject-other/object hierarchy in this new form.

Additionally, the need to demand recognition from the dominant culture or group is a symptom of the pathology of oppression. Oppression creates the need and demand for recognition. It is not just that the injustices of oppression create the need for justice. More than this, the pathology of oppression creates the need in the oppressed to be recognized by their oppressor, the very people most likely not to recognize them. The very notion of recognition as it is deployed in various contemporary theoretical contexts is, then, a symptom of the pathology of oppression itself. Implied in this diagnosis is the conclusion that struggles for recognition and theories that embrace those struggles may indeed presuppose and thereby perpetuate the very hierarchies and injustice that they attempt to overcome.

Overcoming violence is just not a matter of the reciprocal recognition that Judith Butler clearly endorses when she asks us to "consider that the struggle for recognition in the Hegelian sense requires that each partner in the exchange recognize not only that the other needs and deserves recognition, but also that each, in a different way, is compelled by the same need, the same requirement. This means that we are not separate identities in the struggle for recognition but are already involved in a reciprocal exchange, an exchange that dislocates us from our positions, our subject-positions, and allows us to see that community itself requires the recognition that we are all, in different ways, striving for recognition" (Butler 2004, pp. 43–44). On this account, relationships between people are defined as exchanges—which already places them within an economy of property and substitutions whereby all human relations are those of commerce. Moreover, this description of reciprocal recognition makes recognition a universal need that transcends subject positions and therefore cultural or historical context. On this model, recognition sustains itself as the founding universal principle of relationships on the circular logic that recognition presupposes recognition, that our primary recognition is the that of the need for recognition itself. Recognition is seen as a universal desire that motivates all human beings in all cultures throughout human history.

12. Certainly it is not a matter of epistemological or cognitive recognition, but rather of political recognition. We do not respect their humanity even when we recognize them as humans. But we do recognize them on the political level—as our enemies. We call them "dogs" or "beasts" in order to justify mistreating them (as if being an animal was justification for mis-

treatment); the U.S. occupation of Iraq has seen many dogs, both meta-phorical and literal. As we have seen, the us versus them mentality that divides the world into kinds of people—friends and enemies, humans and dogs—both produces and justifies the killing of some but not others. It is not that others are not recognized as human, but rather that they are rec-ognized as enemies, all-too-human enemies. Indeed, the very definition of identity as a struggle for recognition is part of the us versus them logic that views all human relationships as struggles, as fights to the death in which there are necessarily winners and losers. Even if violence and ha-tred can be *partially* explained in terms of recognition, overcoming vio-lence and hatred requires going beyond recognition and toward witness-ing ethics.

13. See Cornell 1995.

14. See Oliver 2004, chap. 4.

15. For a more developed account of this notion of witnessing see Oliver 2001.

16. Davis 2005, p. 89.

17. See Beauvoir 1948.

18. See Hage 1993, p. 86.

19. In my forthcoming book, *Animal Pedagogy,* I examine metaphors of ani-mals in the history of Western philosophy to see how they disguise ambi-guities between humanity and animality.

Texts Cited

Abu-Lughod, Lila. 1998. *Remaking Women: Feminism and Modernity in the Middle East*. Princeton: Princeton University Press.

————. 2002. "Do Muslim Women Really Need Saving?" *American Anthropologist* 104.3:783–790.

Agamben, Giorgio. 1998. *Homo Sacer: Sovereign Power and Bare Life*. Trans. Daniel Heller-Roazen. Stanford: Stanford University Press.

Ahmed, Leila. 1992. *Women and Gender in Islam*. New Haven, Conn.: Yale University Press.

Alloula, Malek. 1986. *The Colonial Harem*. Trans. Myrna Godzich and Wlad Godzich. Minneapolis: University of Minnesota Press.

Alvarez, Lizette. 2006. "Jane, We Hardly Knew Ye Died." *New York Times*, Sept. 24, section 4, page 1.

Aziz, Christine. 2004. "Tank Girls: The Frontline Feminists." *The Independent*, Features section, Dec. 28.

Babington, Charles. 2004. "Senator Critical of Focus on Prisoner Abuse." *Washington Post*, May 12, A18.

Beauvoir, Simone. 1948. *The Ethics of Ambiguity*. Trans. Bernard Frechtman. New York: Philosophical Library.

Bennet, James. 2003. "From Student to Suicide Bomber." *International Herald Tribune*, Paris, May 30, 1.

Berger, John. 1980. "Photographs of Agony." In *About Looking*, pp. 39–45. New York: Pantheon.

Black, Joanne. 2004. "Girls Can Do Anything." Wellington, New Zealand, *Dominion Post*, May 24, B4.

Bragg, Rick. 2003. *I Am a Soldier, Too: The Jessica Lynch Story*. New York: Random House.

Brooten, Lisa. 2004. "The Feminization of Democracy Under Siege: The Media, the 'Lady' of Burma, and U.S. Foreign Policy." *National Women's Studies Association Journal* 17.3 (forthcoming).

Buck-Morss, Susan. 1991. *Dialectics of Seeing: Walter Benjamin and the Arcades Project*. Cambridge, Mass.: MIT Press.

Butler, Judith. 1993. *Bodies That Matter: On the Discursive Limits of "Sex."* New York: Routledge.

———. 2004. *Precarious Life: The Powers of Mourning and Violence*. New York: Verso.

———. 2005. "Photography, War, Outrage." *PMLA* 120.3:822–827.

Carby, Hazel. 2004. "A Strange and Bitter Crop: The Spectacle of Torture." *Open Democracy: Free Thinking for the World*, Oct. 11. www.openDemocracy.net pp. 1–4.

Cavarero, Adriana. 2002. *Stately Bodies*. Trans. Robert de Lucca and Deanna Shemek. Ann Arbor: University of Michigan Press.

———. 2006. "Violent Bodies." Unpublished essay, parts of which will appear in her forthcoming book *Horrorism*.

Center for American Progress. 2004. "Conservatives Justify Torture as 'Blowing Off Stream.'" *Daily Talking Points* at www.americanprogress.org, May 7.

Chatterjee, Partha. 1989. "Colonialism, Nationalism, and Colonized Women: The Contest in India." *American Ethnologist* 16.4:622–633.

———. 1993. *The Nation and Its Fragments*. Princeton: Princeton University Press.

Chaudhary, Zahid. 2005. "Phantasmagoric Aesthetics: Colonial Violence and the Management of Perception." *Cultural Critique* 59 (winter): 63–119.

Chow, Rey. 1989. "Violence in the Other Country: China as Crisis, Spectacle, and Woman." In *Third World Women and the Politics of Feminism*, ed. Chandra Talpade Mohanty, Ann Russo, and Lourdes Torres, pp. 81–100. Bloomington: Indiana University Press.

Cloud, Dana. 2003. "To Veil the Threat of Terror." *Quarterly Journal of Speech* 90.3 (August): 285–306.

Coady, Tony, and Michael O'Keefe. 2003. *Terrorism and Justice: Moral Argument in a Threatened World*. Melbourne: University of Melbourne Press.

Cocco, Marie. 2004. "Scandal Shows Women Acting Like men." Long Island *Newsday*, May 13, A51.

Collier, Jane. 1995. "Intertwined Histories: Islamic Law and Western Imperialism." In *Contested Polities: Religious Disciplines and Structures of Modernity*, ed. N. Reynolds and S. Mahmood; special issue of *Stanford Humanities Review* 5.1:162.

Cooke, Mariam. 2002. "Saving Brown Women." *Signs: Journal of Women in Culture and Society* 28.1:468–470.

Cornell, Drucilla. 1995. *The Imaginary Domain: Abortion, Pornography, and Sexual Harassment*, New York: Routledge.

Cross, Gary. 2004. *The Cute and the Cool: Wondrous Innocence and Modern American Children's Culture*. Oxford: Oxford University Press.

Cuniberti, Betty. 2004. "Women soldiers face extra scrutiny." *St. Louis Post-Dispatch*, May 23, E1.

D'Amico, Francine. 2004. "Women of Abu Ghraib." Syracuse *Post-Standard*, May 23, C1.

Danner, Mark. 2004. *Torture and Truth*. New York: New York Review of Books.

Daraghmeh, Mohammed. 2003. "Women as Bombers Test Tenets of Islam." *South Florida Sun-Sentinel*, Fort Lauderdale, June 1, A22.

Davis, Angela. 2003. *Are Prisons Obsolete?* New York: Seven Stories Press.

———. 2005. *Abolition Democracy: Beyond Empire, Prisons, and Torture*. New York: Seven Stories Press.

Derrida, Jacques. 2005. *Rogues: Two Essays on Reason*. Trans. P.-A. Brault and M. Naas. Stanford: Stanford University Press.

Dewar, Helen, and Spencer Hsu. 2004. "Warner Bucks GOP Right on Probe of Prison Abuse." *Washington Post*, May 28, A01.

———. 2004. "Lott Defends Treatment of Iraqi Prisoners." *Washington Post*, May 28, A6.

Dodds, Paisley. 2005a. "Report: Sex Tactics Used on Detainees at Guantánamo: Account Describes Grilling by Women." Associated Press, *Chicago Tribune*, Jan 28, 11.

———. 2005b. "Women Used Sex to Get Detainees to Talk." Montreal *Gazette*, Jan. 28, A15.

Dowd, Maureen. 2005a. "Torture Chicks Gone Wild." *New York Times*, Jan. 30, A17 (op-ed).

————. 2005b. "W.'s Stiletto Democracy." *New York Times*, Feb. 27, section 4, column 6, Editorial Desk, 13.

Dreyfuss, Robert, and Dave Gilson. 2007. "Sunni, Shiite? ... Anyone? Anyone?" *Mother Jones* (March/April), pp. 57–65.

Edwards, Linda N., and Elizabeth Field-Hendrey. 1996. "Home-Based Workers: Data from the 1990 Census of Population." *Monthly Labor Review* 119.11 (Nov.): 26–34.

Ehrenreich, Barbara. 2004. "Feminism's Assumptions Upended." In *Abu Ghraib: The Politics of Torture*, pp. 65–70. Berkeley, Calif.: North Atlantic Books.

Eig, Jonathan. 2003. "Why You've Heard of Jessica Lynch, not Zan Hornbuckle; As Sentiment About War Evolves, Victims Grab Attention, not Fighters." *Wall Street Journal*, Nov. 11, A1.

Engelhardt, Tom. 2004. "What Do We Call the Enemy?" At www.TomDispatch.com, posted August 18, 2004.

————. 2006. "9/11 in a Movie-Made World." *The Nation*, Sept. 25, pp. 15–21.

Enloe, Cynthia. 1990. *Bananas, Beaches, and Bases: Making Feminist Sense of International Politics*. Berkeley: University of California Press.

Espenshade, Linda. 2004. "Self-Injury: Why Pain Offers Relief." *Intelligencer Journal*, Lancaster, Penn., Sept., Lifestyles section, B6.

Fanon, Frantz. 1967. *A Dying Colonialism*. Trans. Haakon Chevalier. New York: Grove.

Fattah, Hassan. 2006. "Growing Unarmed Battalion in Qaeda Army Is Using Internet to Get the Message Out." *New York Times*, Sept. 30, A6.

Follman, Mark. 2004. "The Year of the Sucker Punch." Salon.com, Dec. 30.

Foucault, Michel. 1979. *Discipline and Punish: The Birth of the Prison*. Trans. Alan Sheridan. New York: Vintage.

Franks, Mary Anne. 2003. "Obscene Undersides: Women and Evil Between the Taliban and the United States." *Hypatia* 18.1:135–233.

Freud, Sigmund. 1900. *The Interpretation of Dreams*. Trans. James Strachey. New York: Avon, 1967.

————. 1913. "The Theme of the Three Caskets." In *The Freud Reader*, ed. Peter Gay, pp. 514–522. New York: Norton, 1989.

————. 1919. "Three Essays on the Theory of Sexuality." In *The Freud Reader*, ed. Peter Gay, pp. 239–293. New York: Norton, 1989.

Fuoco, Michael. 2005. "England Faces New Charges on Abu Ghraib." *Pittsburgh Post Gazette*, May 24, A-1.

Giddens, A. 1990. *The Consequences of Modernity*. Cambridge: Polity.

Givhan, Robin. 2005. "Condoleezza Rice's Commanding Clothes." *Washington Post*, Feb. 25, C01.

Golden, Tim. 2006. "Memo on Detainees Fueled Deep Rift in Administration." *New York Times*, Oct. 1, A1.

Gregory, Derek. 2006. "Vanishing Points: Law, Violence, and Exception in the Global War Prison." In *Violent Geographies: Fear, Terror, and Political Violence*, ed. Derek Gregory and Allan Pred, pp. 205–236. New York: Routledge.

Haddad, Yvonne, and John Esposito, eds. 1998. *Islam, Gender, and Social Change*. Oxford: Oxford University Press.

Hage, Ghassan. 2003. "'Comes a Time We Are All Enthusiasm': Understanding Palestinian Suicide Bombers in Times of Exighophobia." *Public Culture* 15.1:65–98.

Hampf, M. Michaela. 2004. "'Dykes' or 'Whores': Sexuality and the Women's Army Corps in the United States During World War II." *Women's Studies International Forum* 27:13–30.

Harris, Francis. 2005. "U.S. Army Woman Admits Abu Ghraib Prisoner Abuse." *Daily Telegraph* (London), May 3, 12.

Hart, Lianne, and Richard Serrano. 2005. "Abu Ghraib Plea Is Dismissed." *Los Angeles Times*, May 5, A-1.

Hartigan, Richard. 1982. *The Forgotten Victim: A History of the Civilian*. Chicago: Precedent Publishing.

Harvey, D. 1989. *The Condition of Postmodernity: An Enquiry Into the Origins of Cultural Change*. Oxford: Blackwell.

Hawthorne, Susan, and Bronwyn Winter, eds. 2003. *After Shock: September 11, 2001: Global Feminist Perspectives*. Sydney, Australia: Spinefex Press.

Herald Sun. 2005. "We Did It for Fun: Female Guard Explains Iraq Abuse." *Herald Sun*, May 4, 35.

Herbert, Melissa. 1998. *Camouflage Isn't Only for Combat: Gender, Sexuality, and Women in the Military*. New York: New York University Press.

Herman, Eric. 2006. "More Kids Dying for Drug-Free High." *Chicago Sun Times*, April 16, A3.

Hesford, Vicky. 2005. "Feminism and Its Ghosts: The Spectre of the Feminist-as-Lesbian." *Feminist Theory* 6.3:227–250.

——. 2007. "Securing a Future: Transformative Time Against Nation Time." In *Transformative Time Against Nation Time*, ed. Lisa Diedrich and Victoria Hesford. Lanham, Md.: Lexington Books.

Holmes, Robert. 1989. *On War and Morality*. Princeton: Princeton University Press.

Hoskins, Andrew. 2001. "New Memory: Mediating History." *Historical Journal of Film, Radio, and Television* 21.4:191–211.

———. 2004. "Television and the Collapse of Memory." *Time and Society* 13.1:109–112.

Huyssen, Andreas. 1995. *Twilight Memories.* New York: Routledge.

Jaber, Hala. 2003. "The Avengers." London *Sunday Times*, Dec. 7, 1.

Jacoby, Jeff. 2005. "Saying Nothing Is Torture in Itself." *Boston Globe*, Jan. 30, K11 (op-ed).

Kant, Immanuel. 1795. "Perpetual Peace: A Philosophical Sketch." In *Kant's Political Writings*, pp. 93–130. Trans. H. B. Nisbet. Ed. Hans Reiss. Cambridge: Cambridge University Press, 1970.

Kaplan, E. Ann. 2005. *Trauma Culture: The Politics of Terror and Loss in Media and Literature.* New Brunswick, N.J.: Rutgers University Press

Kellner, Douglas. 2005. *Media Culture and the Triumph of the Spectacle.* http://www.gseis.ucla.edu/faculty/kellner/.

Kilborn, Peter. 2005. " 'Relos': America's Domestic Expatriates." *New York Times*, June 2, A1.

Kolhatkar, Sonali. 2002. " 'Saving' Afghan Women." *Women in Action* (April): 34.

Kristeva, Julia. 1998. *Visions capitales.* Paris: Réunion des musées nationaux.

———. 2002. *The Portable Kristeva.* Ed. Kelly Oliver. New York: Columbia University Press.

———. 2005a. *La haine et le pardon.* Fayard: Paris.

———.2005b. "Thinking About Liberty in Dark Times." In *The Holberg Prize Seminar*, 2004. Holberg Publications: Bergen, Norway. This lecture, delivered in English, is also the first chapter of *La haine et le pardon* (Kristeva 2005a), as "Penser la liberté en temps de déstresse."

———. 2005c. "For Teresa." In *Living Attention*, ed. Alice Jardine, Shannon Lundeen, and Kelly Oliver. Trans. Shannon Hoff. Albany: SUNY Press. This chapter appears in French in *La haine et le pardon* (2005a), as "Peut-on faire la paix?"

Kristof, Nicholas D. 2003. "A Woman's Place." *New York Times*, April 5, A31 (op-ed).

LaCapra, Dominick. 1994. *Representing the Holocaust: History, Theory, Trauma.* Ithaca, N.Y.: Cornell University Press.

Larzeg, Marnia. 1994. *The Eloquence of Silence: Algerian Women in Question.* New York: Routledge.

Lloyd, Genevieve. 1984. *The Man of Reason: "Male" and "Female" in Western Philosophy.* Minneapolis: University of Minnesota.

Lury, C. 1998. *Prosthetic Culture: Photography, Memory, and Identity*. London: Routledge.

Luthra, Rashmi. 2007. "Framing Gender in Afghanistan and Iraq: Unveiling the Gaze of Empire." In *Media and Political Violence*, ed. Annabelle Sreberny, Hillel Nossek, and Prasun Sonwalkar, pp. 325–339. Cresskill, N.J.: Hampton Press.

Marshall, Lucinda. 2004. "The Misogynist Undercurrents of Abu Ghraib." *Off Our Backs* 34.5–6:10–12.

Massing, Michael. 2004. *Now They Tell Us: The American Press and Iraq*. New York: New York Review of Books.

Mazzetti, Mark. 2006. "Spy Agencies Say Iraq War Worsens Terrorism Threat." *New York Times*, Sept. 24, A1.

McAlister, Melani. 2003. "Saving Private Lynch." *New York Times*, April 6, 4.2.

McClintock, Anne. 1995. *Imperial Leather: Race, Gender, and Sexuality in the Colonial Contest*. New York: Routledge.

McLuhan, Marshall, and Q. Fiore. 1967. *The Medium Is the Message: An Inventory of Effects*. New York: Bantam.

Mcveigh, Karen. 2005. "Amnesty Dossier Condemns a World of Deepening Brutality." *The Scotsman*, May 26, 20.

Mohanty, Chandra Talpade. 1987. "Feminist Encounters: Locating the Politics of Experience." *Copyright* 1 (fall): 30–44.

Murphy, Jeffrie. 1986. "The Killing of the Innocent." In *War, Morality, and the Military Profession*, ed. Malham Wakin, pp. 341–364. Boulder, Colo.: Westview.

Najmabadi, Afsaneh. 2000. "(Un)Veiling Feminism." *Social Text* 18. (fall): 29–45.

News Journal. 2005. "Torturers' Tricks Debasing Country's Missions at Guantánamo Bay." Daytona Beach, Feb. 7, 04A.

Novak, Viveca. 2005. "Impure Tactics." *Time* New York 165.8 (Feb. 21), p. 33.

Oliver, Kelly. 1997. *Family Values: Subjects Between Nature and Culture*. New York: Routledge.

——. 1998. *Subjectivity Without Subjects: From Abject Fathers to Desiring Mothers*. New York: Rowman and Littlefield.

——. 2001. *Witnessing: Beyond Recognition*. Minneapolis: University of Minnesota Press.

——. 2004. *The Colonization of Psychic Space: Toward a Psychoanalytic Social Theory*. Minneapolis: University of Minnesota.

Ollove, Michael. 2004. "Women in Photos of Abuse Intensify the Shock." *Baltimore Sun*, reprinted in *South Florida Sun-Sentinel*, Fort Lauderdale, May 13, A18.

Parker, Kathleen. 2003. "In Search of a Face for the ERA: Saving Pfc. Lynch from Artificial Legacy." *Chicago Tribune*, April 9, 21.

———. 2004. "Why Were Women at Abu Ghraib Anyway?" *Grand Rapids Press*, May 30, D2 (editorial).

Pollitt, Katha. 2005. "Virginity or Death!" *The Nation*, May 30, p. 9.

Reuter, Christopher. 2004. *My Life as a Weapon: A Modern History of Suicide Bombing*. Trans. Helena Ragg-Kirkby. Princeton: Princeton University Press.

Rich, Frank. 2003. "Pfc. Jessica Lynch Isn't Rambo Anymore." *New York Times*, Nov. 9, 2.1.

Richter, Paul. 2005. "Support for Guantánamo Eroding in Bush's Circle." *The Nation*, June 13, p. A10.

Rutenberg, Jim, and Helene Cooper. 2006. "Presidents Spar Over Iran's Aims and U.S. Power." *New York Times*, Sept. 20, A1.

Ryan, Joan. 2002. "Women Hold the Key to Future in Kabul." *San Francisco Chronicle*, March 31, D3.

Saar, Eric, and Viveca Novak. 2005. *Inside the Wire*. New York: Penguin.

Saffire, William. 2001. "Coordinates: The New Location Locution." *New York Times Magazine*, Oct. 28, p. 22.

Scott, Joan W. 1992. "Experience." In *Feminists Theorize the Political*, ed. Judith Butler and Joan W. Scott, pp. 22–40. New York: Routledge.

Scripps, Bonnie Erbe. 2004. "Don't Blame Abuse on Women in Military." Salt Lake City *Desert News*, May 23, AA04.

Shanker, Thom. 2006. "In Bill's Fine Print, $20 Million to Celebrate Victory in the War." *New York Times*, Oct. 4, A1.

Shay, Shaul. 2004. *The Shahidas: Islam and Suicide Attacks*. New Brunswick: Transaction Publishers.

Sontag, Susan. 2003. *Regarding the Pain of Others*. New York: Farrar, Straus, and Giroux.

———. 2004. "Regarding the Torture of Others." *New York Times Magazine*, May 23, pp. 24–28.

Spivak, Gayatri Chakravorty. 1988. "Can the Subaltern Speak?" In *Marxism and the Interpretation of Culture*, ed. Cary Nelson and Lawrence Grossberg, pp. 271–313. Urbana: University of Illinois Press.

Steward, Nkrumah Shabazzz. 2005. "Gitmo Interrogators Reportedly Relied on Sex Humiliation." *I'm Juxtaposing* by Eightheadz, creator of 8Bm.com. www.8BM.com.

Stoler, Ann Laura. 1995. *Race and the Education of Desire: Foucault's History of Sexuality and the Colonial Order of Things*. Durham: Duke University Press.

Suskind, Ron. 2004. "Without a Doubt." *New York Times Magazine*, Oct. 17, pp. 44–51, 64, 102, 106.

Thomas, Cal. 2004. "Sexual Politics Behind Whorehouse Behavior at Iraq Prison?" *Los Angeles Times*, reprinted in *Grand Rapids Press*, May 25, A10.

Victor, Barbara. 2003. *Army of Roses: Inside the World of Palestinian Women Suicide Bombers*. New York: St. Martin's.

Viner, Katherine. 2002. "Feminism as Imperialism." *The Guardian*, Sept. 21.

Virilio, Paul. 1994. *The Vision Machine*. Trans. Julie Rose. Bloomington: Indiana University Press.

Wark, M. 1994. *Virtual Geography: Living with Global Media Events*. Bloomington: Indiana University Press.

Warner, Brooke. 2004. "Abu Ghraib and a New Generation of Soldiers." In *Abu Ghraib: The Politics of Torture*, pp. 71–86. Berkeley, Calif.: North Atlantic Books.

Waxman, Sharon. 2005. " 'Friends' and Enemies: The War as Situation Comedy." *New York Times*, Jan. 16, section 2, Arts & Leisure, 1 and 23.

Weisman, Steven. "Ex-Powell Aide Moves from Insider to Apostate." *New York Times*, Dec. 24, A1, A4.

Whitlock, Janis. 2006a. "The Virtual Cutting Edge: The Internet and Adolescent Self-Injury." *Developmental Psychology* 42.3:407–417.

———. 2006b. "Self-Injurious Behaviors in a College Population." *Pediatrics* 117.6: 1939–1948.

Wyatt, Edward. 2006. "Now on YouTube: Iraq Videos of U.S. Troops Under Attack." *New York Times*, Oct. 6, A1, A19.

Yamani, Mai, ed. 1996. *Feminism and Islam: Legal and Literary Perspectives*. New York: New York University Press.

Zernike, Kate. 2005. "Behind Failed Abu Ghraib Plea, a Tale of Breakups and Betrayal." *New York Times*, May 10, A1 and A14.

Žižek, Slavoj. 2001. "Welcome to the Desert of the Real." *Re:constructions*, Sept. 15, 2001. http://web.mit.edu/cms/reconstructions/interpretations/desert-real.html.

Index

on quest for meaning, 140,
180n50; on *shahidas,* 143–44; on
sicknesses of imagination, 91; on
split between law and desire, 113–
14, 176n8; on vulnerability, 8,
138–39, 180n50
Kristof, Nicholas, 42, 44

Lacan, Jacques, 90
LaCapra, Dominick, 107
language: as social institution, 120
Last, Jonathan, 87
law: disassociation with pain and
pleasure, 113; disconnect between
letter and spirit of, 112–13; disconnect with experience, 119;
failure to integrate with desire,
113–14, 176n8; as impediment to
righteous revenge, 118; interpretation as finding loopholes, 112;
legal vs. moral guilt or innocence, 119; as management of
bodies, 111–15, 120; prison industry and, 111, 176n2; as punishment vs. regulation, 161–62;
restricting natural instincts, 119;
surveillance technologies under-
mining, 114–15; symbolic, 115,
120–21
legitimate force: definition of, 14, 26,
63; high-tech weaponry and,
126–27
lesbianism, 61
Levinas, Emmanuel, 89
liberation of women: freedom and
consent in, 57; as freedom to
shop, 51–54, 64, 160; at home vs.
abroad, 49–50, 55; impact on

everyday lives, 54–55; imperialist
discourse of, 64; justifying military action, 5, 39–40; protection
of women as goal of, 63; rhetoric
concealing women's oppression,
47; as sexual freedom, 54; unveiling of women, 39, 47, 50–51,
53–55
Liberation Tigers of Tamil Eelam
(LTTE), 36–37
Limbaugh, Rush, 26
Link, Kathy, 58
lives, value of, 133, 135
loopholes: law as interpretation of,
112
Lott, Trent, 152
LTTE (Liberation Tigers of Tamil
Eelam), 36–37
Lynch, Jessica: as "amorous disaster,"
147; changing image of, 40–41;
desexualization of, 62–63; King
Kong syndrome and, 43; propaganda about, 41–42, 63; rescue
of, 5, 19, 40–42, 77
lynchings (U.S.), 69, 71
Lynn, John A., 41

Marshall, James, 28
martyrdom, 143. *See also shahidas*
(female martyrs)
Massing, Michael, 79–81
materialism and insecurity, 111–12
maternal body: defining women, 160;
suicide bombers and, 37; as
threat to autonomy, 27; as
weapon, 35, 36
McAlister, Melani, 42, 43–44
McLuhan, Marshall, 97